CHASING
DOCTOR
DOLITTLE

Also by Con Slobodchikoff, Ph.D.

Prairie Dogs: Communication and Community in an Animal Society

CHASING DOCTOR DOLITTLE

LEARNING THE LANGUAGE OF ANIMALS

CON SLOBODCHIKOFF, PH.D.

ST. MARTIN'S PRESS ✿ NEW YORK

www.stmartins.com

Design by Steven Seighman

Library of Congress Cataloging-in-Publication Data

Slobodchikoff, C. N.
    Chasing Doctor Dolittle : learning the language of animals /
Con Slobodchikoff. — 1st U.S. ed.
        p. cm.
    Includes bibliographical references and index.
    ISBN 978-0-312-61179-8 (hardcover)
    ISBN 978-1-250-01205-0 (e-book)
  1. Animal communication.   2. Language and languages.   I. Title.
    QL776.S596 2012
    591.59—dc23

                                                    2012033696

First Edition: December 2012

10 9 8 7 6 5 4 3 2 1

CONTENTS

AUTHOR'S NOTE

Animal language is a controversial topic, and many scientists and animal behaviorists believe that animals are not capable of having language. In this book, I present evidence for what I consider to be animal language, assembled from my own (and a number of other) scientific studies. I need to point out that these are my own interpretations, and not necessarily those of the authors of the studies that I discuss. In a number of cases, the authors would probably disagree with my interpretation of their work, and by discussing their studies, I do not intend to imply that they either agree with or endorse my interpretation and my point of view. If you are interested in reading the original studies and drawing your own conclusions, I have arranged a chapter-by-chapter bibliography at the end of this book.

CHASING
DOCTOR
DOLITTLE

1. DOCTOR DOLITTLE AND ANIMAL LANGUAGE

Do animals have language? When they make sounds, are they really speaking? Can you imagine how the world would change if we found out that they really do have something to say? People have long been fascinated with the idea that animals can talk. I have been interested in this idea for a long time, which has prompted me to spend many years decoding the language of prairie dogs through experiments in the field and the laboratory. As far back as 2,500 years ago, Aesop's fables featured animals talking to one another. Even today, we might watch two dogs barking and think that they might be talking about how strong and fierce they are, or they might be telling each other about the humans they have to live with. We have longed to know if there is any meaning behind the barks, meows, whistles, raised feathers, chemical sprays, and all the other elements that are grouped by scientists into the general category of animal communication. When our cat looks up at us and meows, wouldn't it be wonderful to know what the cat means? And when we tell our darkest secrets to our dog, wouldn't it be wonderful to know that our dog really understands us like no human friend could? This is the Doctor Dolittle fantasy—that we can learn to decode animal signals and find that underneath, there is language we can understand.

In the books by Hugh Lofting, Doctor Dolittle learned to interpret the whistles, grunts, groans, and body postures of different animal species from his parrot, Polynesia, who in her long life of more than 160 years had learned all animal languages. She dictated to Doctor Dolittle a complete dictionary of all of the words that animals use, telling him that each species of animal has its own language, but all of the animals can understand one another's languages. With that dictionary, Doctor Dolittle was able to speak to his dog, to a pig, to white mice, to monkeys, and to a variety of other animals, leading him on to many adventures around the world.

In this book, I invite *you* to be Doctor Dolittle. Dare to imagine that animals say meaningful things to one another. Let me play the role of Polynesia while I show you the many signals that animals use to increase their success at locating food, telling friend from foe, escaping danger, and finding a mate. After reading this book, you might not be able to set up a practice like Doctor Dolittle's, but you will have a much better idea of what animals may *really* be saying to one another.

Let me begin by explaining that my using the term *animal language* is equivalent to waving a red cape in front of a bull for many scientists and academics: It's very controversial. That's because, according to many scientists and linguistic professionals, language is the last gulf that separates us from all of the other animals. Over time, all of the other barriers have fallen by the wayside. Not too long ago, people thought that we were the only tool users, the only ones with culture, the only ones with a sense of self. All of that has crumbled as we have found out more and more about other animals. We can't even claim that we are the only ones with warfare who indiscriminately kill one another, because ants have been doing that for millions of years before us. So all we have left to cling to—that makes us special and separate, that sets us apart from all of the rest of the natural world—is language.

In my view, that separateness does not exist. We are all part of the natural world. We are the product of the same evolutionary process that has shaped every species on earth. I believe that animals might have languages that are designed to fit their needs, just has we humans have languages that are designed to fit ours. We simply don't know enough about the lives of animals to make the sweeping assumption that language is outside their capabilities. To study animal communication systems most effectively, we need to be able to understand the world from the animals' point of view, and the context may not yet be apparent to us because it might be too subtle for us to recognize with our current limited sense of understanding.

The idea that animals have language is frightening to some people, but it is also empowering to animals. When people find out that an animal species has a language, they often look at that species in a more compassionate way. The prairie dogs that I have studied for many years are considered by many people to be pests and vermin, suitable only for eradication, despite the fact that they are a keystone species in grassland ecosystems, who prop up some two hundred other vertebrate species that depend to a greater or lesser extent on the activities of these animals. In just one hundred years, human activities and a disease introduced by humans have caused prairie dogs to decline to about 2 percent of their previous numbers. Many people would like to see that 2 percent decline to 0, despite the fact that it would rip to shreds the ecological functioning of grasslands.

But when I tell people that prairie dogs have a sophisticated language, opinions change. I have given a number of presentations to city councils and citizen groups about both the ecological value and the language of prairie dogs, and what really causes them to rethink their attitudes about these animals is the language aspect. It's as if they suddenly start to empathize with this creature, not as some kind of mindless pest that is bent on destroying agricultural crops and grass intended for cattle, but as a living, breathing partner in the natural world that surrounds us. And with that realization, people are far more willing to extend the opportunity to prairie dogs to coexist with humans. Instead of poisoning or shooting the animals, they suddenly become receptive to other alternatives, such as relocating them to places where they are not interfering with human activities.

Changing our attitudes in order to rebuild the bridge linking our species with other species is a risky business because of its enormous implications on our own attitudes and behaviors. We might have to start looking at animals in a different light, but it is possible to do so.

However, even with a change in attitude, that still leaves the challenge of how to design scientific experiments to determine the language capabilities of any given species. If we back off from our initial judgments about animals and open ourselves to the possibility that they don't just signal, but they actually might have a language, how do we design experiments that would allow us to determine whether or not they do?

Looking for language in animals involves questions about whether they have some awareness of themselves as individuals, because one of the main driving forces in the use of language is its power to affect the behavior of others, usually to the advantage of the speaker. Many species make signals, but as we will see, some of these signals are hardwired in an animal's genetic code and are given involuntarily when the proper cue triggers them. Other animal species can decide to produce signals that are specific to different contexts. We tend to think of language as something that is just verbal, but my view of language includes a variety of signals, such as body postures and mixes of chemical odors. Once we open ourselves to the possibility that an individual animal has the capability of distinguishing itself from the other animals around it, then we also open the door to the idea that animals might actually intend to communicate with one another. It is this intentionality that separates mere signaling from language.

Fortunately, attitudes about animals are now starting to change and many more scientists are willing to ascribe emotions, personality, and individuality to at least some species. And it turns out that once we look at animals with an open mind, we can find a lot of evidence to show that they intentionally communicate with each other, deliberately selecting the best signals in their repertoire to transmit a lot of information about the world around them and often using their signals to influence others.

It's my contention—one that I will expand upon in this book—that those communication systems can be considered *"language."* To avoid the barriers and pitfalls that have stalled animal language debates up until this time, I am drawing upon my extensive scientific experience in studying animal behavior to present a new theory of language—the Discourse System—that shows how language is part of a series of structural and physiological adaptations that animals have for communicating information to others. I will explain the Discourse System in more detail in chapter 3, but its chief highlight is that it takes language off its ethereal cloud as some sort of angelic gift granted only to humans, and places it back where it belongs—as part and parcel of a functioning physiological and structural system, a system common to many species.

Although down the road, many species may eventually prove to have language, we have to keep in mind that these languages need not be the same, or even operate in the same way, as ours. (Even Doctor Dolittle knew this!) This is because, as I emphasize when I talk about the Discourse System, language can be shaped by evolution. As such, our language evolved to meet our ecological needs, just as other animal languages serve the ecological needs of other species.

After I explain some of the characteristics of language and share my Discourse System Theory, I'll take you on a tour of the situations where animals use language—in avoiding danger, feeding, mating, fighting, and greeting. These examples are based on my own judgments. There are hardly any studies done that explicitly say that they are dealing with animal language, simply because the prevailing scientific paradigm is that it's not possible for animals to have language. After all, if something doesn't exist, why should anyone try to study it? But I believe that someone has to stand up and pose the possibility that animals might have language. We have to get off our human-dominated pedestals and begin to open our minds to the idea that we have more in common with other species than we'd like to think. Language is the last bastion separating us from all other living beings on earth, and I say, let's have a go at breaking down that wall. Doctor Dolittle, here we come!

2. WHAT IS LANGUAGE?

My interest in language stems from the time when I had to learn English as a five-year-old child. My parents left Russia around the time of the Communist Revolution, and made the trek across Siberia to live in exile in China. I was born in Shanghai, and spent my early childhood speaking Russian with my parents and grandparents. Then my family moved to the United States and I was enrolled in school in San Francisco, where of course no one spoke Russian.

I came into the school in midyear. On my first day, the teacher said something—it was incomprehensible to me—and everyone turned toward the American flag, put their hands over their hearts, and started speaking in a strange language. I was totally clueless, so I just stood there. The teacher stopped the class, came over to me, and jabbered something in my face. Since I didn't understand, I was punished, and the class went on with their recitation of the Pledge of Allegiance. From that time on until I learned the words, I stood there with my hand over my heart and moved my lips, which apparently satisfied my teacher. I looked like I was speaking, but I certainly wasn't communicating.

English did not come instantly. I was already fluent in Russian, so I would slowly and painfully translate sentences that I had formulated in Russian into whatever English words I knew that seemed to come close to what I wanted to say. Because I would hesitate as I translated both my outgoing and my incoming sentences, the teachers assumed that I must have some kind of speech impediment. I was sent to a speech expert for testing, who concluded that I must be a latent stutterer, because I could not instantly express my words. So I was enrolled in special training where I was taught how to take a deep breath and snap my fingers whenever I could not articulate a particular word. Unfortunately, I did not know enough English to be able to tell them that I could not articulate a particular word because I did not know that word. Later, when I could speak fluently enough to share this concept with my teachers, none of them would believe me—an expert had pronounced that I was speech-impaired.

After several years of my enduring those speech-correction classes, my family doctor, who had seen me speaking Russian to my parents without stuttering, wrote a letter to the school administration demanding an end to my special lessons and pointing out that he was prepared to raise the issue with the school board. My family doctor was willing to give me the benefit of the doubt. He looked at my speech from a more open perspective, and came to a different conclusion from that suggested by the prevailing thinking of the time.

In retrospect, this was a valuable lesson. It taught me that experts can be wrong. The speech expert came to a conclusion on the basis of faulty assumptions and no real data. My teachers and the speech expert apparently assumed that everyone in that school system would automatically know English by the time that the students started school. That a person might not know English did not, apparently, occur to them. It was the 1950s, and it was totally outside their paradigm of the time. Now, of course, years later, many more immigrant children go to school who don't speak English, and teachers and speech experts are sensitive to the fact that not knowing English does not imply anything about the linguistic abilities, let alone the intelligence of a particular child. At the time, however, no amount of evidence that either my parents or I could provide would change the minds of the teachers and their speech expert that I belonged in special classes.

ANIMAL LANGUAGE

Just as the speech expert was wrong about me because he was blinded by the prevailing wisdom of the time, the current experts who assert that animals cannot have language might be blinded by their own assumptions. To declare that animals cannot have language, with no evidence to show for it, is not very convincing. Much more convincing would be conclusive scientific evidence that animals either did not have language or are completely incapable of understanding anything even remotely related to language.

But when we look for a lack of language among animals, we do not find that evidence. Instead, as I will explain in detail in the following chapters, there is a considerable body of evidence that suggests that animals do have language, and that they can use this language very successfully to warn each other about predators, tell each other about sources of food, tell each other about possible aggression, and signal their intentions to mate. If we approach the premise that animals *might* have language from an open perspective, then we start seeing all kinds of bits of evidence that it might be true.

Let's do a *thought experiment*—an experiment where we are thinking through the consequences of a set of conditions, without our actually having to be there to perform the experiment ourselves. Let's say that we arrive at a remote village in the South American jungle. The people come out of their huts and greet us with a series of clicks using their tongues. We assume that because they are people, they have a language. How do we go about testing whether these people have a moral philosophy of right and wrong, an understanding of the world around them? Easy, you say. We learn their language. Then we can ask them. I reply, well, what if you assume that the clicks are not a language, but are merely indications of the peoples' emotional states? Can we know anything about their capabilities and belief system? Of course not, you reply. Yet this is exactly the situation we have with animals. If scientists assume that animals cannot communicate in a meaningful way, they do not bother to look any further.

Finding evidence of language is not easy. Let's go back to our South American village. How do we go about learning their language? We point to things, use our facial expression to show puzzlement in body language, and make it clear that we want to know what something is called. When they tell us, we add that new "word" to our lexicon for their language. Eventually, we build up a store of words that designate familiar objects—man, woman, house, child, tree. We build a dictionary of semantic terms, words that have particular meanings. Even then, we can't be really sure that the words mean what we think they mean to the people in the village. This situation is quite common when we deal with another culture.

Some years ago, I was trying to do a research project in an

English-speaking African country. I needed to get a research permit, and I had applied for the permit about a year in advance of arriving in the country. By the time I landed at the airport, there still was no sign of the permit. So I went to the office that issued the permits and asked about it. I was told to come back tomorrow. The next day, bright and early, I went to the permit office, only to be told once again to come back tomorrow. Several tomorrows later, the clerk at the office finally told me, "What are you doing here? I told you to come back tomorrow." This is tomorrow, I explained. "No, no," said the clerk, "I said come back tomorrow—not the next day!" Apparently I had failed to understand that "tomorrow" meant go away and don't bother me again in the near future. I finally got my research permit by talking to my African colleague who had sponsored the trip. My colleague, a personal friend of the president of the country, picked up the phone, called the office, told them to have my permit ready in ten minutes or he would see to it that there were serious consequences, and my permit was ready in fewer tomorrows than the ten-minute limit.

With this added layer of complexity, how do we decide if the South American villagers have a language? Clicks are not that easy to hear for someone who hasn't grown up listening to them all their life. We can maybe record on tape a click for "go." We can play the tape on a machine that analyzes sound, and we can generate a sonogram, a pictorial representation of the frequencies and time elements in a vocalization. But there are going to be subtle differences between individual speakers—some have higher pitched voices, some have lower pitches, some slur their clicks a little more than others. And plurals—let's say that "go" changes to "gos" when many people go. This is represented by a minute lengthening of the click for "go," a lengthening that everyone in the native village can hear. Unless we have unusual abilities to detect sound, chances are we would not be able to detect this difference without knowing more about the language.

In the face of these difficulties, we might hit on a winning strategy—teach these people our language! If they can learn our language, then they must have a language themselves. After a while there would be some common basis for communication. If the village people are very good at learning a different kind of language, then we might be able to decipher key elements of their communication system and conclude that they really do have a language. On the other hand, if they cannot understand the concept of a language that is composed of sounds other than clicks, we might conclude that it is not possible to determine whether or not they have a language. The important point in this circumstance is that we failed to find a way to adequately test whether the village people have a language. To conclude at this point that they do not have a language would be ridiculous—yet that is just how some people approach the idea that animals might not have a language.

Actually, some psychologists, biologists, and anthropologists have tried just the strategy described above—teaching animals either human languages or languages designed by humans. The goals of this have been multifaceted. Some researchers wanted to communicate with another animal species, others wanted to determine whether some animal species had the cognitive capabilities to understand language and grammar and respond appropriately, and still others wanted to know if animals had concepts of numbers, shapes, and colors. I discuss some of these studies in chapter 9 of this book.

To understand why it has been difficult to gain scientific evidence of language in animals, we need to know a bit about how scientists do research. The scientific method places great store in observable, repeatable phenomena that can be tested with experiments. Particularly in the field of animal behavior, statistical analysis is extensively used to analyze results, requiring that multiple animals be tested. For any behavior to be considered statistically significant, it must be observed multiple times in different animals under controlled conditions. Single instances of a spontaneous behavior—such as that observed by people with their pets—are scoffed at as being *anecdotal*—something that cannot be tested with experiments or statistically oriented observations. Generally, anecdotal information is considered mildly interesting, but without scientific merit.

Traditionally, scientists have believed that the best place to conduct experiments is within the confines of a laboratory, where they can control many of the factors that might confuse the results—such as extraneous noises, other people or animals wandering by, or changes in light intensity or humidity. Unfortunately, laboratory environments aren't necessarily conducive to animals expressing their full range of behaviors— when you sit in a cage all day and then are taken out for an hour by technicians wearing white smocks, you might not choose to display any behavior other than fear. Experiments done under natural conditions, such as those found in the habitats where wild animals live, are much more difficult to arrange, but can lead to much better results.

While the scientific method is certainly good for science, it raises difficulties for asking questions about whether animals have language, are self-aware, or have consciousness. How do we go about designing experiments that will test for these attributes, and still retain the rigor of the scientific method and statistical analysis? Behavioral research in humans is so much easier. The experimenter can simply ask questions of the subject, who can respond in a language that the researcher can understand.

The open-endedness and flexibility that are part of the chief characteristics that distinguish language from communication are exactly what make testing for language in animals so difficult.

The scientific way of looking at any experiment is to get repeatable, predictable results that can be analyzed statistically—if the results are mostly the same in a series of repetitions, then scientists conclude that the results are valid. The goal here is to conduct an experiment under controlled conditions, with no surprises, which is exactly the opposite of the situations that language is designed to deal with.

Let's say that an experimenter puts you in a room with a table, and on this table is sitting an item you've never seen before, a chayote. You don't know its name, and although it looks something like a vegetable or some large seed pod, you don't know whether it's edible or not. The experimenter is trying to determine whether you have any linguistic skills by recording the vocalizations you make and analyzing the sounds for consistency and repeatability, doing the same experiment over the course of three days.

The experimenter points to the chayote and waits for your response while a recorder is picking up everything that you might say. The first time, maybe you will say, "green vegetable." The experimenter gives you no clues as to what this item really is, which is *not* what usually goes on in language. If you were speaking with someone in the room about the chayote, he or she would give you feedback to help you better understand what it is. But not during this experiment. So next time, maybe you will say, "squash." A third time, maybe you will say, "Can I eat this?" All of these responses are valid utterances about a chayote in your language. But there is nothing consistent about these responses, and a statistical analysis will prove that there is absolutely no similarity among any of the sounds that you made, leading the experimenter to conclude that you do not have a language.

More to the point, if you were shown something that you *did* know, say, an apple, forty times and each time you correctly called it an "apple," the researcher could say that there was no evidence that you understood the concept of apple beyond some simple, hardwired association between the sight of a round red fruit with a short stem and the word "apple," or that you could distinguish between the apple and yourself as separate beings, or that you showed any intentionality in using the word "apple." Even being able to distinguish between a MacIntosh and a Golden Delicious wouldn't necessarily convince a researcher that you possessed language. Your ancestors could have been eating these apples for thousands of generations, and you just could have inherited the instinctive ability to assign the different descriptors based on color and shape cues. This is the kind of wall we are up against because of the very nature of the scientific method.

So how do we test for language? One way is to vary a known context in slightly novel ways. For example, let's say that you have consistently told the experimenter that the apple that was on the table was a "red apple." Now the experimenter can substitute a green apple and see what happens. The experimenter can tease out the sounds for "red" and for "apple," and if you say, "green apple," the sound for "apple" is going to be the same, but there will be a different sound for "green." The signals change as the context changes, and if we know something about the different contexts, we can begin to test for language.

My team of researchers did this with prairie dogs when one of us walked a number of times through a prairie dog field. Each time, the researcher walked the same path, at the same speed and pace, with eyes straight forward, and wearing the same clothing, except for one thing: We varied the color of the T-shirt she wore. Every time she walked, we recorded the alarm calls that the prairie dogs gave.

We already knew the basic structure of the alarm call that prairie dogs give for humans. We digitized it and measured thirteen different aspects of each call. As we analyzed the calls given for the human wearing different colored T-shirts, we could then get closer to understanding which aspects were involved in describing the different colors, because the sounds for the different colors varied, but the sounds for "human" stayed the same.

Another way to test for language is to make more use of anecdotes. People love anecdotes about animals doing unusual things or responding in amazing ways during crisis situations. Science usually ignores these anecdotes, fobbing them off as meaningless because they are considered as just stories. However, another step would be to assemble enough anecdotes about animal language use so that we could begin to see patterns emerge, and use those anecdotes to set up experiments.

The general public, especially pet owners, know from experience that animals have an intention to communicate. To understand where the scientists are coming from, we need to get an idea of how a simple communication system works, and how it applies to animal species over evolutionary time.

SIGNALS AND EVOLUTION

The most basic model of communication has three components: a sender, a receiver, and a signal that passes between them. A sender usually produces a signal with some part of its body, although, like the building of a mound or the crushing down of grass (or the writing of a book or the painting of a picture), a signal can have an existence independent of a sender's body.

In terms of animal behavior, a signal can be a movement of a sender's body, such as the flap of a wing, the swish of a tail, or the stomp of a hoof. In these cases, the movement creates a visual signal that can be seen by another animal, called a receiver. Other bodily movements can create sound or auditory signals, such as the singing of a bird, the chirping of a cricket, or the drumming of a woodpecker. Still other movements, such as urination, or the deposit of body chemicals on nearby surfaces, can produce scent or olfactory signals. In fact, animals can produce signals in the form of every sensory modality that we know of—sight, sound, smell, touch, taste—and even some that we as humans don't use, such as electrical current, underground vibration, and sounds produced above or below our range of hearing.

But how do we know in the case of animals, whether the information has been received? We can't just ask, as we would do in humans. For this dilemma, animal behavior comes to the rescue with the *Operational Definition of Communication*, which says that we know that communication has taken place when we are able to detect a signal produced by a sender animal and that signal produces a predictable response on the part of the recipient animal. So, for example, a dog produces a low, menacing growl, and another nearby dog tucks in its tail and retreats, telling us that the first dog produced a signal that resulted in an observable response on the part of the second dog. Our experience with dogs tells us that growls are produced in an aggressive context and from that experience we can deduce something about the meaning of the signal.

So what is the difference between communication and language? Communication can be viewed as a closed system, totally controlled by instinct. Which signal to give, and what response to make in return, are behaviors that are hardwired into animal brains. The initial signals can either be triggered by the sender's internal emotions, such as fear or anger, or they can be triggered by some cue it receives from the environment around it, such as the approach of a predator.

In the traditional communication model, an animal receiving a particular signal gives a specific response to that signal, determined purely by instinct. However, a small number of possible responses can evolve to allow for what appears to be some flexibility in response, but in actuality, what is happening is that slight differences in external stimuli will trigger different responses.

Take, for example, the wild rabbit. If a predator is viewed at some distance away, the rabbit's response is to freeze in place. This is because many predators will only attack or chase a moving prey item. So becoming motionless reduces the cues the predator might receive as to the rabbit's whereabouts, especially if the rabbit can blend in with surrounding vegetation and completely avoid being noticed.

However, should the predator keep approaching, once it gets close enough, the rabbit will switch to a different tactic: running away. The distance that triggers this change of strategy probably evolved as the perfect distance to allow the rabbit enough time to escape before being snatched into someone's jaws. It might seem as though the rabbit made a decision to run, but actually its brain was simply shifting from one preprogrammed behavior (*freezing*) to another (*running*) because the external cue (*distance of the predator*) changed. So in this case, there is no flexibility in the response. The white tail of the disappearing bunny, as well as the white tails of fleeing deer, might have evolved as a "don't bother" signal to predators. It's likely that deer and rabbits aren't even aware of the signal that evolved, literally, "behind their backs."

Language, on the other hand, can be viewed as an open system, where both the production of a signal and the response can vary according to both the internal condition of the animal and circumstances that are external. Language evolved to process information about a changing set of conditions and to allow a variety of responses that could not be encoded purely through instinct. Information that affects an animal's behavior can come from within—its internal physical, mental, or emotional state—or from the world around the animal.

The best chance we have of distinguishing between simple instinctive communication and language is in the case where an animal produces signals that refer to a specific context or to external events happening near the animal, which we can also observe and evaluate. This linking together of something happening near an animal, who then produces a certain signal, is the first step in developing an *Operational Definition of Language*.

But it's not enough that a given animal produces a signal. To be eligible as part of a language, that signal has to have meaning—it has to communicate some information to other animals nearby. Because animals aren't interested in telling us directly that they've received a signal and understood it, we deduce that they did when they respond to the information contained in the signal in predictable ways. This is the basic way that much animal communication research is designed.

For example, my research has shown that prairie dogs, the chubby ground squirrels found in grasslands across the West, give a variety of alarm calls for different predators. The way we teased apart which call meant what, was to observe and record the sounds that prairie dogs made when a coyote hunted in their midst, or when a hawk dove in for the kill, or when a dog was running loose. We recorded many prairie dogs in many locations (including capturing some and presenting them with images of predators in the lab), over multiple breeding seasons, to make sure that what we were hearing applied to all prairie dogs, not just certain individuals. We also analyzed the structure of each call digitally, to allow us to do statistical comparisons. This took years of effort, but it's typical of most scientific research on animal communication.

To show that both the production of a signal, and the response to it, are *not* hardwired, we need to show that as the external context changes, the production of the signal changes as well. The growling dog may suddenly recognize that the other dog is an old friend, and the growls change into a whine of greeting.

Just as people in my earlier examples started with the premise that human language is the "epitome" of all languages, to which the signals of other species must aspire, so, too, have communication researchers sought to set the bar to which all other animal systems measure up.

Charles Hockett, writing in 1960, defined thirteen design features of human language that would be important to find in an animal language, and these design features are still cited today by biologists interested in the question of whether animals have language. These design features are as follows:

- *A sensory channel for sending and receiving messages.* Hockett defined this feature as "a vocal-auditory channel," meaning that the signals have to consist of sounds. Although this is true of spoken human languages, it completely omits sign languages such as American Sign Language (ASL), and closes the door to the possibility that language might use other sensory channels.

- *Broadcast transmission and directional reception.* Signals are broadcast from the signaler and are capable of being received by another person.

- *Rapid fading.* The signal does not stay in the environment for a long time, but disappears quickly, allowing other signals to be produced.

- *Interchangeability.* Animals that are capable of producing signals are also capable of understanding or decoding these same signals when produced by another member of their species.

- *Total feedback.* Signals that are produced by an animal can also be detected by the animal that produces them.

- *Specialization.* The communication system is specialized for the transfer of information.

- *Semanticity.* The communication system is composed of symbols that have meaning, just as words have meaning in human languages.

- *Arbitrariness.* The symbols are arbitrary in their form, rather than iconic. An iconic symbol is a faithful representation of something, the way that a road sign with a car skidding from side to side is a representation of slippery road conditions. An arbitrary symbol is one that has no obvious connection to what it represents, the way that the word "red" has no obvious connection to the color red.

- *Discreteness.* The symbols have to be in discrete units, the way that words are discrete units in a sentence.

- *Displacement.* The communication system can provide information about events that are separated in space or time, such as an event that occurs somewhere away from an animal, or that has occurred in the past or will occur in the future.

- *Productivity.* This is also known as an open system, where new words can be coined at any time.

- *Duality.* The symbols must be made up of smaller discrete units, the way that words are composed of phonemes or computer code is composed of bytes.

- *Cultural or traditional transmission.* The communication system must have a strong component of learning, and through learning, the symbols are passed down from one generation to another.

Let's take a look at how these features might apply to other species. The first six of these design features are common to many communication systems and are not exclusive properties of language. The remaining seven design features become the challenge to demonstrate in animal language. Since Hockett wrote his seminal analysis of language, several other design features, such as recursion and information exchange, have been added. Let's take a look at some of the main features that animal behavior researchers have been exploring.

Two major design features of language reflect the *meaning* contained in a signal. Those design features are: semantics and arbitrariness. *Semantics* is the meaning of a word. *Arbitrari-*

ness refers to the use of arbitrary sounds or signals (words in human speech) that stand for external objects, events or concepts.

For example, in English, "puce" is an arbitrary semantic label that stands for a particular color. There is nothing about the sound, length, or pronunciation of the word "puce" that gives the slightest clue what kind of color it is. As a matter of fact, relatively few people know that "puce" is a brownish purple. A nonarbitrary word is "bowwow" for dog; the onomatopoeic sound of the dog's bark gives even a nonspeaker of English a clue to its meaning.

So, if we can find that animals have arbitrary semantic labels for external events, then it would be a step forward in showing that animals are capable of language.

More recently, the suggestion has been made that *recursion* is a fundamental property that distinguishes human language from the more limited communication systems of other animals. Recursion involves putting extra clauses into sentences. For example, we can say: "John went to the store." Then with recursion, we can add: "John, who is Mary's brother, went to the store." We can continue this recursion with: "John, who is Mary's brother and Julie's uncle, went to the store." Although the authors of the recursion suggestion asserted that this is a unique human property, other animals such as chickadees and starlings have recursion in their calls. I talk in more detail about recursion in chickadee calls in chapter 8.

Two other major elements that enter the picture are syntax and grammar. *Syntax* is the order of words in a sentence. In some languages, you can change the order of words and change the meaning of the sentence. For example, in English you could say: "The man robbed the bank." Then, by transposing bank and man, you could say: "The bank robbed the man," and change the meaning of the sentence. In that respect, the syntax also reflects *grammar*, which is a series of rules that dictate how words (the semantic components, such as nouns, verbs, and adjectives) are combined into sentences. We'll talk more about grammar later, but at this point it's important to realize that all true languages are governed by some sort of grammar, and in the case of human language, all fluent speakers of any given language follow the grammatical rules of that language in order to be understood.

If animals can string several arbitrary semantic labels together in some form of syntax, then it would suggest that they are conveying information that is more complex than simply expressing their emotions. And because grammatical rules are difficult to determine if you don't speak the language, the presence of syntax may be an indirect clue that there may be a grammar.

A recent concept that is being discussed in linguistic circles is that of *computational efficiency*. This concept speaks to the precision of language—if you can convey a specific idea with a single, very accurate word or phrase, it is more effective than a whole paragraph that may come close, but not convey the idea clearly. Interestingly enough, this dovetails nicely with the *Law of Parsimony*, which dictates that the shortest, simplest explanation is the best. Computational efficiency nicely supports the open-ended aspect of language, because it leads to the origin of new, accurate terms to describe new things in the environment. For example, if I say, "cell phone," you know exactly what I'm talking about, and you know it more quickly than if I said, "miniature portable battery-operated signaling device for audio communication with persons in another location."

What I find intriguing about computational efficiency is that animals have it in spades. A single bark from a prairie dog can tell listeners: "Watch out, a hawk is diving! Run for your burrow!" That's so much faster than our explanation. Yes, we can shout, "Watch out!" Or "Above you!" Or even "Hawk coming!" Yet it seems that the prairie dog's single bark, that takes just a fraction of a second, is so much more efficient. And a prairie dog can condense other information about the rate of a predator's approach, its coloring, and perhaps even its individual identity, into its warning barks. Other animals have short signals with what appear to have lots of information packed in. So it seems that computational efficiency can apply to animal language, as well.

THE LANGUAGE GRIDLOCK

Animal behaviorists vigorously debate whether animal signals have any meaning or convey any information. Some suggest that animals produce signals to influence the behavior of other animals. Others suggest that information is coded into a signal by the signaler, and then decoded by the recipient. Still others suggest that there is no information or meaning in animal signals.

Part of the difficulty stems from the definition of *information*. In the 1940s, Claude Shannon, a physicist working at Bell Laboratories, came up with a way of linking information with uncertainty. Originally, Shannon was interested in describing how words were carried over noisy telephone lines, but his concept of information is now used in a variety of different fields, from computers to genetics.

Here is how it works. Let me play a Shell Game with you. Let's suppose that we have two walnut half shells, which we will call A and B, and we have a pea under one of them, and you have to find the pea. If the pea is always under shell A and never under B, you can always be certain that if you pick shell A you will find the pea 100 percent of the time and always win the game. There is no uncertainty under this condition, and in Shannon's view, no information.

Now let's suppose that there is an equal chance that the pea is under shell A or shell B. If you pick shell A, you only have a 50 percent chance of being right. Here we have more uncertainty about where we would find the pea, and in Shannon's view, more information.

Let's make the game more complicated and add another walnut shell, which we will call shell C. If there is an equal chance that the pea will be under A, B, or C, there is more information than there is if we have only two shells, because we have even more uncertainty about where we can find the pea. You now have only a 33 percent chance of picking the right shell, and you are more uncertain about winning the game. This is why people who offer to play a Shell Game with you are confident that most of the time they will take your money.

We can extend this out to any number of walnut shells: six walnut shells with an equal chance of a pea being under any one of them contain more information than five walnut shells with a pea, because we have six alternatives to be uncertain about instead of only five. In Shannon's view, there is the most amount of information in a system when there is the greatest amount of uncertainty about which alternative is correct.

Let's now apply this to a communication system. If an animal has only one signal for a particular context, the Shannon view would say that there is no information present. We know that the animal is going to make that signal, every time. If the animal has two signals for a particular context, and makes either one with an equal probability, then there is more uncertainty in the communication system, and according to the Shannon viewpoint, more information.

But this view of information is not particularly useful in

understanding the behavior of animals. We are interested not only in how many different alternatives there are to a particular message, but whether a signal has been understood by another animal. And the function of signals in a biological communication system is to reduce uncertainty and not to create it.

In this sense, my view of *information* is different from Shannon's definition. I see information as anything that reduces the uncertainty of an animal when it receives a signal and increases the probability of a predictable response to the signal by that animal. When the prairie dog hears a "hawk" alarm call, it is no longer concerned about coyotes or humans or other predators lurking around, but instantly performs the correct evasive maneuvers that would allow it to escape getting caught by the hawk.

This view of information processing is similar to the model that Hockett described for human language. But there are naysayers who argue that the information transfer approach cannot be correct, because it implies that an animal has some kind of mental representation of the external world and conveys that mental representation to another animal, who decodes the signal and comes up with the same mental representation.

Most of these arguments are built on two fundamental points that pretty much sum up the position of many scientists. One is the stimulus-response theory that insists that animals can only do one genetically determined, hardwired thing in response to a stimulus; they don't have a choice. The other is the position that animals do not have any intentions and are not conscious of what they do. By espousing these two basic beliefs about animals, most scientists conclude that animal signals cannot possibly be language. As a result, they're highly unlikely to ever set up an experiment to explore the *possibility* that animals might have language, because they've already ruled out any willingness to be open to it being true.

I have a different way of thinking about this. Let's take a look at this situation: You are approaching an intersection and you see a yellow light. Does that light convey any information to you? I hope you answered yes. Now what is your response? You could stomp on the accelerator and try to beat the red light. Or you could step on the brake pedal and stop the car. Or you could look around, and if the streets are empty, you could keep going without accelerating and hope that you will be OK. Did the light influence your behavior? I would say yes. Did you have only one response to a yellow light, regardless of the circumstances? Maybe, but most likely no. In some circumstances there might be too much traffic to risk running the red light, or there might be a policeman stopped at the curb. Your response to the signal is most likely going to be very flexible, depending on the circumstances around you, the kind of car you're driving, whether your parent or child is in the car, or one of many other possibilities. To put it in a different way, you can slow down, speed up, or slam on your brakes, depending on the context of the situation and your assessment of it. In the same way, animals can have different responses to a particular signal, depending on the context and how they assess it.

The assertion that animals are not conscious and have no intention to communicate has been around for a long time. I remember being at a meeting of animal behaviorists where a speaker was saying that a female bird wanted her offspring to survive. A person in the audience raised his hand and asked, "Do you mean to say that natural selection has shaped the female's actions to make it seem to us like she wants her offspring to survive?" The question was clearly intended to embarrass the speaker, who committed the unpardonable offense of *anthropomorphizing,* or attributing human thoughts, feelings, and motives to animals. This is a huge no-no in the scientific world.

It's this unwillingness to attribute any conscious intent to animals that has led researchers to coin the term *functional reference* to describe animal signals that *seem to* refer to events occurring outside the animals. *Functional reference* means that while *it looks like* these signals refer to something in the outside world, we can't really be sure that they do, so we are going to call it a more neutral term that shows that we don't really believe that animals could actually refer to something external to themselves. That's because, scientists say, animals aren't even conscious of their *own* existence, much less anyone else's.

This scientific view of the world has its roots in the belief that there is a huge gulf between our species and every other species: We are the only species who is self-conscious, and we are the only species that has language. Over and over again, perfectly rational people who strongly espouse the Theory of Evolution, where life developed in the primordial ooze and gradually evolved, sometimes in fits and starts, sometimes having to recover from catastrophic events, but still, with species linked to one another with shared characteristics and common genetic heritages, gradually changing over thousands of generations and millions of years, those same people will stand up and shout their belief that our species somehow "leaped" across a great chasm to be totally unique. How could that have happened? How are we suddenly exempt from being directly connected to the rest of life on earth?

Yet that's what's implied by the scientific paradigm. And it becomes a gridlock of thinking, with no one getting very far because animals have refused to weigh in on the issue. Scientists who have pets and interact with them on a daily basis are literally surrounded with evidence that each dog or cat is a distinct individual, most of whom are plenty aware of themselves and their needs and spend much of their time trying to communicate those needs and desires to their owners. Yet perfectly sensible scientists will dismiss that evidence as anecdotal. In other words, it doesn't count because it's not shown in a scientific, exactly replicable, manner.

While Hockett's criteria for animal language are good for organizing people's thinking about the qualities of language, they make things unnecessarily complicated. Two fundamental steps, showing that animals have semantic signals in different contexts and the signals are arranged according to a syntax (with the implication that syntax might reflect some form of grammar), are a start in demonstrating that animal species have language. For example, prairie dogs have different calls that they produce when they see different predators: one type of call for a coyote, another type of call for a red-tailed hawk, a third type of call for a domestic dog, and a fourth type of call for a human. These calls differ in their semantics: Each call stands for a different type of predator. When we look at the acoustic structure of each type of call, we find that the different component sounds are arranged in different ways for each of the predators. The arrangement of these component sounds represents a syntax that reflects an underlying grammar.

The basics of a language involve a semantic signal by one animal (or a person), that is received by another animal (or person) within a particular context. As the context changes, so does the signal. Whether the signal is learned or produced by instinct is a red herring. The signal can have an instinctive component, a learned component, or a mixture of both. The response of the receiver can also have learned or instinctive components. For example, human visual signals that are called body language have instinctive components that occur in many different cultures and societies, such as smiling and frowning, but many of these signals can be learned as well and used intentionally. Multiple signals can be strung together through syntax, modifying the messages that are produced. The way that the signals are strung together, as for example in a courtship sequence between a man and a woman, can be very precise, showing that there is a grammar involved in the production of these signals. The grammar could have an instinctive component, both in animals and in humans. Human linguists routinely rely on Noam Chomsky's concept of a Universal Grammar, which says that all human languages have a certain grammatical structure in common because this structure is determined by our being human, by our genetic commonality or instinct. In the next few chapters, I show that we already have the evidence to conclude that a number of animal species have semantic signals and that these signals are arranged according to rules of syntax within different contexts.

3. A NEW THEORY OF LANGUAGE

Several years ago, my wife and I were driving from Phoenix back to Flagstaff. To those familiar with the trip up I-17, it's an uphill haul. The last big leap is a three-thousand-foot climb out of the high desert scenery of the Verde Valley on to the seven thousand-foot top of the Mogollon Rim, where clumps of junipers give way to stately forests of Ponderosa Pine. We made it up to the rim at dusk, just when darkness was beginning to thicken the air and make it difficult to see. So when my wife suddenly shrieked "NO-o-o!" at the top of her lungs, I immediately switched my foot from the gas to the brake and quickly slowed down.

Good thing that I did, because before she could explain her outburst, there emerged from the gloom ahead the largest bull elk either of us had ever seen, standing calmly in the middle of the road. Had we hit it at 65 miles per hour, no one would have survived. As we approached, the elk majestically moved off into the woods, and I realized that my wife had saved our lives with a single, shouted word.

Shaken, we talked about the incident the rest of the way home. She said that she didn't actually *see* the elk; instead, she perceived enough of the *shape* of the elk looming ahead, for her brain to assemble the image into the awareness of an elk. Not even having enough time to blurt out its name, she instead called out the first word that came into her head: a big "No!" which I could have taken a variety of ways, but, with its force and tone, plus the universal meaning of "No," I translated it to: "Whatever you're doing right now, stop it!" And I'm really glad that I got the message.

There is a group of words that can contain a world of warning and implied instructions within them: "Fire!"; "Snake!"; "Avalanche!"; even "Car!" There are other words and very short phrases that also work well in times of danger: "Jump!"; "Duck!"; "Run"; "Move!"; "Stop!"; "Look out!"; "Get out of the way!"; "Watch out!"; etc. Speakers of the same language know the meanings of these words and are able to send and receive these signals to warn one another about danger in enough time to take evasive action.

Interestingly enough, each of these signals is either a single word or a very short phrase. To someone from another planet watching such interactions, they would see little evidence of sentence structure. What we know as nouns, pronouns, adjectives, adverbs, and overall sentence construction are not verbalized; rather, they are implied. And yet, we certainly conclude that these utterances are language. So isn't it possible that a bark, a howl, a chirp, or even a whistle from the mouth of an animal could be seen the same way?

Warning signals in general tend to be pretty brief, so as to convey the message as quickly as possible and thus buy the listener extra time to take the appropriate evasive action. The warning signal, like my wife's shout about the elk standing in the road, is crucial to survival. Viewed from this vantage point, it is pretty obvious that this ability to send and receive warning signals, as well as to send and receive signals about the location of food, or mates, or what's up ahead or behind, is just as important as the ability to judge distance, or run fast, or recover from an illness. This ability is vital to not only human survival, but also the survival of any organism, and it needs to be recognized as such.

That's why I'm proposing that we start considering language—the ability to send and receive signals, and to adapt those signals to fit changing situations—not just as a product, but as a biological *system*. By *system*, I'm referring to the parts of an organism that are composed of tissues and cells that share a common, specialized function. Fulfilling that function depends on *behavior*, from the internal movements such as the beating of the heart, the peristalsis of the bowel, and the pumping of blood through arteries, to the external behaviors of muscles moving limbs, eyes scanning, and lips and tongue coordinating to produce speech.

My many years of doing science convinces me that we have a system that we share with many other species, a system made up of physical parts that have a specialized, vital function—to receive, process, and produce signals that contain information about our internal and external conditions; signals that may affect the behavior of others in ways that increase our fitness. This biological system is one that we share with other species, and like our other bodily systems, it has been shaped and molded by evolution. I call it the Discourse System, and I believe that it is as integral to the development and success of any species as all the other systems of an organism's body.

To understand how the Discourse System functions, let's first take a look at the other biological systems of the body.

Here are some systems that we humans have: skeletal/muscular, cardiovascular, digestive, sensory, endocrine, limbic, nervous, immune, and reproductive. All of these systems found in humans have their roots in other species. Our internal skeleton is based on a design that developed hundreds of millions of years ago, when endoskeletons separated out from exoskeletons as a way to provide structure for a moving body. The hindbrain, or lowest portion of the human brain where it meets the spinal cord, is a basic structure that we share with reptiles. Awareness of danger and the fear response are capabilities we have in common with them.

All of these systems can be placed on a continuum from internal to external. In other words, when thinking of them in terms of design, some systems seem to function entirely internal to the body—such as the cardiovascular and the immune systems. Yes, of course, they are affected by external events, but in most cases, those impacts are conveyed by another system. For example, if left alone, the cardiovascular system will work at a baseline level. At rest, the heart will beat rhythmically at a certain rate, blood will be pumped through the arteries under a certain pressure, and air will be drawn into and expelled from the lungs a certain number of times each minute. But when the sensory system picks up information about approaching danger, the brain and spinal cord trigger the release of adrenaline from the endocrine system, which results in tensed muscles and an elevated heartbeat, higher blood pressure, and more rapid breathing. By the same token, the immune system's role is to protect the body from the invasion of germs that can make us sick. It mounts defenses as soon as the skin is opened by a wound, or when we are exposed to microorganisms that cause disease. All of the immune system's activities take place within our bodies.

Other systems have a greater focus externally. For instance, the sensory system has been adapted to totally focus on the outside world. As predators, our eyes have evolved from our mammalian ancestors' position along the sides of our heads (a design common to prey species, who need to see what's approaching from above and behind them) to a position on the front of our faces, which provides binocular vision so that we can perceive depth and hunt more efficiently as a result. Our hearing is also binaural, and our sense of taste/ smell is refined enough to detect the smallest bit of evidence that an item of food is unfit to eat. The footpads of our four-legged ancestors have evolved into hands, with long, grasping fingers and an opposable thumb—all equipped with touch sensors to enable us to handle and manipulate objects.

As we move through the world, we constantly receive information about external conditions through our sensory system. That information is processed by our brain—the CEO of the nervous system. The brain also directs responses to both internal and external cues. Actual physical movements are made possible by the nervous system, which triggers the appropriate muscles to engage in behaviors as simple as an eye blink and as complex as playing a Mozart piano sonata.

The reproductive system sits somewhere in the middle of this continuum. It is responsible for determining and maintaining our maleness or femaleness, and has reproductive organs tied in to the external world via the sensory system, mediated by the release of hormones. Yet, there is a huge component of external focus to the reproductive system. Without the presence of members of the opposite sex, a reproductive system such as ours would be pretty useless.

It's important to remember that all these systems function in an integrated manner, and they also operate in a certain *context.* In nature, an organism can't be separated from its context: What are the surrounding conditions? Is the temperature, the elevation, the visibility ideal or not? What other organisms are present? Do they pose danger, a source of food, or some other opportunity to advance a particular individual's fitness? How can an individual find out about what's going on around it in context, and evaluate it? How reliable is a certain environment around an organism? How will the environment change and how will that affect the organism?

Suddenly, it becomes evident that *information* is crucial. That's essentially why brains evolved—as a way to receive and process information about context, and to direct the behavior of an organism to respond in the most advantageous way. Where other members of the same species are part of the context of an individual organism, *the control, sharing, or withholding of information* becomes vitally important, and language is the way that this is achieved.

All of this leads me to propose that we stop thinking of our ability to learn and use language as some sort of behavioral product, and start thinking of it as another of our vital *systems,* just like the cardiovascular, nervous, and other systems. I've named this system the Discourse System, referring to the ability to produce and understand signals. Here's what it has in common with other systems:

- It has a physical component.

- It is controlled by a special area(s) in the brain.

- It is linked to the Central Nervous System and to the sensory system, and involves musculature, breathing, and a variety of physiological processes.

- It can encompass a number of different signals, produced acoustically, visually, and chemically, or through other sensory means.

- It contains both voluntary and involuntary signals.

- It is influenced by context (i.e., other individuals, external events).

- It can be shaped by evolution.

- It is essential to achieving individual fitness in social contexts.

The Discourse System has both physical and behavioral components. Let's discuss each in turn.

The first of the physical components of the Discourse System are the organism's senses, used to pick up information from the context, or environment around the organism. This often can include other members of the same species or of different species.

Senses involved in detecting the information upon which language is based can be: hearing, vision, smell, touch, even feeling vibration. Whatever senses are most efficient in picking up signals from outside the animal, signals that contain information, are going to be the senses that play the largest role in that species' Discourse System. In humans, these are primarily our eyes and ears. Animals who are heavily dependent upon receiving certain types of signals will tend to develop specialized structures for this purpose, such as the large ears and high-frequency detection system found in bats.

The second physical component of the Discourse System involves the brain. The brain is the organ that translates an incoming signal, categorizes it, weighs its urgency and importance in light of past memories and experience, and directs a response. In humans, the Discourse System has a specialized area within the human brain, Wernicke's area, whose sole purpose is to understand language. Also part of the Discourse System is a specialized brain structure called Broca's Area, primarily devoted to speech and the production of language. Undoubtedly, there are related Discourse areas in other species' brains, but we haven't teased out that knowledge yet.

The third physical component of the Discourse System is the structures involved in signal production. In humans, these are the vocal chords, the palate and tongue in the mouth, and our lungs and breath, all of which work together to give us the ability to pronounce words. In birds, the double syrinx in the throat allows some species such as the wood thrush (*Hylocichla mustelina*) and the western meadowlark (*Sturnella neglecta*) to sing two notes at once. Still other species might have specialized body parts evolved just for the purpose of producing signals, such as the structure of cricket wings that allows them to produce sound when rubbed together.

Also part of the Discourse System are the structures for the reception of signals. The melon of dolphins is a fatty structure that allows these animals to pick up sound signals under water with such fine-scale discrimination that they can tell whether a small ball is solid or hollow in the middle. Dog noses are one million times more sensitive than ours, leading to a whole world of scent messages that we cannot even begin to perceive. Ants and other social insects receive complicated chemical messages from one another that can inform them about the presence of food or of individuals who do not belong in their social group.

In general, evolution pushes for the specialization of signal production and reception to fit the ecological circumstances in which animals live. For example, subterranean mole rats drum messages with their heads on the roof of their tunnels to alert other individuals because vibrations carry well in the hard-packed dirt in which the rats dig their burrows. Hyena bands leave packets of scent on vegetation because their territories are large and scent acts as a semipermanent signpost informing other hyena bands that a territory is already occupied. Elephants produce and receive low-frequency sound (infrasound) messages that we can only perceive as pressure on our chest if we are nearby, because the elephant groups are widely scattered and low-frequency sound travels farther than higher frequencies.

An additional benefit of the Discourse System specialization is privacy. The natural world is a cacophony of sounds, colors, light and shade, and odors. Any given habitat is shared by hundreds, possibly thousands of species with individuals who need to locate and connect with one another, keep in touch, engage in activities together, and avoid danger. So although there is a lot of signal production or noise occurring at any one time, there is some evidence that species who share the same habitat can divide it up, either spatially or temporally, by producing slightly different signals from different places in their habitat, or varying the time intervals between signals, in order to get a better chance of being heard, seen, or smelled.

Some species go one step further with extremely unusual design strategies for their Discourse Systems: a specialized modality of communication—sounds produced in a unique pitch; odors that are imperceptible to anyone else but a fellow species member; colors that are only visible if one can see certain wavelengths of light; vibrations that can only be felt underground; or electrical charges that can only be felt by certain body types in water. Each species carves out a relatively private channel for members of the same species to communicate exclusively with one another.

In our own species, the Discourse System can draft the services of many other body parts to help convey a particular signal. We can add (sometimes intentionally, sometimes not) hand gestures, facial expressions, even body posture and position to get our message across. We call these expressions and behaviors *body language,* and they play such an important role in human communication that at times when the message conveyed by body language comes into conflict with a verbal message, the receiver often chooses to believe the nonverbal message over the spoken word.

In addition to gestures and expressions, the actual position of the body—turned toward or away from the listener, with eyes staring, gazing, relaxed, or occasionally closing—also communicates information. How many people do you know who talk with their hands, waving and moving about, adding further emphasis to their words? Deaf people talk constantly with their hands, and their signing is certainly considered a language.

Even when speaking on a phone where our body language is not visible, we often can convey our feelings and attitudes by modulating the tone and the loudness of our voice. There are also people who are skilled in reading the tone of someone's voice; they can tell whether the stress or irritation level of the speaker has risen by listening for the tightness in their voice. Humans also have a complex skill of voice recognition, where someone we know well doesn't have to identify themselves on the phone by name; we know it's that person by the unique timbre of their voice.

The functioning of the Discourse System is also influenced

by our emotions, which act as filters and lenses, affecting the interpretation of what we experience as well as coloring our responses. This is exactly why people who get extremely upset are encouraged to cool down before continuing a discussion or argument, so as to clear their heads and temper what they say and how they say it. Our emotions can either make our communications more effective (such as people who are convincing because they speak with great passion), or they can trip us up, as in the case when people get so frustrated that they're not getting their point across that they burst into tears. And who has not had their mood changed by a few negative words spoken to us? The strong emotional component to our speech is clear evidence of how the Discourse System ties in our emotions to our language through the nervous and endocrine systems.

Linking this triumvirate of physical equipment—brain, senses, and signal receiving/production anatomy, is the invisible component of the Discourse System: Language. Language is the glue that we use to hold together thoughts. It's the paint that we use to bring ideas to life and give them dimension. Language is the way we often categorize information in our brains.

We know so little about the origins of our ability to speak and understand language. The subject has been mired in controversy for years. Anthropologists have suggested that language started in humans from linking sounds with gestures, and that the evolutionary impetus arose from our highly social nature. Language facilitated cooperation. This approach doesn't shut out other species, but the theory that language started with a mutation that was unique to humans, does. Other people, including linguists, who see language as belonging solely to humans, postulate that a great leap forward was made possible by the human brain.

That there suddenly arose an unbridgeable gap between us and the rest of life just doesn't make sense. After all, every other system in humans has its roots in other species, and can often be traced up the evolutionary line. So why not the Discourse System? If the Discourse System is used to organize, categorize, and integrate information coming in from the environment, and uses that information to produce signals that influence the behavior of others to one's own advantage, then why wouldn't this system have evolved in other species? Is there any real evidence that the Discourse System has a genetic basis? Turns out, there is.

Recently, what has been called the *language gene*, dubbed FoxP2, has been discovered in the human genome. And in support of the theory of the Discourse System, it has been found in other species as well. The connection between the FoxP2 gene and language first was discovered in 2001 in a family known only as KE, in which half of the family members had severe problems with producing speech and understanding language. A mutation in the DNA coding of the gene rendered the gene nonfunctional, and as a result, the people with the mutated gene could not speak or understand language. At the time, people thought that this was the key to finding out that language was coded by a specific gene, giving support to theories that language in humans was the result of a genetic mutation that no other animals had.

However, other studies quickly discovered that this same gene was found in many other animals—perhaps all of the vertebrates—and coded not only for language, but also a whole host of structural and anatomical features, such as the plasticity of neurons in the nervous system. Abnormal expressions of this gene interfered with the ability of mice to learn how to move properly, disrupted the ultrasonic vocalizations of rodents, and interfered with the ability of songbirds to learn how to sing. The structure of this gene is remarkably similar across all of the vertebrate groups that have been studied, having only one or two amino-acid substitutions in different animal species out of the thousands of amino acids making up this gene. So it's not too much of a stretch to hypothesize that this gene might contain the coding for some of the main aspects of the Discourse System—not only the ability to receive and interpret a signal, but also to make an effective response.

Curiously, this gene was found among fossil remains of Neanderthals, indicating that it existed in the human lineage at least 300,000 years ago. The FoxP2 gene gives genetic support to the Discourse System Theory, and it also gives evolution some genetic structures to shape.

I am suggesting that language is not some kind of isolated adaptation possessed by humans, but is part of a larger structure that is possessed by a large number of animals. That structure is reflected in the anatomical and morphological adaptations that animals have for producing, receiving, and interpreting complex signals. For this kind of system to evolve, there has to be a genetic basis that is subject to the effects of natural selection. Finding that the FoxP2 gene is so prevalent among at least vertebrates suggests that we might find other genes that contribute to the development and maintenance of Discourse Systems in animals. Perhaps insects and other invertebrates have their own equivalent of FoxP2 genes leading to a suite of structures that facilitate the development and use of language. As we explore the genetics, anatomy, and behavior of other animals, we may well find that language is not an isolated phenomenon, but a common occurrence. In my view, language in animals has been evolving for a long time, and our human language is just one manifestation in a long chain of evolution.

In the chapters that follow, I will explore how animals use their versions of language to deal with the challenges of alerting one another to predators, finding food, finding mates, signaling their aggressive intentions, and offering greetings.

4. WATCH OUT!

Once, when I was in Kenya, I was walking at night through a part of the Rift Valley with two other biologists. All around us were catclaw acacias—shrubs that have thorns shaped like cat's claws—that can rip through flesh at the slightest touch. In that part of the world, night closes in on you like a dark wet blanket. There are no other lights from cars, nearby villages, or highways, so you can barely see a few feet in front of you. As you move along, the ghostly shapes of the acacias suddenly loom and seem to leap out at you in the darkness. All is quiet except for the occasional high-pitched chuckling laughter of hyenas, or the distant roar of a lion. You are intensely aware that at this time, in this place, you are prey, at the mercy of animals who can see and smell better in the dark than you. Every bit of rustling in the bushes makes the hairs on your neck rise up, and every single one of your senses is on high alert. You are well aware that in addition to the big predatory mammals, there are also dangerous snakes in this area.

We were walking single file, because we had only one flashlight among us. Suddenly we heard a rustling grinding sound coming from about twenty feet off the trail to the right. The person with the flashlight swung the beam to focus on the source of the sound, and the beam lit up a six-foot-long black mamba, which had been traveling parallel to our group, but going in the opposite direction. Black mambas are called "five-minute snakes" by the locals because their bite is so poisonous that it takes just a short while to die. This huge snake had been stretched out to its full length and was zipping along at an incredibly fast speed, looking almost as though a spear had been thrown along the ground. But as soon as the beam of the flashlight hit the snake, it shifted direction and barreled directly toward us.

As that snake covered half the distance toward me with lightning speed, I felt a moment of sheer terror. A surge of heat went through my body and I felt my hair standing up on my head. The world seemed to close down to only two objects: me and the snake that was rapidly approaching my legs. I screamed out, "Aaargh!" and jumped away from the snake through a stand of acacias. My companions did the same. The fear response was something primal. None of us stood there and said to the others: "I say, old chaps, there appears to be a black mamba approaching us at a terrifying speed. Don't you think we should do something about it?" Sometimes there is no time to respond, and a cry of fear is the only thing an animal can do.

When an animal sees a dangerous situation, such as the approach of a predator, it can produce an alarm signal alerting other animals that danger is nearby. Most often alarm signals are sounds, but sometimes they are visual and sometimes they are chemical. Exactly *why* an animal might produce an alarm signal is not known, especially if you consider that making noise when a predator is near is a risky act because it can draw the predator's attention directly to you. What makes this all even more difficult to understand is that many scientists insist that animals are not consciously aware of themselves or others. In that case, why even produce an alarm call?

In the past, traditional behaviorists have claimed that alarm calls are just *motivational signals*, meaning that they are unplanned expressions of the internal state or emotions of an animal. So, according to the *motivational hypothesis*, my yelling "Aargh!" as I jump away from the snake is just my expression of my internal emotional state, which in that moment is one of extreme fear. Yes, my outcry can be heard by others nearby, but it's basically a meaningless sound that's pretty useless because, other than alerting them that *something's* wrong, it doesn't give them any information about what it is.

So let's change the circumstances a little bit: What if you're there with me in Kenya. And instead of it being pitch dark in the middle of the night, it is just before sunset so that you can see. And this time, instead of walking along with me, what if you are perched on a rock looking down at me and two other people walking through the acacias. Then you could see the approach of the black mamba from a distance, and you would have time to let us know about the approaching danger. What would you do then?

Well, you could climb down from your rock and run over to us and try to lead us away, but that would use up too much precious time. Mambas travel much too fast to do that. Yelling "Oh, my God!"—or just screaming—would express your terror and draw our attention to you, but then we'd be focused on you and not the snake. So the motivational hypothesis doesn't seem very helpful to us in the line of fire. But calling out a warning, with sound traveling to listeners at 600 miles per hour, would buy us precious time that we could use to take evasive action and get out of there.

What would you yell? "Danger!" or "Watch out!" might be the first warning that comes to mind, but is it as helpful as saying, "Black mamba! Coming toward you from the north! Run!"? As long as we can hear you, the more information you can fit into a short signal, the more helpful it will be to our survival. And from an evolutionary point of view, if we're related to you and you help save our lives with your warning, there is a big evolutionary payoff because as your relatives we share your genes.

Let's look at what kind of information can be encoded into an alarm signal to make it work well. Since we've been talking about snakes, let me give you another example about another snake with whom I shared a close encounter.

Not too long ago a five-foot female rattlesnake took up residence outside our house in Arizona. The back porch of our house has wooden planks that are level with the surrounding ground and cover some of the concrete foundation upon which the house sits. These planks have several knot holes in them, allowing access to a space below. The rattlesnake decided that the space below the porch was a wonderful place to sleep, out of the sun and away from any potential predators. Because rats get into the crawl space underneath our house it was also a wonderful place for the snake to hunt for her dinner. In the early morning she would crawl out through the knothole and stretch herself across much of the porch, absorbing the sun's rays and warming up. As the day got hotter, she would move away from the porch and curl up under a nearby bush where the brown patterning on her back made her virtually disappear against the brown background of the desert sand.

Sometimes I would forget that she might be out there. I would start to walk out the back door and there she would be, lying practically under my feet. Even though I was used to having her around, I would always yell something like, "Aargh!" This reflected my fear of stepping on her and getting bitten. She on the other hand would rattle a few times, not very vigorously, but enough to let me know that she was there. This in turn probably reflected her fear of getting stepped on and perhaps crushed by a clumsy biologist who wasn't watching where he was going. Eventually I had to ask a friend who specialized in rattlesnake behavior to come and help me move the snake several hundred yards away into an area where there were lots of rocks and lots of rodents, but no people. It was fortunate that I did that because my friend determined that the rattlesnake was pregnant and soon would have had many baby snakes crawling around for me to step on.

As we can see, several different types of information can be encoded into alarm calls. Probably the most useful message can be the name or type of the predator. "Snake!" is a lot more useful message than "Eek!" Yet I'm sure you'll agree that "Black mamba!" or "Rattlesnake!" is even more useful, especially if the listener knows the different attack styles of these two snakes.

Another type of information might be directional, such as "It's over here!" or "Coming down at you from the tree!" Also helpful would be information about how quickly the danger is approaching. For instance, if you were a prairie dog, being alerted to a hawk circling lazily high overhead would produce a very different response than being told that the hawk is dive-bombing directly toward you. An additional type of information could involve directions on how to avoid getting hurt. So, with the rattlesnake I might yell, "Everyone stand very still and don't move!"

From this standpoint, warning signals and the information that they contain can mean the difference between life and death for animals in the wild. That's why I don't believe that the signals are simply motivational—involuntary "Eeks!" and "Aarghs" that have no meaning or intention to communicate anything. No, I believe that these calls are *referential* because they refer to and provide meaningful information about something going on outside the caller.

If an animal takes the risk of warning others about danger, that risk has to be worth *something*. In my opinion, the risk becomes worthwhile because the call conveys meaningful information to the listeners, and this meaningful information raises that call from a mere exclamation into the realm of semantic communication. In other words, these alarm signals have semantic content, just as our words and phrases do. *Semantic content* is a fancy term for meaning, meaning that is encoded into a signal and decoded by the listener. Semantic content is what makes our language work. It transfers understanding from a speaker to a listener. It is the way that information is spread. And in the case of dangerous situations, it is the way that one individual can warn and help others.

The alarm calls given by a species of animals can be a Rosetta Stone for cracking the code of their communication system. This is because most alarm calls evolved as warnings about specific predators. Experimenters can go into the field with video and audio recording equipment and wait for real predators to show up. They can then record both the alarm calls given in response to a predator as well as the behavior of the prey animals as they try to escape. Later, they can play back these alarm calls when no real predator is present. If the listening animals respond appropriately, it's evidence that the alarm calls contain meaningful information about that type of predator. Additional testing can be done to explore whether the calls encode information about directions of approach or rates of approach of a given predator.

THE WORLD OF PRAIRIE DOGS

Some of the most exciting discoveries about alarm calls have been done on very humble animals—prairie dogs. Prairie dogs used to live by the millions across the grasslands of the West. Today their numbers are down by 98 percent, but if you travel to the high prairies of the Midwest and the Southwest, you still might be lucky enough to see these fascinating creatures.

Imagine what it's like to be a prairie dog. First of all, although it seems weird to humans, who tend to prefer bright, sunlit spaces, as a prairie dog you'd live the vast majority of your life three to ten feet under the surface of a grassy plain. Your underground domain would include several rooms—some for sleeping, some where you pee and poop—all connected by tunnels dug through rock-hard ground. You would live there with several other prairie dogs who make up your social group. Some of these are your relatives, some of these are just your friends. Without being able to see in total darkness, you would recognize your family members and friends by kissing them, a behavior called the *greet kiss*, which the prairie dogs do aboveground as well.

At about six weeks of age, you and your brothers and sisters would emerge out into the sunlight. As far as you can see in all directions, raised mounds show the burrow openings of your family's territory as well as those of your neighbors. One of the most distinguishing facts about your life is that you don't travel for much of it—you stay put in your little territory. And lunch would be growing everywhere—all kinds of plants whose seeds and leaves you would be able to eat. But you wouldn't be able to go very far in getting the food, because the next door neighbors, other social groups, defend their own territories just the same way that people in cities defend their yards.

The unfortunate aspect of this is that everyone knows where you live, and most of the predators in the area come to your house for lunch, where you are on the menu. From the sky, red-tailed hawks or golden eagles can swoop down without much warning. On ground level, foxes, badgers, and coyotes wait to pick off anyone who is not paying attention. Not knowing or not realizing where these many predators are can quickly result in death. Responding to an alarm call can make the difference between dying in a predator's talons or jaws or staying alive to enjoy another day.

In my laboratory, my students and I have been decoding the meaning of the alarm calls of one of the five species of prairie dogs—the Gunnison's prairie dog (*Cynomys gunnisoni*). Picture a peaceful, sunny day on a prairie dog colony. Prairie dogs are up out of their burrows. Many are foraging. You can pick out exactly where they are because a sunflower stalk will suddenly tremble and wave back and forth, and even get shorter—a prairie dog is having it for lunch. Prairie dog pups are playing together, rolling and mock fighting in the dust of their home mounds. Every once in a while, two animals approach and greet each other with a kiss. Several animals scattered around the colony are sitting erect on top of their burrows, just watching.

This peaceful scene is often interrupted by the arrival of a predator. As soon as they catch sight of it, one or several prairie dogs start to produce an alarm call, which sounds something like a bird chirp. I have often taken visitors to my field sites and asked them to walk with me through the prairie dog colony. Usually one or two prairie dogs give the cry of alarm, and this is taken up by others in the colony as the cry is repeated at farther and farther distances from us. When I ask people if they can hear the prairie dog alarm calls, they often look puzzled and say, "No, we can't hear the prairie dogs, but we can hear a lot of birds chirping." The word "dog" in prairie dog seems to lead people to believe that the alarm call should be something like a bark, rather than a higher-pitched chirp.

However, this alarm call is the basis for the name *prairie dog*. When American settlers moved into the western plains, they thought that the alarm calls sounded like distant dogs yipping. The alarm call is repeated many times, sounding like the rhythmic barking of a dog. Within a colony, the males, females, and juveniles can call, although females with young tend to call more often than either females without young or the adult males.

So with death lurking around them, what kind of information do the prairie dogs have in their calls? Is it just the fear response, the "Aargh!" that I might yell on seeing a snake? Or is it something more complicated?

TALL, THIN HUMAN WEARING A BLUE SHIRT!

It turns out that prairie dog calls contain a lot of information. Through careful statistical analysis, we have found that the alarm call for each predator is different. There is one call for a human, another call for coyote, a third call for hawk, and a fourth call for domestic dog. These differences are so distinct that people with no musical ability, such as myself, can clearly hear the difference between, for example, a coyote call and a human call. When we are working with the prairie dogs at our field sites, we will often hear an alarm call, and then all the field people will look around to find the coyote, human, or domestic dog that the prairie dogs had spotted off in the distance well before we saw it.

One time, we thought that the prairie dogs had made a mistake. They started giving a coyote call when my field team and I, sitting in a blind raised six feet above the colony, saw a German shepherd. The colony that we were studying was in a semirural area of northern Arizona, with a scattering of houses on one- to five-acre plots surrounded by a mountain meadow. The prairie dog colony was at one end of the meadow, and the nearest houses were about one mile away. The German shepherd was coming from the direction of the houses, so we assumed that it was somebody's pet—in that area, people let their dogs roam wherever and whenever they want.

We were excited because we thought that the prairie dogs couldn't tell the difference between a German shepherd (*Haliotus leucocephalis*) and a coyote (*Canis latrans*). On the face of it, the two look fairly similar. Coyotes tend to be somewhat more slender, with a bushier tail. But there are some coyotes that are fairly robust, with thin tails. We started speculating that there must be limits to how the prairie dogs categorize predators, and German shepherds and coyotes must fall into the "coyote" category. As we were talking the German shepherd got closer and closer to our blind. When he was about 150 yards away, one of my field assistants looked through her binoculars and said, "Whoops." The rest of us said, "What do you mean, 'Whoops'?" We all looked through our binoculars, and guess what? It was a coyote. The prairie dogs got it right.

Knowing the identity of the predator doesn't do you much good if you can't do anything about it. But it turns out that this information can be a lifesaver. Depending on the predator, the prairie dogs take different evasive actions. We did an experiment in which we played back the alarm calls elicited by coyotes, domestic dogs, and humans to the prairie dogs when no predator was actually present.

First, we recorded on video the escape behaviors of prairie dogs when a predator was actually going through a colony. This was not an easy task. Predators such as coyotes and hawks don't show up on cue, so you sit in the blind that you have built to hide yourself from the prairie dogs and the predators, and wait. And wait. And wait. Sometimes whole days go by without anything happening. Other times you get hungry, reach for a sandwich, and just when you have your mouth full and your hands covered with sticky mustard, a hawk swoops in from nowhere, grabs a prairie dog, and is gone before you can turn on the video camera. Usually there are two or three people in the blind with you, one person watching the prairie dogs, one person watching for predators. Your job is to run the video and audio recorders. But you can't talk to anyone. That might spook the prairie dogs, and it might keep the predators away. So you sit there through long periods of boredom, punctuated by short periods of excitement when a predator shows up, the prairie dogs scatter, and you feel a sense of triumph that you got another piece of valuable data.

We found that humans produce a colony-wide response to escape, with all the prairie dogs in the colony running to their burrows and jumping inside as soon as the human appears at the colony's edge. Coyotes produce a response in which all the prairie dogs run to the lips of their burrows and stand in an upright alert posture as they watch the progress of the coyote through the town. Domestic dogs produce a milder response—the prairie dogs stand upright in place, wherever they happened to be feeding, and watch the dog until the dog gets relatively close. Then they run to their burrows and disappear inside. Dogs really aren't that good at catching prairie dogs and are more of a nuisance than a threat. Hawks that are diving into the colony produce a response in which all the animals in the immediate flight path of the hawk run to their burrows and dive inside. All the animals outside the flight path stand up and gawk at the hawk like spectators at an accident site.

After documenting the escape behaviors, we played back calls that were previously given by the prairie dogs to live predators, and recorded the responses of the prairie dogs on video. All the playbacks of the calls produced exactly the same responses as the live predators. This told us that the prairie dogs understood the information encoded in the alarm calls and took evasive action appropriate to each species of predator.

Much to my surprise, the amount of information that the prairie dogs encode into their alarm calls does not stop with the species of predator. We have also found that within a predator category, such as an alarm call for a human, the prairie dogs incorporate information about the color, size, and shape of the individual predator. To figure this out, we set up some experiments using graduate students and volunteers. As you can imagine, these people differed in their size and shape. We mapped a route through the prairie dog colony, and told each person to walk exactly that same route every time they walked. We also worked with our people to make sure that they all walked at the same speed, something that took a lot of practice. Then we sent them out, one at a time, to walk the route while we recorded the responses and alarm calls of the prairie dogs from our blind. Because we didn't want the prairie dogs to get used to this situation and perhaps stop calling, we could only do one or two of these walk-throughs a day, so it was a pretty time-consuming process.

In one experiment, we had different people wear different-colored T-shirts. One person wore a blue shirt, another wore a green shirt, a third wore a yellow shirt, and a fourth wore a gray shirt. The prairie dogs incorporated information about the general size and shape of the different people, and also had information in their calls about the different shirt colors.

In the next experiment we had two graduate students walk

through a prairie dog colony at different times, one wearing a yellow shirt, the other wearing a gray shirt. Once again, the prairie dogs produced calls that contained information about the general size and shape of the people, and also about the shirt color. We then had the two people switch shirts. Now the prairie dogs had the same size and shape descriptions for the people, except that that color descriptions were switched, mirroring the switch in shirts. Each call is a combination of different frequencies of sound, and as we switched the shirts, the frequencies that were associated with colors changed to reflect the different shirts, while all of the other frequencies associated with general size and shape stayed the same.

Finally, we wanted to see if we could fool the prairie dogs by keeping color constant and making it harder to see any size and shape differences. So, we used the same four people and had them wear blue jeans, sunglasses, and a large floppy white laboratory coat. This time the prairie dogs had a much harder time detecting any differences. For most of the people, they could not tell the difference. Only one person, who was much shorter than the other three, was identified correctly in the calls of the prairie dogs.

We did similar experiments with dogs. I got several people to volunteer their dogs. On different days, each person drove up to the edge of the colony with their excited dog and waited while the prairie dogs settled down from the disturbance of the car. We gave each person a two-way radio, and signaled when the dog could be released from the car. As soon as the dog left the car, we started our recording. The dogs behaved very differently from one another. One dog ran straight at any prairie dog he could see. Another dog simply ambled around, paying no attention to the prairie dogs, but smelling all of the flowers. A third dog tried to stalk the prairie dogs just like a cat, lying down on the ground and then creeping up slowly toward a prairie dog. As with the humans, the prairie dogs incorporated information about individual dogs based on the size, shape, and coat color of each dog. But because the different dogs behaved so differently, we found out that the prairie dogs also incorporated information about the speed of travel of a dog—the faster the speed, the closer together the alarm barks were given.

When dogs were in the colony, it seemed as though the prairie dogs didn't take them too seriously. But coyotes were another matter. Hawks, too. Here was the dilemma: Staying near the burrow entrance was the safest place to be. But venturing farther out might reap the rewards of getting better things to eat. Only, the farther out you go, the farther you have to run to your burrow. So one crucial thing you as a prairie dog would want to know if a predator appears, is how fast is it coming? Knowing that information tells the prairie dog how far it can venture from the safety of the burrow, and how fast it has to run to return to safety. What's more, if danger is right on top of you, you might not have the time to call continuously.

So, when a predator is approaching very rapidly, the animals give a single-note call that is different for each predator. This is similar to some ground squirrels who give a single note call in response to a predator who is approaching them rapidly, regardless of whether it is an aerial or a terrestrial one, except that with other ground squirrels the call seems to be a more general one meaning "rapid approach," rather than specifying the predator. If a human runs toward a prairie dog, it will give a single-note call. This single-note call for a human is acoustically different in structure to the single note that prairie dogs give for a diving hawk. Also, when a human appears, usually only a single prairie dog gives an alarm call. In contrast, when a coyote or a domestic dog appears, many prairie dogs call simultaneously. And, the faster the coyote or dog is traveling, the closer together the barks are. This means that there are multiple sources of information about the type and behavior of the different predators that are attacking the prairie dogs.

When we start putting all these items of information together, it appears as though the prairie dogs have something like a grammar. They have parts of their calls that are noun-like: human, coyote, dog, hawk. They also have parts that are adjective-like: yellow, blue, green, big, small. And they have verb-like and adverb-like parts: running fast, walking slowly. These parts can be recombined in different ways, depending on the identity of the predator, the physical description, and the speed of travel.

Another surprise was that the prairie dogs can also describe novel objects that they have never seen before. We found this out by doing a series of experiments using plywood cutouts. We used three types of cutouts, each painted black: an oval silhouette, a coyote silhouette, and a skunk silhouette. The coyote and skunk silhouettes were life-sized, and the oval was the size of the coyote. As you have seen from our results with humans and dogs, prairie dogs can pick up individual differences of size, shape, and color. With the silhouettes, we wanted to make sure that we didn't have such differences. Each silhouette was concealed behind camouflage material, and then was pulled out from behind the material by a set of pulleys across about a third of the diameter of the colony. We then recorded the alarm calls. Each silhouette resulted in its own type of alarm call. The coyote silhouette produced a call that was similar to, but not exactly like, a real coyote. This was not surprising, since the silhouette was two dimensional, and real coyotes come in three dimensions, with more realistic coat colors than jet black.

More surprising, however, was that the oval silhouette produced an entirely new kind of call. There aren't any oval silhouettes creeping through prairie dog colonies waiting to pounce on a prairie dog, so the animals would not have had a chance to develop a call for such a strange item. Instead, they seemed to reach into their store of descriptive labels, a vocabulary in their brain, and use that to put together a description of a completely novel thing that they had never seen before.

Another species of prairie dog, the black-tailed, has a call that has been described as a "jump-yip." Black-tailed prairie dogs (*Cynomys ludovicianus*) are slightly bigger than the Gunnison's prairie dogs, and have a black tip on their tail, unlike the Gunnison's, who have a white tip. Black-tailed prairie dogs live in the western Midwest states, from south-central Canada to Texas.

The prairie dog making the jump-yip call stands up on its hind legs, stretches up its front legs, arches its back, and produces a piercing yip call that sounds something like, "Whoeeep!" The call is contagious. When one animal gives this call, others stand up and give it, one after the other, kind of like a wave at a football game. I have seen some black-tailed prairie dogs get so excited about giving this call that they stretched out as far up as they could toward the sky with their front paws, arched their back, gave the call . . . and fell over backward. They then got up, looked around to see if anyone saw them, and seemed to pretend that nothing happened.

No one knows why black-tailed prairie dogs give the jump-yip calls. A lot of times they do it when nothing seems to be happening in the colony. But sometimes they give the call when a predator has just left, or when a territorial dispute breaks out. The acoustic structure of the jump-yips for the different contexts has not been analyzed, so there may be different kinds of jump-yips. But one context in which they give this call is in response to snakes. There seem to be some differences in the structure of the jump-yip with different snakes—more venomous snakes such as rattlesnakes produce more bark-like jump-yips than nonvenomous snakes such as gopher snakes. In prairie dog country, a common way to know whether a snake is dangerous is to look at the shape of the head. Rattlesnakes, which can kill prairie dogs with their venom, have triangular heads, while nondangerous snakes that are too slow to catch a rapidly moving prairie dog have cone-shaped heads. We don't know for sure at this point whether prairie dogs can tell different snakes apart, but my guess is that they can. Remember, to a ground squirrel who stands less than a foot tall, the head of a rattlesnake is about the same size as a soccer ball is to us. I would be willing to bet that prairie dogs can tell the difference between a venomous rattlesnake and a harmless gopher snake, because those who couldn't see the difference probably didn't survive long enough to tell the tale to their kids.

In addition to the jump-yips, the black-tailed prairie dogs have the same kind of complex alarm calls as the Gunnison's prairie dogs. We learned this from some experiments in Texas, doing the same kind of experiments that we did with the Gunnison's prairie dogs in Arizona. Not surprisingly, the call structure of the alarm barks changed according to the size, shape, and color of clothes of the people used in the experiments. There was one new wrinkle, however. In these experiments, when one person fired a shotgun, the prairie dogs produced a distinctly different call for that individual person after he fired the gun. This call was different from the one that the prairie dogs made for that person before he shot the gun, as if they tacked onto their call some information about how potentially dangerous he now was to the animals.

NO TIME TO CALL

Other ground squirrels do not seem to have as complex a communication system. Or, maybe it's just that no one has found such a system yet—more investigation might show that they, too, have similar complexity. A number of the ground squirrels and one species of tree squirrel have two different kinds of alarm calls, one for aerial predators and another for terrestrial. The acoustic structure of the call for aerial predators is usually different from the structure of the call for terrestrial ones. The aerial predator call has been described as a sharp, short yelp, while the terrestrial predator call has been described as a long trill.

One hypothesis for why there are two kinds of calls has been called *response urgency*. The idea here is that some predators, such as aerial ones like hawks and eagles, attack with such speed that the animal making the alarm call doesn't have enough time to produce a long call. It simply has time to yell, "Aargh!," and then the hawk is right there on its doorstep. Remember my experience with the rattlesnake. Other predators, such as coyotes, are visible for a long time as they approach the squirrels, and so the animals have a lot of time in which to call. So, according to this hypothesis, they have the luxury of producing meaningless wails of fright over a long period of time.

But this fails to explain why the animals have two acoustically different types of calls for the different predators. If it were merely a matter of fright, as well as solely response urgency, then we might expect only one type of call, given as a short, sharp single note for aerial predators, and as a series of the same short, sharp notes repeated over and over for terrestrial predators, where there was more time to express fear of the approaching predator.

The calling patterns of the animals producing the alarm calls can give others information about the whereabouts of a predator. Richardson's ground squirrels (*Urocitellus richardsonii*) that live in Canada can provide information about the flight path of an aerial predator. When an aerial predator flies over the colony, multiple animals give the aerial predator call. Because each animal's voice is distinct from all of the other animals' voices, at least to other squirrels, in the same way that our voices are distinctive, other animals in the colony can get an idea of the direction in which the predator is flying by listening to the calls of the different animals who are in the flight path of the approaching raptor.

Some of the ground squirrels, such as the marmots (*Marmota flaviventris*), do appear to use only one sound as their predator call. Marmots tend to live in mountainous country at higher elevations. Not too long ago some friends and I were hiking along an old mining trail in a mountainous region of south central Colorado when we came across a few marmots. I wanted to record their alarm calls, but to do so we would have had to walk across a ravine and up a steep, rocky slope covered with loose rocks. At elevations of ten thousand feet or more, it becomes something of a challenge to run down a ravine and up a steep hillside just to get a marmot to give an alarm call, and none of us was willing to volunteer. Fortunately, my friends had Iris, their female Jack Russell terrier with them, who was willing to do anything and go anywhere. If you have ever had any experience with Jack Russell terriers, you know that they seem to be wired up to a high-energy battery that never quits. They're always on the go. We tried to get the dog to run toward the marmots, but she was too interested in all of the smells that were along the old mining trail. Then a marmot gave an alarm call. Iris was off like a flash. She ran straight for where the marmot was, and then ran all around the area while several nearby marmots were calling out their alarm. I got some great recordings that day. When Iris was far away from the marmots, they called quite frequently, but as she got closer to the animals, they called less and less until finally they stopped calling altogether when she was practically on top of them.

As predicted by the response-urgency hypothesis, several studies have shown that marmots seem to produce fewer calls when they are in a high-risk situation, and more calls when they are in a low-risk situation. Marmots typically produce anywhere between one and twenty chirps within an alarm call. The number of chirps is not related to the type of predator, but rather to the perception of risk by each individual animal. Most of the time, since aerial predators are more of a risk than terrestrial ones, this leads the marmots to produce a single chirp to flying predators, and multiple chirps to terrestrial ones.

One of the ground squirrels, the eastern chipmunk (*Tamias striatus*), combines calls that contain information with calls that express fear. This chipmunk produces three types of calls when it interacts with a predator: a chipping call, a series of high-frequency notes given when it detects an aerial predator; a chucking call, a series of lower-frequency notes given when it detects a terrestrial predator; and a trill, a low-amplitude multinote call given only once as it is running away from the predator. The chipping and the chucking call contain information about the different predators, aerial or terrestrial, and the trill is an expression of the animal's fear as it runs to escape.

Another ground dweller, the meerkat (*Suricata suricatta*), also has distinctly different calls for terrestrial and aerial predators. Meerkats are about the same size as prairie dogs and live in large family groups in East Africa, where they are preyed upon by eagles, hawks, and a variety of terrestrial predators. A family usually lives in an abandoned termite mound, which in Africa can be a huge structure rising four or five feet above the ground. The meerkats live and sleep inside tunnels within the mound, and go off looking for insects and other small prey, just like the prairie dogs leave their burrows and go off looking for grass and flowers to eat. Like prairie dogs, meerkats can stand up on their hind legs and watch for anything that they might consider to be dangerous. When a meerkat spots a predator it gives either an aerial or terrestrial alarm call, depending on the type of predator that it saw, and all of the other meerkats living in that group take appropriate evasive action. Meerkats also incorporate response urgency into their calls, providing information to other animals about the immediacy of the response that is required. Here we have a clear combination of motivational factors, such as fear of the predator, combined with referential factors, such as a description of the type of predator. Meerkats and chipmunks show that alarm calls don't necessarily have to have either motivational or referential communication. Instead, they can easily have both, just like I can yell, "Black mamba!" with fear in my voice.

WHEN BIRDSONGS BECOME ALARMING

Bird alarm calls have also been assumed to be expressions of fear, rather than calls that contain any information about a potential predator. Often, when detecting a predator, songbirds produce a vocalization that has been termed the *seet* call, because it is a relatively high frequency, almost pure tone that sounds like *seet*. This was assumed to be a good call for the birds to give, because it was assumed that predators of songbirds, such as hawks and owls, could not locate the bird making the call very easily. The logic of this was based on our own human abilities. We have a difficult time locating the origin of high-pitched pure tones.

Next time you hear a cricket chirping, try to find it quickly. Although crickets don't produce pure tones in their chirps, the frequency band is narrow enough so that the sound has, to our ears, a ventriloquistic quality. We can't find its source very readily. One time I was in a shopping mall that was completely enclosed in a large building. I sat down on a bench next to some plastic vegetation modeled after some indeterminate species of plant and heard a cricket chirping from the base of the fake vegetation. I tried to find it, but try as I might I could not locate it. So I got down on my hands and knees and started looking around for where the cricket might be hiding. Other people stopped and asked what I was doing. I told them I was looking for the cricket that was chirping. Some people helpfully got down on their hands and knees and also started rummaging around near the base of the plant to see if they could flush out the cricket.

But no cricket was to be found. I started explaining to the people around me about the ventriloquistic aspect of cricket calls and how difficult it is to locate the source of the calling cricket. Around that time my hand ran across a small, half-buried speaker in the dirt near the plastic vegetation. As I brought my ear close to the speaker, I heard the speaker making the chirping sounds. *Oops!* Apparently, to enhance the experience of fake nature, cricket sounds were played back through speakers around the mall. That cleared up the question in my mind of how a cricket could survive in such artificial surroundings. It did not, however, endear me to all of the other people who were on hands and knees helping me find the cricket, when I explained what was actually making the noise.

After the idea of the seet call had been proposed and accepted by the scientific community, someone decided to see if hawks and owls really could not locate the origin of the seet sounds very accurately. A series of experiments showed that both goshawks and barn owls could turn their heads toward the source of a seet call with considerable accuracy. Not all hawks and falcons seem to be equally good at locating the seet sounds, so perhaps the birds gain a small measure of protection from some predatory species.

Typically, the behavior of other birds, even different species, is to freeze on the ground or in a bush when they hear a seet call. Some birds exploit this freezing behavior through a form of deception. In Europe, in the wintertime, food such as seeds are difficult to come by, particularly during snowstorms. When great tits are feeding on a concentrated food source and are displaced by more aggressive sparrows, they sometimes give false alarm calls. These calls cause the sparrows to leave the seeds and fly into a bush where they freeze, allowing the great tits to pick up as many seeds as possible before the sparrows realize that there isn't any predator in sight and come back to feed.

Many birds have another type of alarm call, the mobbing call. Unlike the seet call, the mobbing call is not a mostly pure tone, but is a broad spectrum of tones, and has a harsh, rasping quality to it. When a bird gives a mobbing call, other birds fly to the area where the call was given, and if there is a predator there, all the birds start to attack or mob the predator. A hawk can easily kill a single bird, but when it has to deal with ten or more birds buzzing around, it quickly leaves. Mobbing calls are often given by nesting birds as a way of summoning help when a nest is under attack.

As I was writing these words, I heard some mobbing calls outside my window. We have some Say's phoebes (*Sayornis saya*) raising little chicks in a nest perched on an outdoor light fixture next to our front door. The chicks have gradually been growing larger and larger as the parents have been bringing in a constant stream of insects that they caught from who knows where. I marvel at the variety of insects the birds catch, most of which I never see outside a bird's beak. We have been watching the chicks like proud parents, waiting for the day when they take flight. But, like human empty nesters, this will also bring us freedom, because while the chicks are growing, we don't want to disturb them and so we use the garage door rather than the front door. We are eagerly waiting for our chance to use the front door again.

The rasp of mobbing calls was very distinctive. I got up and went outside. There were the two parents, the Say's phoebes, sitting on a nearby branch and screeching their lungs out. There was also a house finch that was nesting in a nearby cactus, also calling. And sitting on a nearby bush, the target of all of these calls, was a huge raven. The raven had evidently planned on flying up to the nest and snatching one or more of the nestlings. Like a parent chasing off bullies who were about to beat up his little kid, I yelled at the raven and ran toward him. The raven flew off to another nearby bush with a "you've got to be kidding" sort of languor. I yelled and ran at the raven again. This time the raven decided that a few nestlings weren't worth the trouble when faced with an obviously deranged human, and flew off to try his fortune hunting somewhere else.

At one time, biologists thought that the structure of the mobbing call was pretty much the same across a number of different bird species, so that a bird hearing the call would respond to it even if it was given by another species of bird, because the call was the same as that given by members of its own species. However, once people started to look at the structure of the mobbing calls, they realized that the calls were different for each species, with different sound frequencies making up each species' calls, even though they superficially looked the same. Now it appears that birds can learn the mobbing calls of other species, and learn to associate the mobbing call with the presence of a predator that can attack them.

The mobbing calls of black-capped chickadees (*Poecile atricapillus*) are particularly complex. These calls are produced by the birds when they see a raptor who is perching. The call consists of a "chick" part and a "dee" part. The "chick" part has one or more of each of three syllables, labeled by convention as A, B, and C, and the "dee" part has one or more repetitions of the same one syllable, labeled by convention as D. One study analyzed the D syllable's acoustic properties while the birds were giving mobbing calls to different-sized predators, such as gyrfalcons, peregrine falcons, Cooper's hawks, and pygmy owls and found that there was a direct correlation between the number of D syllables in the call and the body length and wingspread of the aerial predator. Another study with a related species, the Carolina chickadee (*Poecile carolinensis*), showed that these birds produce more "chick" calls when they see a larger predator, such as a red-tailed hawk, and more "dee" calls when they see a smaller predator, such as an eastern screech owl. Conceptually, this is similar to the descriptive information that prairie dogs provide about the size, shape, and color of a potential predator.

As with the ground squirrels, some birds have calls for both aerial and terrestrial predators. The chicken (*Gallus gallus*) is one example. In many cultures around the world, chickens lead a semiwild existence and are attacked by both hawks and terrestrial predators. They also have a variety of other calls. From 1942 through the 1970s and 1980s, the San Diego

Zoo had a lot of semiwild jungle fowl, close relatives of domestic chickens, living on the zoo grounds. Researchers recorded the calls of these jungle fowl in different contexts and found that there were twenty or more different vocalizations, including alarm calls. At the time, the fowl could be seen everywhere around the zoo, and it was fun for visitors to try to interact with the birds. The fowl did not seem to mind people, letting little kids get up close before proudly walking off behind some fence where the kids couldn't follow. Sadly, when I visited the zoo this year, I found the jungle fowl to be gone.

Studies of chickens caged in outdoor aviaries showed that they had different calls for aerial and terrestrial predators. The aerial alarm calls were given for hawks, crows, vultures, and blue jays. The terrestrial calls were given mostly for humans walking by the aviaries where the chickens were housed. This highlighted a problem. Because the calls were collected while the chickens were in an outdoor aviary, the chickens could have been responding to some factor other than the aerial or terrestrial predator—possibly to simple motion, or to the speed with which the predator passed by the cage, or to the size of an image on their visual field, or to the relative closeness of the predator to them.

To solve this dilemma, experimenters designed a way in which chickens could watch predators on a television monitor. They projected computer-generated images of a soaring raptor and a raccoon, and recorded the alarm calls produced by the chickens for each of these images. They then played back the calls of the males to female chickens. The aerial-call playbacks produced crouching down and looking up, an entirely appropriate behavior for a chicken receiving information about the presence of a soaring hawk. The terrestrial calls produced an erect vigilant posture, as though the chickens were trying to see the whereabouts of a terrestrial predator.

The chickens, however, were not labeling specific predators, but were labeling the mode of attack of the predator. When the experimenters made the computer-generated raccoon seem to fly through the air, the chickens gave an aerial alarm call, suggesting that they did not necessarily recognize the raccoon as a specific predator, but just saw it as something that is flying through the air and might be a potential predator.

MONKEY SEE, MONKEY SPEAK

There has long been a persistent belief that if we are to find the origins of human language in other animals, we will find these origins among primates, because primates are most closely related to us in evolutionary time. When I talk about my work with prairie dogs, people are always surprised that a lowly rodent can have such a complicated language. These same people probably would not be surprised to find that some primates have complicated alarm calls.

Just like the chickens and ground squirrels, some primates have calls for aerial and terrestrial predators. Two species of lemurs living in Madagascar, the ring-tailed lemur (*Lemur catta*) and Verreaux's sifaka (*Propithecus sifaka*), have different calls for raptors and for terrestrial predators. Although the two species have overlapping ranges, the calls of each species to the two categories of predators are acoustically different. In playbacks of the two kinds of calls, both the ringtails and the sifakas look upward when they hear their own species' call for a raptor, and run up into a tree when they hear their call for a terrestrial predator. Interestingly enough, a free-living population of ring-tailed lemurs in Madagascar can recognize the two different calls given by sifakas, but a captive population of ring-tailed lemurs in Japan could not tell the difference in the calls of the sifakas when they were played back to captive lemurs. This of course raises the question: Did the ring-tailed lemurs in the wild learn the call of the sifakas, and did the captive population lose the recognition of the call because they had no sifakas to listen to? My guess is, yes.

Similarly, like the prairie dogs, some species of primates can provide information about the categories of predators. Vervet monkeys (*Chlorocebus pygerythrus*) are the best-known example among the primates. Vervets live in east Africa, in grassland savannas punctuated by acacias and other trees. They are preyed upon by a variety of predators, just like the prairie dogs. And, like the prairie dogs, they are social. However, unlike the prairie dogs, they travel around in small groups, so they come across a variety of predators by chance. Among the predators that they encounter are eagles, leopards, and pythons (snakes). When they see these predators, they give alarm calls. Studies have found that the vervets have different calls for each of the above predators: one call for eagles, another call for leopards, and a third call for pythons.

After I read about the vervet studies, I decided to go and see the monkeys for myself. I drove from Nairobi to Lake Nakuru in Kenya, where there was a large troop of vervets around the lake. Lake Nakuru is huge. Where the vervets live, there are large acacia trees that cast their shade on grassy meadows. Nearby are granite cliffs that rise for hundreds of feet from the edge of the lake. At the base of these cliffs a population of baboons would go by on the road every morning, making their presence known from a large distance by their constant yelling and squabbling. Baboons are as noisy as teenagers at a mall.

In the acacia trees lurk leopards, whose favorite food is monkey. In the grass lurk pythons, whose favorite food is also monkey. And in the air lurk eagles, whose favorite food happens to be . . . did you guess it? Monkey.

I camped in the grass underneath the acacia trees, pitching my two tents in the soft earth. That evening, I was startled by hearing the cries of one or more leopards. A leopard cry is a rasping whining sound, sort of like a combination of a chainsaw and a whistle. My field assistant, a Kenyan, was so frightened by the leopard cries that he insisted that we sleep in the truck all night. I refused. He got in the truck and locked the doors. Although big cats do sometimes munch on people, humans do not seem to be a preferred food. Most of the time cats will attack people only when they are starving, possibly because people taste bad. Sometimes, big cats will learn that people are easy pickings: the lions of Tsavo in Kenya would go into the tents of railroad workers at the beginning of the past century, grab a person and haul him off to eat for dinner. However, this seems to be an acquired taste, kind of like eating stinky cheese. Around people these days, even in the wilds of Kenya, cats that munch on humans usually don't have much chance to acquire the taste before some hunter shoots them.

The following morning I woke up with leopard tracks around the two tents. My assistant seemed to be surprised that I was still alive, but despite my having been unmolested, would not come out of the truck. This soon presented a problem. The acacias around Nakuru have long defensive spikes on their branches, spikes that can instantly puncture a tire. This is why I traveled in my Toyota truck with four tires strapped to the roof. It's not unusual to have all four of your tires punctured simultaneously by the acacia spikes, and without four spares, you are up the proverbial creek.

When I got up that morning, I saw that the right front tire had gone flat during the night. I needed my assistant to help me get a tire down from the roof, jack up the truck, and put on the new tire. He would not budge. He told me that some leopards are really shamans who take on animal form and can cast a spell on people, causing people to die of horrible stomach pains. His own father died this way, he said, after encountering a shaman in leopard form. I might be immune because I was not African, my assistant said, but he was certainly not immune.

Finally, after much pleading and cajoling, he consented to get out of the car and help me. I think the telling point was my saying that if he didn't help, I would stay there for a week or longer, as the truck was full of food and water and I had all of the camping supplies that I needed. If he helped, however, we would look at the vervets and leave.

Tire changed, I drove out to find the vervets, my assistant in the back seat. They were in a small troop about a mile from my camp. I drove slowly up to the monkeys. It was already stifling hot, with the temperature over 100 degrees and fairly high humidity. Our clothes were sticking to us, and sweat was pouring down my face. I tried to let in a little bit of a breeze by keeping my window open. As I drove up to a female vervet who was sitting under an acacia tree with her little baby, I was startled to see her start to run toward my truck. She leaped into the open window, brushed past my head, ran into the back of the truck, rummaged around for about a minute while my assistant and I sat there open mouthed and not knowing what to do, and then ran past me again holding a box of crackers that she had found among my supplies. Once out of the car, she ran up to her baby, dug into the box with her hand, took out a couple of crackers, and mom and baby settled down to have lunch while watching the antics of the tourists.

But predators are serious business for the monkeys. The

experimenters who studied the monkeys played back each type of alarm call, and the monkeys did different things. When an eagle call was played back, the monkeys ran up into an acacia tree and to the center of the tree where the eagle would have a difficult time getting at them because of all the branches on the outside of the tree that would be in the way. When a leopard call was played back, the monkeys also ran up into a tree, but now they ran to the periphery of the tree, where the branches were thin. These branches could support the weight of a monkey, but not the weight of a heavier leopard, so the leopard had a difficult time getting at the monkeys. When a snake call was played back, the monkeys generally stood up on their hind legs and scanned around, apparently trying to identify the location of the snake.

The scientists tried to find out how much the monkeys understood about the different calls. Were the monkeys merely responding out of fear, and just happened to have three different fear-related calls? Or, were they aware that they were calling to try to warn other monkeys? The researchers tried to address this by playing back calls of different monkeys, using a technique called habituation-dishabituation.

In learning theory, habituation is a simple sort of learning that occurs whenever there is a constant stimulus always present in the environment. The nervous system learns to filter out this constant stimulus, so that after a while the animal is no longer aware that the stimulus is there. As I sit writing these words on a hot summer day, there is a constant noise of an air-conditioning fan whirring in the background. Much of the time, I am not aware of this noise—my nervous system has filtered out the noise through habituation. If something about the noise changes—i.e., the fan gets a sudden, harsh-grinding sound—then I would be instantly aware of that sound, as well as the whirring noise of the fan, through dishabituation. This principle of habituation extends to any situation in which animals or humans become used to something, so that it no longer bothers them. People who study animals in the wild can often get relatively close to the animals because the animals habituate to the people, and are not bothered by them as long as nothing about the situation changes.

In the habituation-dishabituation experiments, the researchers played back a previously recorded individual monkey's call in response to a leopard, multiple times whenever the leopard was no longer present. After several playbacks, the other monkeys tended to ignore that particular alarm call—the caller had become unreliable. When a leopard call from a different monkey was broadcast, however, the monkeys all ran into trees and out to the periphery of the branches. This suggested that the monkeys could identify the calls of specific individuals and assess whether those calls contained useful information. When we had the "little-boy-who-cried-wolf" call from a particular monkey, the other monkeys learned to ignore that individual's cries, but not the same cries from other individuals. From this, the researchers deduced that the monkeys are not merely calling out of some internally generated fear while other monkeys are responding through some hardwired instinctive program (although fear may be a component of what the monkeys feel when they see a leopard), but are calling in an attempt to convey meaningful information to other fellow monkeys.

Similarly, work with Diana monkeys (*Cercopithecus diana*) and Campbell's monkeys (*Cercopithecus campbelli*) in the Ivory Coast of Africa has shown that these monkeys have distinct calls for eagles and for leopards. A series of playback experiments showed that both the Diana and Campbell's monkeys respond to the predator category of the call, rather than to the distance that the predator is from the caller (the way that some ground squirrels respond with a single chirp to a predator that is near them, but with a trill to a predator that is farther away), or the height of a predator (the way that chickens respond with an aerial call to anything that is above them or a terrestrial call to anything that is level with them). Each species of monkey has its own acoustically distinct calls, but both the Campbell's and Diana monkeys can recognize each other's alarm calls and give their own alarm calls in response. For example, if a Campbell's monkey hears the alarm call of a Diana monkey for a leopard, it will give its own acoustically distinct leopard call.

Campbell's monkeys have a modifier in their alarm calls that stands for less dangerous situations. If, for example, they see an eagle and perceive that the eagle is not an imminent threat, they will produce an eagle alarm call, but preface that with a pair of loud "boom" sounds. In effect this is like having an adjective precede a noun. And Diana monkeys have learned this rule. When they hear a Campbell's monkey alarm call that is preceded by a pair of "boom" sounds, they do not give their own alarm calls in response. They have learned that the syntax of the Campbell's monkey alarm call is important.

Campbell's monkeys can also use an aspect of human grammar called *affixation* to modify the meaning of their calls. In human speech, adding a suffix to a word or word stem can change the meaning of that word. This process is called affixation. For example, we can add the suffix "hood" to the word "mother" to change the meaning of "mother" to "motherhood." The alarm calls of the male Campbell's monkeys have two parts: a beginning, and an ending that acts like a suffix. This suffix can change the meaning of a call. By adding the suffix, an eagle call can become a call meaning that there is some kind of general disturbance related to birds, or a leopard call can become a general alert call.

WHAT'S YOUR ALARM SIGN?

While we are starting to know something about the language-like properties of acoustic alarm signals, we know almost nothing about the linguistic properties of visual signals. We know that visual signals are frequently used in human communication. American Sign Language (ASL) has a grammatical structure as well as semantic content, although for years linguists argued that ASL did not have enough of the criteria to qualify it as a language. But among animals it is very difficult to decode the semantic nature of visual signals, and even if we could do that, it is very difficult to replicate the signals in the same way that acoustic playbacks can be done.

Many times, I have seen prairie dogs standing up in an alert posture on their hind legs when they see something that alarms them. They don't just stand up in a smooth motion, but instead stand up in a very jerky fashion, rising partway up, hesitating for a fraction of a second, then rising up again, hesitating again, until finally stretching out their body full-length, standing on their hind legs. I am guessing that this is some kind of visual signal that may very well have the same kind of semantic meaning that the acoustic alarm calls have, but quantifying the differences in posture as well as displaying those differences to other prairie dogs in order to get a predictable response is next to impossible.

SOMETHING SMELLS ALARMING

Just as we don't know very much about visual signals, we know very little about the linguistic properties of chemical signals. Perhaps because our language is an acoustic one, and because we aren't very good at consciously smelling odors, we tend to be somewhat at sea in dealing with *pheromones*, the chemical signals that animals send out to influence and provide information to other animals. In my local mall, there is a department store with an entrance that walks you past all of the perfumes. When I walk in, I am swamped by many different odors coming from a lot of different tester bottles and from a lot of different people trying out different perfumes. But if there is an odor that I particularly like, I am completely unable to describe it. I simply don't have any words for it. If it were a color, I could perhaps come up with something like "mauve." I still don't know what this color is, but if I tell my wife that the shirt is mauve, she knows exactly what I mean. But I lack the mauve equivalent when it comes to describing odors. We all do. We humans aren't very good at it, although some people who taste wine or use their nose for food preparation can get better at describing odors than most of us. For a long time, we didn't even know how much of a role odors were playing in our lives.

On a descriptive level we know that many insects use pheromones for communication, including sending signals of alarm. But we don't know very much about whether those signals have semantic content or a grammar. Among the animals that produce chemical alarm signals, we know the most about honeybees, because honeybees are very important to us economically, pollinating perhaps more than 70 percent of the fruits and vegetables that we regularly include in our diet. Without honeybees our diet would be bland indeed.

My house in the Arizona desert is a place where many animals share my living space. I mentioned the Say's phoebes previously, nesting on top of the lamp at our front door. Large harvester ants have nests that open up in the cracks of the concrete near the garage door, so that we have to step around them as we walk to and fro. Sometimes they swarm, a surefire indication that a storm with lots of rain is on the way. When we are able to turn on the front porch light—when no birds are nesting there—a lot of insects are attracted to the lights, along with a couple of resident bark scorpions that come to eat the bugs. These scorpions are potentially dangerous. Their sting has a neurotoxin that can be fatal to people. One night my wife and I arrived from a shopping trip with a rolla-way cooler stocked with ice and things that we bought at the grocery store. As I was unloading other groceries, my wife was wheeling the cooler into the house. I heard her scream, and arrived on the scene to watch her and a bark scorpion rac-ing each other to see who got into the front door first. She won.

A couple of summers ago, some honeybees found a crack in the roof tiles. Enterprising bees must have discovered that this crack let them have access to the attic, and so an entire hive moved in and set up shop. Soon the bees were coming and going. As long as they left us alone, we were willing to leave them alone. All of the honeybees were pretty good-natured. When we walked past that part of the house, they would casually fly past us, checking us out, but otherwise were unconcerned.

Last summer, things changed. The first thing that I noticed was that the bees were flying really fast. The typical Euro-pean honeybee (*Apis mellifera*) lumbers along, flying slowly, looking like a cargo plane that is struggling to get up into the air because it is overloaded. These new bees zipped. I thought: *This is bad.* When I was doing fieldwork in Africa, I would sit quietly at my field site watching hyraxes and record their vo-calizations as the males gave territorial calls that announced their claim to their piece of real estate, a rock pile called a *kopje*, that had a dominant male, several females, and all of their young. Each male had his own distinctive voice, and each one let loose with volley after volley of screams around sunup and sundown, letting all the other males on other rock piles know that there was no point in trying to move to better turf, because the rock pile was occupied and any intruder would have a fight on his hands. As I sat there with my recorder humming, an African honeybee (*Apis mellifera scutellata*) would often come to check me out. These bees flew really fast. They would come barreling in and hover an inch in front of my nose, smelling me and assessing my level of threat to their colony. I had to be very, very still, because African bees are very short-tempered, and if they get mad, they let out alarm pheromones that call all of their hive mates, who gladly give up their lives stinging the creature that irritated one of their hive members. Drop for drop, honeybee venom is more toxic than rattlesnake venom, so this was serious business.

This crop of bees at my house acted like the African bees that I had seen before. I knew that Africanized bees were moving from southern Arizona into the central desert where I live, so I suspected that somehow these bees displaced the docile bees with whom I had happily shared my roof. Soon these bees were buzzing my car, slamming themselves against the windshield, and flying in circles around my head. I knew that it was only a matter of time before my wife and I got stung, and if that happened, hundreds of bees would respond to the alarm pheromones by swarming out of the hive, each intent on stinging us. This was not a happy thought.

I didn't want to hurt the bees, so I called a local beekeeper who said on the phone that he could collect the queen and most of the hive to relocate them to one of his hive boxes that he kept on his property. He came out, put on a bee suit, got out a ladder, and said that he would check out the hive. As he came to the door, he looked like some alien from space, with a heavy canvas hood and metal mesh around his face, heavy canvas covering his entire body, and thick gloves that made his hands look twice their normal size. I told him that I had to go to a meeting in an hour, and would there be any problem about my leaving. He assured me that the bees would quickly settle down after he removed the queen, and I had nothing to worry about.

Half an hour later, there was a knock on the front door. Our door consists of two parts. There is an outer screen door and an inner wooden door. When the weather is balmy, we can open the wooden door and leave the screen door closed, so that we can get in the desert breezes while at the same time keeping out the bevy of desert flies, wasps, beetles, and scorpions that seem to relish the thought of living inside the house. I opened the wooden door and looked out through the screen. Standing there was the beekeeper, surrounded by perhaps five hundred bees that were flinging themselves at his bee suit, stinging the heavy canvas and falling to the ground, dead. He was very apologetic. He suggested that it would probably not be a good idea to go out right now. In fact, he continued, it would be a good idea to not go out at all that day, and it would also be a good idea to call up all of the neighbors and tell them to stay inside until nightfall.

He explained that this was definitely an Africanized bee colony, and was the most aggressive that he had ever seen. He could do nothing for us. The bees were too aggressive to keep in hive boxes, and we would have to find some other way of taking care of this colony. As what seemed like thousands of bees flew in a huge swarm around the entire house, I watched him getting into his car and swatting at the twenty or thirty bees that managed to slip inside the car with him as he rapidly slid in the door. He drove off, still swatting and driving somewhat erratically as the bees flung themselves at his head.

The bees kept us prisoners inside our house for twenty-four hours. Even at night, when I thought that they might have settled down and gone inside their hive, I would flip on the porch light, only to see an angry swarm of bees converging on the light, with hundreds more flitting like dim shadows just within the limits of my perception. The next day the bees were up before we were. Time had not modified their desire to sting whoever had disturbed their colony. As we watched from our windows, clouds of bees flew around and around our house, like runners on an endless track or hamsters running on a wheel. Such is the power of the alarm pheromones that the bees put out that it must have still been lingering, potently exciting the bees into a continual frenzy.

I remembered a conversation that I had with Justin Schmidt, an African bee expert then at the Carl Hayden USDA Bee Laboratory in Tucson, Arizona. I had told Justin that I was worried about Africanized bees because I was out in the field a lot, and what could I do if I encountered a swarm of bees when I was out by myself. I had thought of perhaps taking a raincoat or maybe a plastic tarp so that I could cover myself quickly in case the bees attacked me. Justin nixed that idea. He pointed out that the bees are very persistent and hang around for hours. There would be no way that I could stay under the tarp long enough for the bees to give up and go away. Also, Justin pointed out, the bees are so persistent that they would search for any openings in the tarp and come through those to sting me. I would need some air, and any air holes would be highways for angry bees. Now I was watching the persistence that Justin described.

While producing alarm pheromones in response to a disturbance seems like mindless stuff, mere stimulus-response, there is much more to the story. Honeybees have at least twenty different chemical compounds that mediate the defensive response. Five of these chemicals help the guard bees, who are flying around the entrance to the hive watching for any signs of a disturbance, produce a warning that gets other bees inside the hive to come out to the hive entrance. Once there, two other chemicals cause the bees to fly up out of the hive in a swarm. These two are produced in different parts of a honeybee's body. One chemical, isopentyl acetate (IPA), is produced in cells associated with the stinger. The other, 2-Heptanone, is produced in glands associated with the mandibles. And it turns out that the relative concentrations of these chemicals help the bees flying out of the hive determine what to do. Low concentrations of IPA and 2-Heptanone tell the bees that they should attack. However, low concentrations of IPA and high concentrations of 2-Heptanone tell the bees that they should fly out, but not attack.

The different chemical pheromones act as words for the honeybees, conveying semantic meaning as to the kind of response that is required. By varying the concentrations of the chemicals, the bees can give each other precise information about the kind and magnitude of the defense that they have to mount against an attacker, just the same way that we use adjectives and adverbs to modify the meaning of our words. With a lexicon of twenty chemical words and a large number of modifiers in the form of the concentration of each chemical, the bees can convey subtleties of information about hive defense that we cannot even begin to imagine. But because we do not rely so much on odor, it is sometimes hard for us to appreciate the precision of the information conveyed by such pheromones.

Ultimately, much to my regret, I had to get a pest control operator to come out and kill the bees. I was really sorry to do this, but after watching the display with the beekeeper, I knew that I would be putting my life—and my wife's—in the hands of bees who thought that they owned the place and saw no reason for anyone to disturb their home. In fact, because bees die when they sting someone, they were willing to die for their home. I wasn't willing to make the same sacrifice.

WARNING CALLS AND THE DISCOURSE SYSTEM

Even though warning signals might be very short bursts of sound, or short visual signals, or a rapid release of chemical odors, there is a considerable amount of information contained in them. As we have seen, there is semantic information labeling predators and giving information about context. The messages can contain multiple levels of meaning, and the way that the messages are assembled provides a glimpse of syntax. These messages also contain what linguists sometimes call *computational efficiency*, or what is the simplest and most efficient way to say something. As part of the Discourse System, these messages are directly affected by Natural Selection: The animals that fail to receive a message and act accordingly are caught and eaten by predators.

My thinking is that Natural Selection pushed hard on the development of the Discourse System for use in warning of potential danger. Imagine you are a prairie dog out in the open, away from the shelter and safety of your burrow, and you look up and see a giant predator approaching. To a prairie dog, a coyote must look as large and looming as a Tyrannosaurus Rex. This must strike fear in the heart of the prairie dog, and the easiest thing, especially if the coyote hadn't noticed it yet, would be to run to the safety of the burrow and stay there. But adult prairie dogs don't do that. I instead, they give an alarm call to alert relatives and neighbors in the colony. It's a risk, because calling attracts attention to themselves. But often, many other prairie dogs join in, only breaking to run for their burrows when the coyote is very near.

In this situation, here is how Natural Selection works on the Discourse System: First, evolution selects for prairie dogs to have good distance vision to see approaching danger. Evolution also shapes the prairie dog's Discourse System by selecting for the development of a good set of lungs that can project a call so loud it can be heard half a mile away. Then, the prairie dog's brain contains the toolbox of possible calls that are within its repertoire, and the ability to decide which information to encode into a call (remember that not just predator type is encoded; other descriptors such as coloring and rate of approach are included, too). And then, other prairie dogs who hear the alarm must decode it and then decide which evasive move to make to escape predation. The amazing result of fierce selective pressure to cram the most vital information into a series of short barks is an elegant and effective example of computational efficiency.

5. WHAT'S FOR DINNER?

A few years ago I was giving a talk in Morocco at a conference on the biology and behavior of rodents. After the conference, my Moroccan host invited my wife and me to dinner at his parents' house.

Their home was traditional Moroccan. Beautifully tiled walls enclosed a spacious combination living-dining room. Instead of a dining table, banquettes ran along the sides of the room, and a large, low table was pulled up to the corner banquette with comfortable chairs placed on the other side of it. We were invited to sit and were served sweet Moroccan tea with fresh mint. As we chatted, friends and relatives kept arriving until the room was completely full.

My host's mother, a sweet-faced, smiling woman wearing a modest head scarf, had spent the entire day cooking a fabulous meal. There was a mixture of delicious smells, each slightly distinctive from the others, and each promising some mouthwatering delights to come. We all gathered around the table and course by course, the meal was served. In the center of the table was a large shallow bowl filled with couscous. My host explained that Moroccan hospitality dictated that there should be plenty of food for everyone who comes, regardless of whether the person is a friend or stranger, and that the couscous bowl should never be empty. If the couscous becomes depleted, then everyone simply takes a little bit less to make sure that there is still enough food for everyone. We later learned that this generosity and spirit of sharing pervaded the entire country.

We started to eat. Our first course was a salad, and everyone helped themselves with the fingers of the right hand to some of the couscous. Then other bowls were passed around. One was a tagine of chicken, preserved lemons, and olives. Other dishes featured vegetables and lamb, immersed in sauce. Although the food was mouthwatering, no one ate quickly, probably because everyone was participating in conversation. Some people seemed to be having two or three discussions simultaneously, alternating between people on their left, their right, and across the table. A few people were just talking to the person sitting next to them. And at times, the conversation opened up to include everyone, usually with laughter and joking intermingled.

All told, the dinner, which began at 9 p.m., lasted more than three hours. Everyone appreciated the food, and everyone constantly lavished praises on the cook—my host's mother—who shyly smiled and nodded her head, obviously pleased that everyone was having a great time. My host's parents did not speak any English or French, but only Arabic, and yet they managed to convey to us that we were welcome to be in their home, and they were very happy that we were there. Most of the rest of the people spoke at least French, some English, and of course Arabic, and the conversation was often a polyglot mixture of different languages. Most of the time my wife and I could follow much of what people were saying, even though we didn't understand the words that they were speaking. We often were able to glean the gist of a comment from facial features and hand gestures. We were impressed by how this dinner was primarily a social occasion. People got together to share the bounty of food, and to reaffirm social ties by offering food to each other and talking about the food that they were sharing.

In writing this book, I thought a lot about how language has become inextricably tied to the human experience of eating, and our dinner in Morocco was an excellent case in point: For one, language was used to affix labels to different foods. During the meal, we quickly learned a new vocabulary of Moroccan cuisine: tagine, couscous, harira (a spice mixture), preserved lemons. I recall a particularly intense interchange between my wife, an excellent cook, and our hostess, also an excellent cook. My wife wanted to know the name of a particularly succulent vegetable in one of the tagines. The answer came in Arabic, which was then translated into French. Unfortunately, no one in the room knew what the vegetable's name was in English. So they carefully described how the vegetable looked, and they reassured my wife that it was quite common. When she got back to the States, she experimented by buying different root vegetables at the supermarket and cooking and tasting them. The answer was a vegetable she had not used before, but has been included in dishes many times since: The turnip!

But language is much more than just an exchange of basic information about food. Even when a guest compliments a cook on the meal and requests a recipe, what is being actually communicated is so much more than an ingredient list.

Let's take a closer look at that evening's meal. Language, of course, was the medium used to bring all those people together through the initial invitation to come to dinner. However, with three different languages being spoken at the table, and only a couple of guests able to understand all three, it quickly becomes apparent that a verbal language was not what made the evening a success. Rather, what was really important were the other modes of communication that people used: smiles, the general laughter, the occasional gesticulating with hands, the way that people changed the pitch and rhythm of their voices and leaned toward each other as they spoke and listened attentively, the warm embraces as we parted—these modes of communication, more than the specific words that were actually spoken, conveyed and reinforced the social bonds.

Seen from this point of view, it becomes clear that sharing a meal is not only an ideal opportunity to share in relaxed conversation, it also is a way to communicate our feelings and ideas with those who attend. By sharing a meal and a conversation, language and food work together to build and reinforce human relationships.

Once we returned from our trip, we invited our local friends to several dinners where we talked about our travels and our experiences, and served food that was similar to what we had eaten in Morocco. Our dinner parties were generally smaller than the dinner that we experienced at my host's parents' house, so the noise level was a lot less, but we witnessed many of the same elements that we saw before: laughter, smiles, changes in pitch of voice, reaching out and touching someone who is seated nearby—all of the modes of communication that we saw among our Moroccan friends.

So what can this refined activity, honed over thousands of years, possibly have in common with other animal species?

After all, we don't usually see ourselves having much in common with the "tooth and claw" aspect of how animals obtain food. Yes, we eat meat and grains and vegetables, but our food usually originates far away and comes in plastic packaging instead of wrapped in fur or feathers. We don't have to hunt our meal any farther than the local supermarket, and if one kind of fish or fowl is out of stock, there are usually hundreds of other options to tide us over. Other than sushi, salads, and the raw food movement, we tend to heat and cook our food, armed with the latest kitchen gadgets, cookbooks, and even culinary TV shows. For the most part, we see our dining experiences as pretty far removed from what goes on in the rest of the animal kingdom.

Yet from a communication standpoint, we probably have much more in common with certain animal species than we think. Even in wealthy countries, we know that without proper nutrition, people can starve to death. The same is true for animals. Without an appropriate diet, an animal will starve in relatively short order. And in the wild, food is often not readily available or easy to obtain. For many species, finding food is the major occupation that fills their waking hours. Food is a precious resource. So when an individual animal finds food, it has a choice: It can either communicate to other animals that there is food available, or it can eat the food, and let other animals of their same species fend for themselves and possibly starve. And this is what many solitary animals, such as bears and mountain lions, do.

But social animals do things differently. Rather than competing for a meal, snarling or fighting over scraps, or hiding their kill from thieves, many species voluntarily share food with other members of their social group. What's more, they often share information about the location, abundance, and quality of the food.

Why would they do this? Doesn't Darwin's theory of the survival of the fittest dictate that it's every individual for itself? What possible advantage would there be to communicating information about food if it most likely means that in the end, there will be less for you? Well, it turns out that there are several reasons that communicating about food might be a good thing.

YOU GET THIS CHECK, I WILL PICK UP THE NEXT

What if the food supply is unpredictable, hard to locate, and not very abundant? In that case, it pays for an individual who is part of a social group to share any food that it has found, with the expectation that other individuals will also share any food that they have found sometime in the future. If I stumble across some food and share it with you today, I can expect that tomorrow, if you're the one to locate food, you'll return the favor and share it with me. And I can share the food by telling you where to find it. This is the concept of *reciprocal altruism*.

For example, vampire bats (*Desmodus rotundus*) live in social groups containing maybe fifteen to twenty individuals, most of whom are unrelated to each other. They need to drink blood on a daily basis in order to survive. But getting blood from large vertebrates such as horses, mules, or the occasional human is not an easy task, and on average any one bat is able to find a blood meal every two or three days. So the bats who have found blood regurgitate some of that blood to the bats in their social group who have not found any blood and are hungry. That way no one starves.

When I was doing fieldwork in Kenya, Jackson, the Kenyan who worked as my assistant—packing the camping gear, cooking the meals, cleaning up, and helping me with some of my experimental gear—had a cousin who suddenly showed up one day and started living with him. The cousin had no job. I knew that this put a stretch on Jackson's finances. Instead of one mouth to feed, now there were two. While I provided much of the food, Jackson's cousin liked to drink changaa, a powerful alcoholic drink that kicked like a mule and left you feeling the next morning as if an elephant had sat on you during the night (the word *changaa* means "kill me quick," which is pretty descriptive of what the drink does to people). This was expensive and Jackson wisely did not ask me for financial help in buying the stuff. Finally I asked Jackson why he kept feeding his cousin and buying changaa. He replied that now his cousin was out of work and he himself had a job, but in the future after I left, maybe the cousin would have a job and my assistant would be jobless. Then the tables would be reversed, and the cousin would support Jackson. The timescale was different, but the principle of reciprocal altruism was the same as for the vampire bats: feed those who are hungry because tomorrow they might well be feeding you.

CROW AND RAVEN LANGUAGE

My uncle was a mathematical linguist who taught at Moscow State University. I saw him only once in my life when he came to visit the United States, and I talked to him perhaps twice on the telephone. The last time that I talked to him, he immediately began our conversations by saying, "You have to study the language of ravens."

He knew that I was studying questions of animal language, and was excited to share what he had just learned about raven language. When I asked him why he said that I'd have to study these birds, he related the following story.

One day when he was walking along the street in Moscow he noticed that a man was looking up at a light pole and making strange noises. So he stopped to listen and see what was going on. He noticed immediately that there was a raven on top of the light pole, and the raven was responding with noises similar to those the man was making. My uncle was intrigued. After watching this for about five minutes, he could no longer contain his curiosity and went up to the man and asked him what he was doing. The man replied that he was talking to the raven. So my uncle asked him to elaborate a little bit further about how he was talking to the bird. The man responded that it was very simple, he knew the language of ravens.

The man then launched into an explanation of how he learned this language. During World War II he was part of a group of partisans who were fighting the Germans. As it was winter, food for both humans and birds was in very short supply. Ravens rapidly learned that if they hung around people, there would always be scraps that they could eat. And, said the man, when the ravens came around food, they would make calls that would attract the other ravens in the immediate vicinity, and all the ravens would hang around waiting for more food. The Germans noticed this behavior and started to watch for wherever they saw a concentration of ravens, because they realized that this meant that there was a group of partisans nearby. The Germans would then mount an attack and disperse the partisans.

The man said that he listened very carefully to the calls that the ravens made and recognized that some of the calls were given specifically for food and other calls were given specifically for danger. He spent weeks trying to mimic those different kinds of calls. Eventually he found that in giving the food calls, he could get the ravens to fly in toward his camp, and in giving the danger calls he could get the ravens to disperse. After this, when the partisans were around German encampments, he would continually give the raven danger calls and make the birds disperse so that the Germans wouldn't realize that the partisans were nearby. However, when there were no Germans around in the vicinity, he would give the raven food calls and everybody in the partisan group delighted in feeding the birds that came in.

After the war, the man said that he spent years studying other vocalizations of ravens and eventually found that he could communicate fairly extensively with them. Unfortunately, because my uncle was going off to a meeting, he could not take the time to find out exactly what "extensively" actually meant, nor did he get the name of the man, and the man disappeared, never to be seen again by my uncle.

I took my uncle's advice and looked into the communication of these intelligent birds. Both ravens (*Corvus corax*) and crows (*Corvus brachyrhynchos*) make a number of calls, including at least one food call and several alarm calls. Ravens feed on carcasses and these can be found only sporadically. Perhaps for this reason some ravens have adopted the habit of following wolves around and waiting for the wolves to kill their prey. Then they try to jump in and grab pieces of meat while the wolves are feeding. Juvenile ravens will sometimes playfully peck at the hind legs of the wolves, but this can be a dangerous business because the wolves can whip around and grab an unwary raven. Once they get some morsels of meat they go off and cache their morsels in the ground, under branches or leaves, where they can come back and eat at their leisure. When they are caching the food the ravens try to make sure that no other raven is watching them. Meanwhile ravens who didn't get any food watch to see where the ones who were successful cache their food supply.

Like other birds in the family Corvidae—such as pinyon jays and nutcrackers—ravens and crows have an excellent memory and can remember where they left their food. This excellent memory applies not only to food, but seems to apply to remembering possible threats as well. In one study with American crows in Washington state, experimenters wore a particular mask when they were trapping the crows. For more than two-and-a-half years after that trapping experience, the crows scolded with angry vocalizations anyone wearing that particular mask, and had no such responses to humans without a mask or even to humans wearing a different mask.

A raven finding a carcass will often make a "haa" call, which can attract a number of ravens from long distances. One experimental study assessed whether ravens have different food calls depending on the quality of the food and the quantity. The experimenters showed wild ravens in Austria three types of food: meat, kitchen leftovers, and wild boar food, which was presented at different times in either a single bucket or in three buckets. The ravens could only look at the food for ten minutes before they were allowed to feed. During this time the ravens that were looking at the food gave a series of "haa" calls, which had the effect of bringing in other ravens from nearby areas. Ravens gave more "haa" calls to the meat and kitchen leftovers than they did to the wild boar chow, which did not seem to be a particularly preferred food source. There was no relationship between the quantity of the food and the number of "haa" calls that the ravens made. However, once a number of ravens arrived at the food source, there were other calls that they were making, which the experimenters labeled as appeasement and intimidation calls based on the behavior of the birds, but could have related to the quality and quantity of the food.

One of the problems of studying the vocalizations of ravens

and crows is that the birds make so many different kinds of vocalizations that it is sometimes hard to figure out the exact context. Crow vocalizations have been studied for a long time and some of the authors writing about these vocalizations have called it their language. At least twenty-three different kinds of vocalizations have been identified in American crows. Ravens have been shown to have at least twelve different calls. Some 80 percent of the calls of ravens are found in all individuals, while other calls are clearly learned and transmitted between mated partners or members of the social group, just like we learn the words of our language. But finding specific calls for specific contexts can sometimes be elusive. One study looked at eight different calls of American crows that resulted in the crows flocking together, or assembly calls. The study concluded that it was not just the type of calls that produced the assembly response, but also the way that the calls were patterned in terms of timing and sequence. In other words the calls have a syntax. And without a Rosetta Stone, that syntax is difficult to decipher.

Crows and ravens can benefit from the social aspects of other crows around them. At night many crows and ravens rest and sleep in communal roosts. During these communal roosts there is a lot of vocalization going on, and we have no idea whether this vocalization is meaningful or just idle chatter. But we do know that crows and ravens that have not been able to find food tend to follow individuals in the morning who know where food is located. Such roosts have been called *information centers* because it seems that the birds are getting information from individuals who either are experienced at finding food or know where food can be located.

The interesting thing about raven information exchange is that sometimes it's deliberate, such as when ravens who locate food alert others to its location. This is called *active information exchange.* In the case where hungry ravens follow successful foragers back to their find, the information communicated might not be intentional at all. Then it's called *passive information exchange.* Ravens following wolf packs is another example of passive information exchange.

Passive information exchange happens in humans all the time. For example, when I travel to a new place and want something to eat, I often cruise by a bunch of restaurants and check out how many cars are in the parking lots. I know that if the parking lot is packed, the food is probably good. And when I get shown to my table, I surreptitiously check out the plates of other diners to see what looks the most appetizing.

Active information exchange works when I take out my mobile phone, check the app for reviews of nearby restaurants, and then decide where to go based on the most favorable reviews. People send in reviews most often as a way of instructing others. Of course, neither of these approaches necessarily provide a surefire guarantee of having good food. A parking lot might be empty because of the time of day, and not because the food is bad. A reviewer might not have the same culinary tastes as I. Still, when I don't know anything about the availability of good food, looking to my social peers is a way of finding out.

Ravens deal with food bonanzas. By following large carnivores such as wolves, grizzlies, and coyotes, they can come upon a kill that is too large for any one raven to eat at one sitting. If they feed just themselves, the kill will disappear very quickly as other scavengers descend to get their share. Letting other ravens know about the food is a way of sharing a bounty that no one raven can entirely consume, and at the same time is a way of enhancing the social status of the bird that finds the kill. It's just like us asking our friends over for dinner.

Here we can see parallels between us and them. We ask

people over to our house for dinner so that we can improve our social bonds. If we put out a good spread, with lavish quantities of delicious foods, other people are impressed with what we feed them, and our social status rises. On the other hand, if we invite people over for dinner and offer them only peanut butter sandwiches, our social status takes a hit and no one wants to come over for dinner anymore. In developed countries today, we have the capability of storing food in our refrigerators and freezers, so the food is not going to spoil immediately. When people did not have such technology, food would spoil very quickly. Hunters who killed a deer or bison would be faced with a temporary bonanza of food that would be greater than they could eat before the spoilage set in. So they could either feed their immediate families and throw away all of the remaining food, or they could invite all of their friends and neighbors over for a feast, and in the process enhance their social status as powerful hunters. They could also chalk up credits that could be cashed in for food in scarcer times, like the vampire bats.

I KNOW SOMETHING YOU DON'T

Reciprocal altruism is not the only reason that animals might share information about food. Another reason is much more subtle, and has to do with the value of the information itself. Here the idea is that someone who possesses valuable information gets more attention than others, and if that information is really valuable, having it might actually raise the status of the information holder in the eyes of others. Take the example of food calling in chickens.

When I go to a fancy restaurant I am often amused at the displays of male humans at nearby tables, seeking to impress their females with how well they know the different wines and how well they are able to pronounce foreign-sounding names on the menu. It reminds me of chickens. Not the chickens on the menu, but the different ways that male chickens communicate about food based on whether females are listening.

When I was a child living in Shanghai, my parents had a backyard full of chickens. The chickens provided a ready supply of eggs and an occasional chicken went into the cooking pot. I don't remember very much about the chickens, but one event stands out in my memory.

In Shanghai there were centipedes that were about a foot long, that would get into the house and create general consternation and confusion as they ran around at a high rate of speed. The centipedes could be particularly unpleasant when they would crawl up into bath towels, apparently relishing the moisture of the towels and the opportunity to find a place to hide. One of the functions of the chickens was to keep the centipedes from going into the house.

I remember one occasion when I was sitting outside on the porch steps with my grandfather, and we were both watching the chickens scratching around in the dirt trying to find bits and pieces of seeds. Suddenly a chicken gave a loud clucking sound, and all the other chickens stopped feeding and started to look around. The chicken that gave the vocalization gave another type of cry and started to run toward one edge of the yard. The other chickens ran after her. There was a general commotion and a roiling of chickens. I was watching, completely fascinated. Then I saw that one of the chickens raised her head, as if triumphantly, and in her beak was an enormous centipede. The other chickens were trying to grab the centipede for themselves. There was a short tug-of-war between several chickens, until one ended up with the centipede and quickly gobbled it down.

At the time I was too young to be anything other than impressed by what I saw. Much later on, when I knew something about centipedes, I could marvel at how these chickens were able to eat a complete centipede in spite of its sharp claws and poisonous jaws. Also much later on, I started to wonder about the cries that I heard that chicken make: Were these food calls that alerted the other chickens to the presence of the centipede, or were they merely expressions of the excitement of the chicken upon seeing something that was going to be an excellent meal? Or maybe, could they have been both?

When male chickens, or cockerels, locate food and there are no females around, they don't bother to make any calls. But when females are around, it's a different story. Males then call more often, with a shorter interval between calls, for more preferred foods such as peanuts, and call less often for less preferred foods such as nutshells. Hens call as well. Playback experiments where hens were played food calls have shown that they start looking around for food when they hear the calls. However, if they are already feeding or are in the process of eating some favorite food, they ignore the calls.

We know that white-tailed ptarmigan (*Lagopus leucurus*) hens signal the quality and identification of food to their chicks. Ptarmigans are grouse-like birds that feed on a variety of plants in mountainous areas such as the Rocky Mountains and the Sierra Nevada Mountains of the United States. When the chicks hatch they are precocial, meaning that they can walk around at a very early age. Ptarmigan hens give calls when they find plants that are high in protein, and then give different kinds of calls during a behavior called *tidbidding* where they drop bits of food and bob their heads up and down. The chicks are attracted to this and feed on the foods that the hens indicate. In this way the chicks learn to feed on plants that are highly nutritious and have a lot of proteins, even when these plants are not the most common ones in the surrounding environment. There is a lot of variation in the calls that the hens make, and it is entirely possible that the hens have slightly different calls for different species of plant foods.

GIMME GIMME

Yet another reason for communicating about food is a selfish one, where one animal begs for food from another. This is something that we are familiar with every spring as we watch newly fledged baby birds trailing their parents around, begging for a handout. Those begging calls sound distinctive even to our ears.

When I was in my early teens, I found a baby sparrow that had fallen out from under the eaves of my parents' house. English sparrows always nested under the eaves, and occasionally a baby would get pushed out of the nest and drop down to the ground. Usually, this was fatal for the baby. It was a long drop down to the concrete driveway below, and typically I would find a mashed up, featherless corpse in the early morning hours as I would go off to school.

This time it was different. The baby had some feathers on her, and this probably allowed her to break the force of her fall so that she did not hit the concrete very hard. She was very much alive when I found her. So I took her into the house, put her into a shoebox with scraps of cotton cloth, and hoped that she would survive. I knew nothing at all about what baby sparrows ate, and I had no idea how to go about feeding her, having never seen birds feeding their young.

My mother had an idea. She suggested that we take an eyedropper, fill it up with a little bit of milk, and feed it to the baby bird. There was an immediate problem. The bird would not open up her mouth to drink the milk. We tried putting a little bit of milk on the beak, we tried poking the beak with the eyedropper, we tried moving the eyedropper up and down as if it were the baby's mother's beak, but nothing worked. The baby kept her beak clamped shut. Hours went by and we could see the baby becoming weaker and weaker. We had to do something if we were to keep the baby alive.

Finally, I had an inspiration. What if I made bird chirping noises? I tried some of the raucous chirps that English sparrows typically make. Nothing happened. I tried singing a few more melodious notes. Nothing happened. Then I tried some rhythmic high-pitched chirps, spaced out about one chirp per second. Miraculously, the baby's mouth opened wide. My mother immediately stuck the eyedropper into the baby's beak and squeezed out some of the milk. The baby drank and drank and drank. As long as I kept up the rhythmic chirping, the baby kept opening her mouth and kept accepting food. After a few days we started substituting moistened bread for the milk, using our fingers to stuff it down into the baby's mouth. The baby started to grow and eventually grew into a female adult English sparrow who lived with us for about four years. Without my inspiration about making rhythmic high-pitched noises, I'm sure that she would've starved to death. It was kind of like a lock-and-key mechanism. The high-pitched sounds were the key that unlocked her mouth, and even though she was starving, she would not unlock her mouth without the right key.

But what sounds to us like raucous chirps actually contains some complex information. Begging calls of grey warbler chicks (*Gerygone igata*) are acoustically complex and can communicate different levels of hunger. Although we might think that as a nestling bird gets more hungry it would yell louder, that's not what the grey warbler chicks do. The more hungry they get, the softer the begging calls become. As the chicks age, the acoustic structure of their calls changes, with the chicks calling more frequently and for longer intervals of time. If predators appear, adult parents have a switch-off call that they make to keep the nestlings from calling, and also a switch-on call to signal that the predator is gone and it is safe for the baby birds to resume their begging. White-browed scrub wren (*Sericornis frontalis*) adults have several food-associated calls when they approach their nest. They give a short, high-frequency "chip" call or a "short-buzz" call when they are approaching their nest. Once on the nest, they give food calls that are variable in their structure. The chicks have at least three different kinds of calls: short, high-frequency "peeps"; "noisy whines" that are longer in duration and have a raspy sound; and "tonal whines," which are as long as the "noisy whines," but lack the raspiness. Like the gray warblers, adult white-browed scrub wren have a switch-off call that tells the baby birds to be quiet when a predator is around. Other than the general context of "feed me," we don't know why the nestlings make these different calls.

I like to go out to eat in restaurants, but I confess that if I go into a restaurant that has a lot of babies sitting in highchairs, I sometimes leave and go someplace else. It's not that I don't like babies. It's that I don't like noise when I eat. I can only imagine the aggravation that mother and father birds must feel when they are trying to get some rest from a hard day's work catching bugs and having to deal with squalling kids who are never satisfied.

WHAT'S FOR DINNER?

Is there any species that uses food, eating, and communication in the way that we humans do? It probably won't surprise you to learn that our primate cousins, like us, have a large social component to communicating about food.

Some years ago I attended an animal behavior conference in France. Perhaps because I knew a little bit of French and made some effort to speak the language, the conference organizers invited me to a small dinner party held for some of their friends. The setting was the dining room of an old French château. Arriving somewhat early, I came into the room and saw that there was a long, narrow table that was laid out for about thirty people. Gradually, people started filing in, among them a number of well-known animal behaviorists. After we milled around introducing ourselves, we all sat down at the table and waited for the food to be served. And we waited. And we waited. Still no food was forthcoming. For a while this was fine, because we could engage in interesting conversations with the people seated immediately around us. But gradually the spell of hunger took over and the conversations became shorter, with people anxiously looking in the direction of where they thought the food was going to emerge.

Eventually the room fell into complete silence. Then at one end of the table a primatologist who had been working with chimps surprised everyone by giving a loud series of calls that chimps make when they see food. We were startled. The person kept giving the calls, making them louder and louder.

Somehow this seemed to have the desired effect, because waiters appeared with some morsels of food. When the food was placed in front of us, other people around the table got into the spirit of things and started yelling chimp "pant-hoots," which the chimps make when they are excited. Soon most people around the table were either yelling or, if they were more prim and proper, saying under their breath the chimp "pant-hoots." More waiters rushed in with food and with wine, and pretty soon everyone was feeling fed and mellow. It probably was a coincidence that the food appeared at the time of the chimp food calls, but it seemed like an excellent example of interspecies communication.

Chimps (*Pan troglodytes*) have several calls associated with food. There is the "grunt," which is a relatively low-frequency sound that varies between being tonal and very noisy, there is the "deep grunt," which ranges from a low frequency to a somewhat higher frequency, there is the "aaa grunt," which tends to be somewhat higher in frequency, and there is the "hoo," which is tonal and has a number of harmonics. Occasionally chimps will also make a "hoo grunt," which is a mixture of "hoos" and "grunts" while they are feeding. The problem with identifying the exact context of these sounds is that one sound can integrate with another one, so that often there is no one sound associated with a specific kind of food. For us that should not be surprising. We seldom look at a delicious plate of spaghetti and repeat every time we see that dish only the word "spaghetti." Usually we add other things into our speech, such as, "Here's this delicious steaming dish of spaghetti." Maybe that's what chimps do, too.

Just like us, chimps produce food calls in social situations. Male chimps give food calls when there are important social partners nearby. Rarely do male chimps give food calls when feeding alone. Instead, they give food calls when feeding near their grooming partners, who have a long-term social relationship with them. Curiously, male chimps do not necessarily give food calls when they are around another chimp who has groomed them earlier in the day, nor do they necessarily give food calls when they are around estrus females with whom they could mate. It seems that the value of food sharing lies in the establishment and maintenance of long-term social relationships. That's not much different from what we do with our friends when we share recipes of our favorite foods.

Food calls have been found in a number of other primates, including cotton-top tamarins (*Saguinus oedipus*), marmosets, red-bellied tamarins (*Saguinus labiatus*), and rhesus monkeys (*Macaca mulatta*). When rhesus monkeys living on Cayo Santiago Island in Puerto Rico were presented with two types of food, coconuts and monkey chow, the males mostly did not call for either kind of food. The females, however, called with distinctly different calls for the two types of food: "warbles" and "chirps" for the coconuts, and "grunts" and "coos" for the monkey chow. Monkeys who did not call for the food but were caught feeding, were punished by aggressive behaviors from the other monkeys in the social group, reaffirming the social nature of the calling.

Animals that live in large groups need to have a lot of food. If that food is scattered around—so that there are lots of food bonanzas, but the locations are unpredictable—sharing information about food sources becomes an efficient way of harvesting the food. It allows the mobilization of a large number of individuals in going out and getting the food, and it also prevents individuals from wasting time and energy in searching in the wrong places. Everyone benefits from obtaining food in a timely and efficient manner. This is what happens with stingless bees, ants, and honeybees.

STINGLESS BEES

At the end of a busy day, I sometimes feel like relaxing and turn on my TV. Before too long, the commercials start, selling everything from aspirin to Zoloft. With due apologies to the advertising industry, I usually ignore the commercials and either go do something else during the time that someone is talking about vacations on idyllic cruises or all of the new features on sleek-looking cars, or I zone out completely and think about all of the things that I still have to do the following day. With one exception: If I am hungry, the commercials for fast foods stick in my mind. And if I am hungry enough, just the words about delicious food might be enough to send me to my refrigerator or even motivate me to get into my car and drive someplace where I can get some food. I don't have to be watching the TV to respond that way. Just the auditory cues are enough.

When I was a student at the University of California, Berkeley, I got a summer job that involved going to Mexico and Central America to study stingless bees. One of my professors was interested in how many different species of stingless bees lived in that part of the world, so he came up with a little bit of money to hire me and another graduate student to go and study the bees. He paid for a large university van that we would keep for three months, gave us each $300 toward gas, food, and lodging, and sent us on our way. I wasn't paid a salary, but I thought that it was an excellent deal because otherwise I would not have had the money to make a trip like this by myself. A total of $600 between the two of us meant that we had to be extremely frugal, and many meals consisted of buying bunches of bananas and eating a banana for breakfast, lunch, and dinner. If nothing else, it was a great way to lose weight!

We had two tasks. One was to collect samples of stingless bees from about central Mexico to southern Costa Rica, so that our professor could later determine how many different species of stingless bees lived in each geographical location. The other was to try to find the nests of these bees and take as many pictures as we could of the nest architecture.

For the first task, we adopted a simple procedure. We took a spray bottle, filled it up with a mixture of honey and water, sprayed some leaves on a bush where we thought might be a suitable habitat for the bees, then left for several hours. Upon coming back, we would often find a swarm of stingless bees buzzing around the leaves that we had sprayed, collecting the honey. We could then catch a small sample of bees and label the sample with our geographical location.

The second task was more complicated. Stingless bees have their hives in the holes of trees, in areas of dense jungle vegetation, where the light is often dim and it is difficult to see the bees leaving and coming back to their hive. We tried to follow some of the worker bees that were collecting our honey, but this proved to be an impossible task. Most species of stingless bees are small—about a half-inch long—and are black, brown, or dark red, so once they lift off from a leaf, you can see them for maybe a couple of seconds before they disappear into the jungle gloom. We had some success when a hive happened to be near a place where we sprayed the honey, but in general it was a frustrating process.

Then, purely by chance, we found an answer. Many people would stop and ask us what we were doing, and I would explain that we were studying the biology and behavior of stingless bees. This seemed to satisfy most people, who would nod their heads and go on their way, doubtless chuckling to themselves about the folly of American biologists.

One person, however, started to describe the architecture

and layout of a stingless bee nest. I asked him how he knew about this. He explained that many people in small villages kept colonies of stingless bees for the honey that the bees produced. A villager would take a three-foot-long tree branch that was maybe six inches in diameter, split it into two halves, hollow out the wood inside each half, put the two halves back together, bind them with twine, cut a small hole in one end, and suspend the branch from a nearby tree or house roof. The stingless bees would find this hanging branch and start making a nest inside. Periodically the villager would untie the twine holding the two halves of the branch together, scoop out some honey, and tie up the branch again, so that the bees could repair their hive and start the process of producing more honey. Stingless bee honey tastes somewhat like honeybee honey, perhaps not quite as sweet. I found it delicious to eat until a fellow biologist pointed out to me that the bees commonly incorporate bits of animal droppings such as monkey feces into their honey.

Stingless bees are found in the American tropics, and in Africa, Asia, and Australia. Like the honeybees, stingless bees live in hives, but the hives are not as elaborate. Often the hives are in hollowed-out logs or cavities, and the colonies of bees are not as large as honeybee colonies. Unlike other bees, stingless bee females lack a stinger and so cannot sting in self-defense. Some species of stingless bees, however, have poison glands associated with their mouthparts and can inflict a painful bite onto anyone who raids their hive.

One species of stingless bee (*Melipona panamica*) does a dance and produces sound. When the bee finds a source of food, she returns to the hive and does a dance that consists of a series of clockwise and counterclockwise turns. During the dance, she produces sound pulses. These pulses provide information about the distance to the food. Short pulses mean that food is fairly close by, while longer pulses mean that food is far away. And, unlike the honeybee, she can also inform other bees of the height at which the food can be found. While other worker bees are unloading her pollen and nectar, she makes a series of different sounds that code for height: shorter pulses mean that food is higher up in the forest canopy, while longer pulses mean that food is closer to the ground. Because this bee lives in a forested environment, it is quite important to provide information about height, because some of the forest trees can be quite tall.

Another species of stingless bee, *Scaptotrigona postica*, deposits an odor trail back to the hive. She stops at intervals along her flight path and leaves a packet of chemicals produced by glands in her abdomen. These packets of chemicals serve as signposts for other stingless bees leaving the hive in search of the food source. And, following the odor trail, the workers can go high up into the forest canopy, or can find food on the forest floor. In some other species of stingless bees, the worker who has found the food will also, in addition to leaving an odor trail, lead the workers from the hive to the food.

The chemical trail serves as a semantic signal, since *arbitrary coding* (the combination of chemicals in the odor packet) informs other workers of the direction to the food source. If, on the other hand, the insects were using the smell of the food that they found, this would not be a semantic signal, since it is not an arbitrary coding of a signal. And, in fact, some insects use just that kind of signal. Buff-tailed bumblebees (*Bombus terrestris*) have a recruiting system that depends on the smell of the food that a foraging bee brings back to the nest. As the bee returns, she runs through the entire nest, occasionally bumping into other workers, and occasionally buzzing her wings. The other bumblebees smell the odor of the food, and then go out looking for that odor outside the nest. So far, experiments with bumblebees have been unable to show that there is any directional information conveyed to the workers in the nest. Similarly, in the German yellow jacket (*Vespula germanica*), a type of wasp, fellow nestmates are recruited to food by the food's odor.

ANTS

Smell or odor is a powerful food cue. One of the reasons that I enjoy going to restaurants is sampling all of the delicious smells that are coming from the food on nearby tables. Even though I order only one thing on the menu (all right, sometimes I order two things on the menu when I can't make up my mind and take home the items that I don't like as much), I can sample all of the other smells that combine into a rich aroma containing the promise of many different and wonderful foods.

This is passive information exchange. No one in the restaurant tries to deliberately waft these aromas toward me to get me to follow the smell into the kitchen and snatch up the food. But some animals use odor for active information exchange to get others of their species to come and get the food. These animals are some of the most numerous creatures on our planet: Ants.

One time in Costa Rica, I came across a trail of leafcutter ants snaking along the jungle floor. I watched the ants for a while as they carried bits and pieces of leaves that they had cut from surrounding trees, carrying these leaves down into their nest where other workers would plant fungus spores on the leaves. The fungus that grows on the leaves is the main food of the ants, which gives rise to the notion that these ants are really farmers growing a crop that they eat just like human farmers grow crops. I walked along the ant trail for a little bit, watching ants carrying bits of leaves that were perhaps twice or more their size. At one point the trail went across a piece of loose bark. Just to see what would happen I picked up the bark and put it several inches to one side of the trail. Almost at once there was pandemonium. Ants that were heading toward the nest with the cut leaves started milling around where the bark used to be. On the other side, ants that were heading down the trail toward the tree branches seemed equally lost and were milling around aimlessly. Not more than six inches separated the two groups of milling ants, but neither group could find the location and continuation of the trail that they had been on. My first thought was how stupid these ants are that they can't recognize that their trail is just six inches away. But on further reflection I started to wonder what would happen if a giant came along and picked up a mile of one of our interstate highways and placed that section a couple of miles away. Would we not mill around the same way as the ants, totally lost?

When an ant worker finds a food source, she will lay down an odor trail, depositing odor packets all the way back to the hive. Depending on her assessment of the quality of the food, she will lay the packets at different distances from one another. If she finds that the food source is of excellent quality and is abundant, she will lay down the odor packets very close to one another. If she finds that the food source is relatively sparse, she will lay the odor packets relatively far apart. These odor packets are composed of different concentrations and proportions of several chemicals produced in glands in her abdomen, and can serve as symbolic words signifying the presence and direction of food. When she gets back to the hive, other workers leave and follow the odor trail laid down by her. They get to the food and collect a packet of food to bring back to the hive, and as they leave, they deposit an odor trail of chemical packets on their way back. Their arrival with food excites other workers, who go out to the food source, sometimes laying down a trail of odor packets on the way out to the food, as well as on the way back. Soon there is an odor highway established between the food and the hive, with ants traveling in both directions, some carrying food back and some heading out toward the food. The chemical concentration of these odor packets can be astonishingly low. In the case of some of the leafcutter ants, it has been estimated that 1 milligram of this substance would be enough to cause the ants to follow the trail about sixty times around the circumference of our planet.

Eventually, the ants collect all the food that is there, and newly arrived workers find no more food. These workers return along the odor highway back to the hive, but since they did not find any food, they do not deposit odor packets along their return path. The chemicals in the odor packet volitalize fairly quickly; in other words, the odor dissipates in the air the way that the odor of perfume gets weaker and weaker after you put a dab of perfume on your wrist. Relatively quickly, the odor trail starts to disappear as the odor molecules disperse into the air and no new odor packets are laid down on the ground. Soon the concentration of odor becomes so weak that the ants in the hive are no longer interested in following that particular odor trail, going out and following, instead, newer trails that have higher concentrations of odors.

These odor signals can be quite complex. A number of the trail and recruitment signals of ants represent mixtures of several different chemicals, and the exact blend may function as different words or different types of information. For example, the African ant (*Megaponera foetens*) conducts group raids on termite colonies. When a scout finds a termite colony, she lays down an odor trail back to her nest, and then uses two chemical substances for leading a raiding party of three hundred to seven hundred ants back to the termite colony. One chemical substance is derived from her poison gland, and the other chemical substance is derived from a gland, called the pygidial gland, in her abdomen. Secretions of the substance from the pygidial gland have a very powerful recruitment effect—as long as the scout is in the nest and producing these secretions, other ants are recruited to go on the raiding party. However, these secretions dissipate quickly, so as soon as the scout leaves the nest, the secretions are no longer present and do not recruit other ants. Secretions of the poison gland persist longer in the environment, for up to twenty-nine hours, and help the raiding party find its way to the termite colony and ultimately, back to the ant nest.

Some ants have signals that are *multimodal,* meaning that two or more sensory modalities are combined, such as odor with sound or vision. In the American Southwest, there are two species of ants that use multimodal signals. These species, *Aphaenogaster albisetosus* and *Aphaenogaster cockerelli,* forage for food individually, but when a worker finds an object that is too large to carry, such as a dead insect, she discharges a chemical substance from her poison gland into the air. Other ants from the same nest are attracted to the source of the odor, and when enough ants have come to the food item, they all cooperate in lifting the food and carrying it to the nest. In addition to the poison gland secretion, the worker may produce a sound called a *stridulation.* Such sounds are produced by rubbing a hardened knob against a file-like ridge somewhere on an insect's body. The familiar chirping of a cricket is an example of stridulation, where the cricket rubs a knob-like scraper on one wing against a series of ridges on the other wing, producing a rhythmic chirping sound. By stridulating, the two ant species cause their nestmates to remain in the area of the food item for up to twice as long as when only odor is present, and to circle and lift up the food much quicker. Other ant species combine odor with a visual signal. In the ant species *Camponotus socius*, when a worker finds food, she lays a chemical trail around the food, and then lays an odor trail back to the nest, consisting of the food that she found, processed through her gut and defecated in small packets. When she gets back to her nest, she performs a waggle display. This waggle display involves vibrating her body from side to side for anywhere between half a second and one-and-a-half seconds. After her nestmates see this waggle display, they follow her back to the food that she found.

HONEYBEES

My wife loves to cook exotic dishes that have a variety of flavors. Some of the ingredients cannot be found in the local grocery store, so she depends on information that she gets from friends, neighbors, or the Internet for finding out where she can buy some of these things. Often, getting some of the ingredients involves a long trip to more distant cities that have a variety of ethnic stores. I don't want to equate my wife to a honeybee, but this is exactly what honeybees do in finding their food.

While visiting the Smithsonian Institution's Insect Zoo, I was drawn to the exhibit of a live honeybee colony. Tucked away in the corner of a room, the colony is encased in what looks like a giant vertical glass-fronted cabinet. There are pipes going from the colony to the outside, so the bees are free to go in and out as they please, collecting pollen and honey from the plants surrounding the Smithsonian Institution and the Washington Mall. I stood there and tried to follow a bee that had just arrived into the hive. This is not a simple as it might seem because the hive contains thousands of bees that are all moving around so that the hive is in a constant state of activity. Eventually I gave up the task and started concentrating on bees that were dancing. Some of the bees were dancing in small circles while other bees in other parts of the hive were dancing in figure eights, all attended by many other bees that were clustered around the dancers.

These dances represent a symbolic way of passing along information. Honeybees build wax combs inside their hives that serve as repositories for the queen's eggs, and also for the pollen and honey that the worker bees bring back from their foraging travels. As the workers return from a food source, they dance on the combs, and transfer information about the distance and direction of the food source to other bees in the hive. The combs are arranged vertically within the hive, at right angles to the plane of the horizon. Because the combs are vertical, the bees can't simply point to the direction of the food. (There is a relative of the honeybee in India, *Apis florea*, that builds horizontal combs that are not enclosed by walls, and this bee has a dance that points directly at the food source.) The bees use a series of semantic signals that allow them to transfer the information to other worker bees that are in the hive.

If the food source is close to the hive, within about 300 feet, or the length of a football field, the bees returning from a food source will dance a round dance. In this dance the bees will go around and around in a circle, sometimes changing direction, but always keeping on a circular path. As far as we know, the round dance does not give any specific information about the distance and direction to the food source. It merely tells other worker bees that there is food in the general vicinity of the hive, and that the workers have to fly out and search within a radius of about 300 feet. This may seem like a difficult task, but honeybees have a good sense of smell, and can probably detect the food source fairly easily once they know that it is somewhere in the general vicinity of the hive.

However, if the food source is at a distance greater than about 300 feet from the hive, the honeybees dance a figure-eight dance. The transition from a round dance to a figure-eight dance is apparently under genetic control. Different genetic strains of honeybees make this transition when the food is at different distances from the hive. Some genetic strains make the transition from a round dance to a figure-eight dance when the food is as close as 120 feet from the hive, while others make the transition when food is about 300 feet. Since these differences represent different forms of symbolic communication, some people refer to these differences as genetic dialects. Many of the honeybees that are seen commonly around flowers make the transition from a round dance to a figure-eight dance at about 300 feet.

The figure-eight dance has a number of semantic elements that tell other bees in the hive the specific direction and the distance of the food from the hive. Remember that the worker bee can't simply point to the food source—the vertical nature of the dance surface, the comb, prevents that from being possible. So, the worker uses gravity instead, symbolically transforming horizontal directions into up and down directions. In the symbolic language of the figure-eight dance, there is a straight-line component and two round components. To understand the straight-line component, think of the number 8. Now think of drawing an 8 in such a way that you draw a straight line from the bottom left of the 8, diagonally across to the top right of the 8. This diagonal line is the straight-line component of the figure-eight dance. The two round parts are the loops of the 8.

In the figure-eight dance, the straight-line component contains the distance and direction information. Imagine that the straight-line component is pointing straight up, toward the top of the comb on which the worker bee is dancing, giving us a rather lopsided figure eight. This means that the food source is directly toward the sun, somewhere between the location of the hive and the position of the sun. Now imagine that the straight-line component is pointing straight down, toward the bottom of the comb. This means that the food source is directly away from the sun, somewhere on the other side of the hive along a line that connects the position of the sun, the position of the hive, and the position of the food source. The worker bees that are attending to this dance use their gravity receptors—fine hairs at the top of their thorax that monitor the tilt of the head—to tell them which way is up and which way is down. Using their gravity receptors, the worker bees can easily tell if the food source is toward the sun or away from the sun.

But what if the food source is neither toward nor away from the sun, but is at some angle to the right or left of the position of the sun and the hive? Then the bees turn the straight-line component so that it deviates from straight up by the same angle that the food source deviates from the position of the sun. To visualize this, imagine three points on a map. One point is the position of the sun. The second point is the position of the hive. The third point is the position of the food source. Now draw two lines, one connecting the position of the sun and the position of the hive, and the other connecting the position of the hive and the position of the food source. The angle between these two lines is the angle that the straight-line component of the figure-eight dance deviates from straight up on the comb. The bee translates horizontal information about sun, hive, and food positions into vertical information within the hive. Other workers can understand this semantic information and use it to go out and find the food source.

In addition to direction, the dancing honeybee can also convey information about the distance to the food source. While the bee is dancing, it waggles its abdomen back and forth during the straight-line component in a series of rapid motions. It also produces a series of piping sounds. Both the waggles and the piping sounds correlate with the distance that the food source is from the hive. The longer the distance that the bee had to fly from the food source to the hive, the fewer the waggles and the fewer the piping sounds. Food that is relatively closer produces more waggles and more piping sounds. The bees that attend the dance can feel the sound as vibrations through their feet, and can also monitor the number of waggles that the dancer makes.

Also, the dancing bee can convey to other bees how much nectar can be obtained from the flowers that the bee just visited. The dancer uses the tempo and the duration of the dance as a way of indicating the profitability of the nectar source. The more profitable the source, the faster the tempo of the turns in the figure-eight dance, and the longer the dance lasts. And as they dance, they also provide samples of the nectar that they collected to the other workers attending the dance (this process is called *trophallaxis*). So, the other bees can get not only the semantic information about where, how far, and what quality the food is, but also a sample of what the food smells and tastes like. As the bee dances, it moves over the entire dance floor, so that a large number of worker bees can sample its dance, and can get a sense of all the foraging locations that are available at that time outside the hive.

For many years, some people could not accept that honeybees were capable of conveying information about the direction of the food source. Instead, they thought that the sole function of the figure-eight dance was to get the other bees excited, and to motivate them to go out and look for food. The excited bees in the hive would pick up the odor of the pollen and nectar that the dancing bee was carrying and would go out and find other food with that same odor. According to this view, the fact that some of the workers found the original food source from which the dancing bee had returned was more an accident and a testimonial to the power of smell of the worker bees. A number of experiments tried to show that it was not smell but rather information transfer that was important during the figure-eight dance, but critics of honeybee language could always come up with some possibility that each experiment did not take into account.

The definitive experiment that showed that honeybees did indeed transfer information about the direction of the food source came from a model of a bee controlled by a computer. A group of scientists in Würzburg, Germany, made a life-size mechanical bee model out of brass and covered it with a thin layer of beeswax. For wings, the model had a piece of razor blade glued to a little spindle, so that the razor blade could be vibrated up and down by a small wire. The model was controlled by a computer, and could be made to do a figure-eight dance with waggles during the straight-line component. The model could also be made to produce sounds during the waggle runs of the straight-line component of the dance. The experimenters inserted this bee into a hive and made the computer rotate the bee in a predetermined figure-eight dance, with the straight-line component pointing in a specific direction. They then monitored where the worker bees flew. Although the computerized bee really didn't look very much like a honeybee, the information it conveyed seemed convincing enough to the workers in the hive. The workers that had attended the dance flew in the correct direction, confirming that information about direction really is transferred from the dancing bee to the other worker bees in the hive. The mechanical bee also showed that the waggles of the straight-line component and the sounds that the dancing bee make carry the same information about distance. Like many other forms of communication, these two forms of behavior contain redundant information, so that if one form of information—for example waggles—cannot be monitored or understood, the other form of information—for example, the sound—could be used to determine the distance to the food source.

The round and figure-eight dances are not the only symbolic dances that honeybees have. Honeybees also have three other dances: the tremble, the shaking, and the stop dance. The tremble dance is given by a foraging honeybee when she returns to the hive with a load of high-quality nectar and can't find any other worker bee to unload the nectar. Normally, as a foraging bee flies into the hive, other workers inside the hive take up the nectar and the pollen that the bee has collected, and then transfer the nectar and pollen into cells within the honeycomb for storage as future food for the honeybee larvae. But if no workers are available, the returning forager shakes her body back and forth and rotates around by about 50 degrees every second or so, as she walks slowly across the comb. She can keep up this dance for up to half an hour. The meaning of this dance appears to be that the worker has come from a rich source of nectar, and that no one is available to unload this nectar, so other worker bees in the hive should stop what they are doing and switch over to the task of unloading nectar. Curiously enough, the person who did so much to unravel the meaning of the round dance and the figure-eight dance, Karl von Frisch, who won the Nobel Prize for his work, apparently could not decipher the meaning of the tremble dance. He ended up concluding that it was perhaps some kind of bee neurosis that came from a bee having a bad experience outside the hive!

Like the tremble dance, the other two dances also seem to have symbolic meanings. The shaking dance, in which the bees shake but do not have the kind of rotation that they have in the tremble dance, appears to be given in the morning—before foraging starts—and in the evening—after foraging ends. Its meaning seems to be: reallocate worker activities from what was done before. So, in the morning, it means start foraging, and in the evening, it means stop foraging and start other activities. The stop signal is a short buzz that causes workers to freeze on the comb. The sound that is produced has a frequency of about 380 Hertz (well within the range of human hearing). It seems to signal that there are competing bees from another hive or predators at the food source indicated by the bee doing the figure-eight dance and that the dancing bee should stop its dance.

Honeybees can use the figure-eight dance as a way of communicating about potential sites for nests, as well as for food. In the spring, the colony reproduces by making new queens. New queens are produced by taking an ordinary honeybee larva and feeding it for about thirty days with a substance called royal jelly, which comes from glands in the workers' heads. Usually, to produce an ordinary worker honeybee, a larva is fed royal jelly for about two days after it hatches from an egg, and then is fed a diet of pollen and honey for about twenty-eight days. At the end of that time, the larva turns into a pupa for a few days, and then emerges as a worker bee adult that is usually not capable of laying eggs. However, if that same larva was fed royal jelly for thirty days, it would become a queen, fully capable of laying eggs and fully capable of living for up to five years, instead of a worker bee's lifespan of about one month as an adult. Normally, the queen puts out a chemical substance that she manufactures in glands near her mandibles, and this substance, known as a pheromone because it affects the behavior of other individuals of the same species, inhibits the production of new queens. This substance, known as 9-ODA or by the long chemical name of 9-hydroxy-(E)2-decenoic acid, also has the effect of inhibiting the development of the worker bees' ovaries, so that they cannot lay eggs. But in the spring the queen apparently modifies her production of 9-ODA, and the workers start feeding a few larvae with royal jelly, in preparation for making a few new queens. Eventually one of the new queens turns into an adult before the other new queens. As soon as that happens, the workers kill all the other new queens, because in the hive only one queen is allowed as an adult at any one time.

Before that happens, the old queen and about half the workers leave the hive as a swarm and try to find another site that would be suitable as a hive. As some of the workers form a large swarm around the old queen, other workers go off and investigate holes in trees or other cavities that might make good nest sites. When these workers come back they dance on the swarm, advertising their particular nest site. Other workers leave to check out these sites. If these workers are impressed with a site, they come back and dance on the swarm. At first there might be workers advertising at least a dozen different locations. However, as more workers go out to check out the sites, the workers that come back from sites that they judge to be inferior don't dance, while workers that come back from sites that they judge to be superior dance vigorously with a figure-eight dance that points out the direction and the distance of the site. As several days go by, there are fewer and fewer sites being advertised on the swarm, and eventually all the workers in the swarm come to a consensus about a site, with only one location being danced. As soon as that happens, the entire swarm goes off to the new site and settles in to start a new hive. This kind of decision-making process has been described by some as a true democracy where everybody gets to present their own views until eventually a consensus is reached.

By some accounts, the average high school graduate in the United States can recognize about 40,000 words and has a working vocabulary of about 10,000 words that are used daily or most of the time. Honeybees do much better than that. Consider that honeybees can indicate direction in a circle all around the hive, or 360 degrees, and can indicate distances from 300 feet to several miles, then by conservative estimates we can deduce that honeybees have around 100,000 words for the combination of distance and direction. While the high school graduate wins out through the diversity of words, honeybees win out by the sheer numbers of words.

FOOD SIGNALS AND THE BIG PICTURE

All animals need to eat. If they don't eat, they starve and die. Solitary animals have to find food on their own, trusting to luck to be able to find enough before starvation sets in. But social animals have an advantage. They have access to all of the information gathered by other members of their social group. And it is not surprising that social animals have developed ways of communicating information about food to their fellow group members, just like we have developed ways of communicating about food to our friends and relatives.

I started this chapter by talking about dinner at my Moroccan host's parents' house. Let me tell you another Moroccan story. I was walking through the market bazaar in Marrakesh, Morocco. If you have never been there, imagine coming upon a large open area filled with people. Scattered here and there are people doing various performances. One person has a monkey sitting on his shoulders. Another person is playing some kind of melody on a couple of metal pipes. There are a number of people juggling various objects. A man is sitting cross-legged on the ground with a basket in front of him. He takes out a metal pipe and starts to play some music, weaving back and forth as he does so. A cobra emerges from the basket, inflates its hood, and starts to weave back and forth in the same rhythm that the man is swaying. Throngs of humanity, some dressed in Western European clothes, some in long, flowing Arabic robes, pass by, like waves rippling across a lake.

I stop in front of the man with the cobra. My scientific mind kicks in and I wonder if the man has pulled the cobra's teeth so that the cobra can't bite him. I lean over toward the cobra holding my camera in my hand so that it doesn't swing out on its strap and hit the snake. The man thinks that I am taking a picture of the cobra without his permission and starts to yell at me in words that I, not speaking Arabic, do not understand. My Moroccan host tries to explain to the man that I mean no harm and quickly pulls me away from there toward a narrow street that is filled with baskets full of foods and spices. All of these baskets are a riot of color. Spices are red, yellow, brown. The foods are different kinds of vegetables, fruits, and farther along the street hang slabs of meat that are covered from top to bottom with flies. My nose picks up lots of different smells, from the food, from the stalls, from the street.

Everywhere around me people are buying food. As they

buy the food, they're haggling about prices, about freshness, about taste. I listen and I try to understand what they're saying, but I don't know Arabic. I only know a few words here and there. A word for "apple." A word for "pepper." I stop in front of the stall that sells apples. As I listen I hear the word for apple that I know. The other words are completely lost on me. It is like I hear *"babble babble babble babble apple babble babble babble."* However, I can also see the expressions on the faces of the seller and the buyer, the movements of their arms and body, the way that they reach out and touch each other, the way that they touch and sometimes caress the food that they want to buy or sell.

This is much the same situation that we have with the animals that I have talked about in this chapter. We can associate some of the sounds and signals with a context, but many of them are variable and we don't know what they mean. We have seen that animals as diverse as ravens and chimps have some sounds that we can identify as food calls, but these are mixed in with other sounds and signals that we can't readily identify.

The challenge for us is to try to devise ways in which we can identify and decode what all of the signals are that we currently cannot understand. And while we humans assume that all language has to consist of sound, we miss the other dimensions of signals that are important: touch, taste, smell, and vision. All of these combine into creating signals about food, for us and for other animals as well.

Food signals also offer a glimpse of a linguistic principle called the *agent-patient*. This principle says that in a sentence, the *agent* is the subject, and the *patient* is the direct object. In the sentence, "The man robbed the bank," the "man" is the agent, and the "bank" is the patient. One of my students did some studies with a wild population of black-tailed prairie dogs in which she recorded their calls as she approached them while wearing a yellow shirt and then approached them while wearing the same yellow shirt, but fed them sunflower seeds. The calls for the two situations were different. They both included descriptor components for human and shirt color, but in the case where the seeds were distributed, the calls had another component. It's possible that the differing component might have referred to the sunflower seeds. So the call in the second situation might be viewed as a sentence: "Human bringing seeds." In this case, "human" is the agent, and "seeds" is the patient.

We can see the Discourse System at work in calls related to food. Take the example of chickens, where the male first evaluates the quality of the food he finds, then bases his communication about it on whether or not there are females around. First, the male's taste receptors analyze the quality of the food, providing input to the brain to decide whether the food is even worth eating, much less crowing about. Depending on the quality of the food and the availability of females in his immediate vicinity, he can decide whether or not to vocalize a call about the food. If no females are available and he is all by himself, or if there are only other males around, then he remains silent.

The male's hormonal system is making a contribution to his decision making, because his sex hormones increase his awareness of females as well as his desire to mate. If no other males are present but there's an audience of admiring females, then he vocalizes to tell them about the presence and quality of the food. This announcement, followed by the reward of food, increases his attractiveness to those females. So his clever choice of when to call increases his reproductive fitness and forms yet another example of how the Discourse System is shaped and specialized by Natural Selection.

Like us, the animals in this chapter are social and have a stake in communicating information about food to members of their group or their species. This can be a matter of direct survival, both for them and for us. If they don't inform members of their social group about the presence of food, about its quality and quantity, and about the type of food, then other members of the social group can turn around and be equally reticent to share information. In the end, no one benefits from the situation, but by communicating about food, both we and other animals benefit directly by staying alive and reinforcing our social bonds.

6. LET ME LOVE YOU

I can't sing. I would love to sing, but I can't get two notes to come out right, one after the other. I come from a very musical family where everyone could sing, play the piano and the guitar, but I was never blessed with any of these abilities. My mother tried and tried to teach me to carry a tune, but eventually gave up to the inevitable realization that I just couldn't do it, no matter how hard both she and I tried.

So when I was courting my wife, I kept my mouth shut as I didn't want to scare her off with my lack of musical ability. She, too, comes from a musical background, has a beautiful voice, and somehow seems to remember the words to practically any song that she hears.

I call her my jukebox. All I need to do is say a few words of a song that I have heard, and she is singing it in its entirety. One of our most romantic evenings was when we were driving from Sedona to Flagstaff along the majestic rock formations of Oak Creek Canyon in Arizona. The moon was just coming up, lighting up the rocks with a silvery glow and casting a magical spell on everything around us. I mentioned something about the light of the silvery moon. Instantly, my wife burst into song. During the entire hour that it took us to complete that drive, she was singing song after song about the moon, never repeating a song in that whole time.

She was the one singing to me, but often it is the male who sings to the female. One summer evening during my student days, I was in Venice, staying at an inexpensive *pension*. I had come back to my room from a day's worth of tramping through museums and sitting in cafés sipping Italian coffee, and was so tired that I went to bed and fell asleep, oblivious to the moon rising above Piazza San Marco nearby. I was awakened by a lovely baritone voice singing in Italian somewhere outside my window. I looked out to see a young Italian male in his twenties holding a mandolin and singing his heart out, looking up at what seemed to be my window. After a moment of confusion, I realized that he was looking at the window of the next room, and I heard the laughter of a female voice. The singing went on for at least an hour. Tired as I was, I stayed awake and listened to the melodious voice singing one tune after another. The next morning I found out from the owner of the *pension* that the man was serenading the owner's daughter, hoping that she would accept a proposal of marriage.

It's no secret that communication becomes important between two people in love. There are more love songs, poems, and greeting cards written about love than about any other subject. When we are in love, we want to express our feelings to the other person: how much they mean to us, how frightened we are of losing them, how we love them more than anyone else. But our communicating about love is not the only thing that is going on. We also want to know if the other person feels the same way about us, if we are as important to them as they are to us.

So we communicate and we solicit communication in return. We talk for hours on the phone or in person, we text, we send cards, we send e-mails. We dress up for that person, paying great attention to how we look and how we smell, putting on expensive clothes, jewelry, and perfumes or lotions. We dance. We show off. We spend money. All of this is very costly but is very important.

From an evolutionary perspective, it's pretty much all about mating. We might struggle up the corporate ladder, make a giant investment in a house, condo, or other property, and make every effort to improve our social standing. But whatever we accomplish in those areas is, in the end, seen by evolution as empty victories if we don't have someone to marry and build a family to share our success with. If you don't mate and successfully pass along your genes to the next generation, your fitness is considered zero, no matter how much money you have or how successful you are in other pursuits. In evolutionary terms, if your fitness is zero, it's as if you have never lived, because you failed to pass along your genes to the next generation. This isn't just platitudes; it is the stuff that drives all of life.

This evolutionary impetus has been covered by the veneer of human culture. Coming from the right family, garnering enough resources, appearing attractive to the opposite sex, finding and winning the heart of someone, locating a safe and desirable place to raise a family, and passing along your inheritance to your kids so that they're successful—all of that can be wrapped up under the umbrella of mating.

Mating is the one area of life where communication signals are interwoven with physical appearance and behavior to make a rich tapestry that lures and reassures even the most solitary individuals that it's good to pair up, even if only for a little while. Every step of this process involves some subtle and not-so-subtle cueing, message production, and response—a cross between a language and a dance where both partners get to know each other and step by step, move toward culmination.

Despite the sea of emotions and hormones raging during courtship, some very subtle but important queries are being made. The first step involves locating and approaching a potential mate. Once the potential members of a couple have located and approached each other, the next step of the mating sequence takes place. This is what I call the *discernment phase,* where male and female get to know one another. They learn each other's histories, status, job position, and lifestyle level. They compare likes and dislikes, and exchange confidences about past losses and future dreams. Communication is essential here, because it enables the sharing of information that each person uses to evaluate whether they want to stay and proceed with the relationship. Exactly what is important to discern varies from individual to individual. Whether a woman is willing to ride on a motorcycle, or whether a man likes opera, may be deal-breakers only to a few members of our human population. But there are some broader issues that are important, not only to us humans, but to other species as well. Let's take a look at things first from a female's point of view.

In humans as in all mammals, the female has the higher investment in the mating process. She is the one spending time and energy on being pregnant. She is going to be the one feeding her milk to the children, and the caloric cost of producing breast milk can be double the caloric cost of being pregnant. She is often the one who is going to be spending more of her time caring for and teaching her kids how to behave as they are growing up.

She wants to know how good the male is as a provider. Can he provide her with a safe place to live, with enough food for the family, with the resources she needs to raise her children? Is he healthy? Is he going to pass along good genes to her kids? Is he smart? Can he take care of her?

This is not only a serious question, but it is *the* question that a female wants to know. When I was living in Kenya, a university-educated Kenyan woman asked me for marital advice. She was in love with a penniless student, who had charm, good looks, was fun to be with, and made her laugh. But he didn't have any money. On the other hand, she was being courted by a prominent Kenyan businessman who already had three wives, but had plenty of money, several houses, and regularly vacationed in Switzerland, the United States, and France. Her dilemma was, should she marry for love or should she marry for money and become one of four wives? With my usual idealism, I told her that she should marry for love, and the money would follow. She said that she would think about it. When I next saw her about a month later, she told me that she decided to marry the businessman. Seeing the aghast look on my face, she explained that the businessman could provide her with all of the resources that she needed to educate her kids and keep her supplied with plenty of food and places to vacation. And what about the person she loved, I asked? She could always have an affair with him, she said.

This leads to what things are important to males. In the males of most species, sperm production is much less costly than a female's investment, so from a biological point of view, a male's main energetic concern is that he not get fooled into spending time and effort in raising and protecting young that are not his. That was the fly in the ointment of my Kenyan friend's logic. Her husband would not take kindly to her having a child with her lover, if that situation were to occur. He would not want to invest his resources heavily into a child that was not sired by him.

So the discernment portion of the mating ritual involves the sending of signals that lower fear thresholds, reassure partners that their potential mate will not hurt them, and build mutual trust. Mating is all about trust. The female wants to know if she can trust the male to provide for her, either through resources, good genes, or both. The male's job is to show the female that she can trust him. He has to show that he has intelligence, experience, and either strength and status, or the cleverness needed to succeed. He has to show the female that he will provide her with food, home sites, protection, and good quality of life. He also wants to know that he can trust the female to have his offspring, and not someone else's. Through language, fear thresholds are lowered, aggressive instincts are muted, and lives are changed as the stage is set for producing the next generation.

BODY LANGUAGE

When I was a graduate student at the University of California, Berkeley, one of my fellow students persuaded me to go to a bar in San Francisco to see if we could pick up women. I wasn't really interested in picking anyone up at that point, but I had heard that he had legendary technique and was curious to see what he did. He needed me because I had a car and he didn't. So we went to a bar in the North Beach area.

We sat down and ordered drinks, I, a soft drink because I was driving, and he a martini. We casually surveyed the bar scene. My first impression was that there were a lot of people packed into a fairly small space. Small tables were set very close together, and people from one group were almost pressed into people from other groups. The noise level was really high, so everyone was shouting, but the background noise tended to drown out whatever people were saying to one another. Clearly, extensive communication with words was not possible. I shouted to my friend that I liked to talk to people, and maybe we should go somewhere else. He held up his hand with his palm toward my face in a "stop" gesture and mouthed the word, "Wait."

So I waited. As my eyes adjusted to the gloom, I noticed that all around us were small groups of pretty women, usually in groups of twos and threes. Interspersed with the groups of women were small groups of men, also in groups of twos and threes. Occasionally, one of the men would go up to a woman, lean toward her ear, say something, and then she would lean toward his ear and say something, and this back-and-forth would continue until either the woman shook her head and the man went back to his table with a dejected look on his face, or the woman would say something to her friends and leave the bar with the man.

While I was casually observing, my friend was looking around the bar with a very determined look on his face. Occasionally, he would rest his gaze on a woman for a few seconds, then look away at me or his drink, then swing his gaze back to the woman. This went on for perhaps an hour, with him looking at different women. I was getting bored and was ready to leave. Noisy bars had never been my idea of fun, surrounded by total strangers in an envelope of sound that made my ears hurt.

Suddenly my friend got up and went to a nearby table where three pretty women had recently come in and sat down. Grabbing a nearby chair, he sat, leaned toward the ear of one of the women and said something, she leaned toward his ear and replied, and this went on for maybe ten minutes. Then they both stood up. My friend came over to me and said that he was leaving with the woman, and I was on my own from that point on. He would find his way back to Berkeley by himself, and would give me a call the following day.

So he left with the woman, and I left shortly after that. I was disgusted that he had wasted my time, not realizing at that moment that he had given me a valuable lesson in the mating signals of humans.

The next day he called. I asked what had happened. He suggested that we get together that evening for a beer at a favorite local hangout of Berkeley college students. When he came in he was all smiles, telling me that he had spent the night with the woman. She had driven him back to Berkeley from her San Francisco apartment, and they had a date for later in the week.

I was amazed that all of this came from a ten-minute interaction where extensive conversation was not possible. So I asked him to tell me his technique. He explained that it was all due to carefully choreographed body language.

At the bar, he spent a lot of time looking at women who appealed to him. As he looked, if he noticed that a woman looked at him, he smiled at her. If she simply looked away, he knew that she was not interested. If, however, she smiled back, he knew that perhaps she was interested, and it was time to go on to stage two of the body-language dance. He looked away and she looked away. Then, about forty-five seconds later, he looked at her again. If she did not look at him, he knew that she had smiled before simply to be polite and not because she was interested in him. But if she looked at him after forty-five seconds, he smiled at her, and if she smiled back at him, he knew that he could make his next move, which was to go up to her, say hello and tell her his name. If she responded by telling him her name, he could go on to stage three. The next step was for him to sit down next to the woman, smile, and say something meaningless like, "Nice to meet you." All the while, he was observing the position of her arms, her legs, and her chest. If she pointed her feet and knees away from him, that meant that she was not terribly interested. If her feet and knees pointed toward him, that was a good sign. Now everything hinged on what she did with her arms and her chest. If she touched her neck or her hair or the front of her shirt, these were all good signs of her interest. Another good sign was her swiveling her chest to face my friend's chest. The best sign was if she turned her arm so that the palm was facing up, exposing her wrist. Then he casually touched her arm for a brief couple of seconds, lightly brushing against her wrist. If she was really interested, she would respond by brushing her hand against his arm or hand within thirty seconds. That was the signal that my friend looked for, and that was the signal for him to suggest at that point that they go somewhere where they could talk, meaning in this case her apartment.

What is intriguing about human body language is that it encompasses behaviors that are totally instinctive and universal—such as facial expressions of surprise, fear, and rage—but it also can be consciously used and manipulated. In the example in the bar, the woman's touching of her hair or neck might have been gestures that she was not fully conscious of making, much as the gesture of crossing one's arms tightly in front of one's chest can inadvertently communicate fear, distrust, or the desire to "shield" one's self.

On the other hand, the woman may well have consciously

decided to use her body language to signal her interest in the male by turning toward him when he sat down next to her. In fact, turning to face someone who is speaking to you, looking them straight in the eye, and giving them your full attention, are all body language tricks used by salespersons, motivational speakers, and people who want to convey a positive message to another person.

Body language—the messages sent via posture, attitude, facial expression, movement, and gestures—becomes particularly potent when it is used in combination with other types of signals. For my friend, the body-language exchange was helped along by his verbal patter, the way he engaged the woman in conversation, and the interest he expressed in what she said, expanding and confirming the promise that the smiles, eye contact, and gentle touches started.

THE LANGUAGE OF SQUID

I have seen plenty of squid sliced and diced and served up on plates as calamari. Unfortunately, by that time it's too late to see that this is an animal with amazing language skills, particularly the Caribbean reef squid (*Sepioteuthis sepioidea*).

Reef squid live in shallower areas of the Caribbean and off the coast of Florida. They often swim around reefs in schools of four to thirty individuals, feeding on fish, crustaceans, and mollusks. Like their octopus cousins, squid can change the color patterns on their skin very rapidly because they have pigment-containing cells called *chromatophores*. Muscles attached to the chromatophores can either contract, stretching out the cell and exposing the pigment it contains, or they can relax, letting the cell bounce back to a very small size and making the pigment practically invisible.

Changes in the size of the chromatophores can create striking visual patterns, all done in the blink of an eye. When the muscles leading to the cells are relaxed and all of the cells are contracted to their smallest size, the squid appears as a whitish, almost transparent tube with short tentacles. But by selectively controlling which cells to stretch, the squid can produce a camouflage pattern that will allow it to fade into the background and confuse its predators, or it can send very sophisticated visual signals to other squid.

Like many other marine animals, squid do not survive long after mating. Once a female has mated with a male, she lays a clutch of eggs and dies. Males live a little longer and can fertilize more females before death overtakes them. During that time, they court the females.

As a male approaches a female, he flashes a specific coloration pattern at her, suggesting that they mate. If she changes her coloration to announce her acceptance, he strokes her with his tentacles. Males also have to deal with other males who are also trying to mate, and so they flash aggressive signals at those males. One of the amazing things that males can do is flash a mating signal across half of their body to a female who is on one side of them, and flash an aggressive signal across the other half of their body to a male who is on the other side, away from the female.

Changes in coloration patterns are rapid and numerous. Watching these pattern changes in the space of seconds gives the impression that you are witnessing a conversation, except that the conversation is a visual one rather than one based on hearing. Because there are so many subtle changes, not very many of the visual patterns have been adequately described or deciphered.

Some patterns appear in specific contexts. For example, a white stripe along the length of the body is an invitation to mate. A zebra pattern along the body and tentacles is an aggressive signal, and if this is combined with a darkening of the entire body, it is a refusal of the invitation to mate.

Making things even more complicated is the use of body postures along with the pattern changes. A squid can float head down in a C-posture, with the tentacles curled upward along the bottom part of the C, or the squid can float head downward in an upside-down V-posture, with the tentacles spread outward, or the animal can float in a horizontal position with the tentacles either curled upward or downward. Each of these body postures can be coupled with different patterns, such as a black band across the middle of the body and darkened tentacles.

Observing these patterns led to the suggestion that there was a grammar involved in communicating information. In his book, *Communication and Noncommunication by Cephalopods*, Martin Moynihan suggested that the visual patterns and postures could be viewed as nouns, verbs, adjectives, and adverbs. Nouns and verbs are the main parts of the visual sentence, such as: "Do you want to mate?" Adjectives and adverbs modify the subject, such as providing a measure of the intensity of the desire to mate.

Moynihan and his colleagues spent many hours observing the reef squid and related cephalopods such as other species of squid and octopus, and have drawn a number of patterns that appear in different contexts. But the visual language is fluid and the patterns are constantly changing, so making a drawing or taking a picture is like recording one word out of one of our sentences and then talking about what that one word might mean.

So far, no one has worked out the precise rules of the grammar that Moynihan suggested, partly because of the difficulty of parsing out all of the elements of the visual language. Assigning meaning to broad contexts, such as mating or aggression, is easier than trying to find meaning in more subtle changes. Imagine how hard it would be for someone who didn't know our language to parse out the subtleties between someone saying "I love you" and "I like you," and then you can perhaps begin to appreciate how hard it is to deal with finding exact meaning in visual patterns that are constantly and rapidly changing.

THE DANCE OF THE ALBATROSS

Albatrosses are one of the few animals that mate for life. This huge sea bird spends much of its life soaring over the open ocean, eating fish, and flying hundreds of miles a day. However, for a few brief months each year, albatrosses come to nest on remote islands where they mate, nest, hatch, and raise their chicks.

Young albatrosses have a four-to five-year dating period when they court other birds before finally choosing a mate and settling down to raise a family. During those years the juvenile male and female albatrosses perform mating dances that are very elaborate, combining elements of visual postures and vocalizations.

One study documented the mating dance of the wandering albatross (*Diomedea exulans*) at Bird Island, a tiny place off the western tip of South Georgia, an isolated island located in the Atlantic Ocean between the southern tip of South America and Antarctica. As the albatrosses return to the island where they were born and grew up as chicks, the males usually arrive before the females. Young males who are unmated gather in display areas where they begin with the first step of the mating dance posture, stretching out their head and neck so that their bill is pointing skyward and sometimes spreading their wings. They also produce a guttural-sounding vocalization in this posture, repeating it several times in rapid succession.

Unmated females arriving at the island fly over the males that are displaying, circling over them several times before landing, checking them out to see which one appeals to them the most. When they land, they walk up to the male with a rolling walk, stop a couple of feet from the male, and point their beak toward the sky, mirroring the posture of the male.

At that point the male has to decide whether he likes this particular female. If he doesn't, he walks away. But if he likes her, then he goes on with the next step of the dance, the greeting phase, which is performed by both birds. This involves a complicated raising and lowering of the heads, bills touching and snapping, and head bobs and twists. Each bird usually extends its head in a raised position, then lowers the head. Then they touch bills several times while snapping the bills producing a clicking sound. After that each bird bobs its head and then one or the other does a curl of its head by twisting the head to one side, so that one eye is looking up at the other bird and the other eye is looking at the bird's feet.

Once again, after the greeting phase each bird has the option of walking away. But if they both decide they like what they see, they go on to the next phase. Each bird rattles its beak and then does a series of head maneuvers, bringing its head back toward its own body and then alternating with head thrusts upward, out front, and then along its side.

These head bobs, beak touches, and neck twists are done in a beautifully choreographed duet, with the two birds alternating movements as perfectly as if they had studied with

Balanchine. Each bird vibrates its beak rapidly, producing a rattling sound as the head is drawn back toward the body and then raised toward the sky. Then the head is moved backward toward the body and thrust out forward so that the head is parallel with the rest of the body. One or the other bird can then raise its head, snap the beak, and then move the beak into the feathers on the side of the breast. After the performance, each bird sits back and vocalizes with its beak pointing down to the ground, and emits a series of rapid "waa waa" sounds, with about two to three sounds repeated per second.

During the mating season, young females engage in this dance with a number of males, sometimes selecting a certain male to dance with more than once. Eventually, a female might do this dance more and more with one particular male, before both leave the island for some eight months of wandering around the Atlantic Ocean, feeding.

The next year that male and female might pair up for the dance again more often with each other than they do with other birds, but still they do not breed. Breeding only takes place after some three or four years of dancing together. The male stakes out a nest site, a place a couple of feet wide among the piles of rocks, and dances there. The female comes to this nest site and dances with the male more and more often, until they decide after several years that they want to mate with each other.

Even though most birds follow this generalized courtship sequence and people have described it as stereotyped or invariant, the data do not support the claim that this sequence is totally hardwired. In fact, there is some variation in the sequence. This variation might be due to young, inexperienced birds getting the sequence wrong, and gradually learning to do the sequence in a way that works in attracting the other partner. Seventy percent of the time the courtship sequences ended when the female walked away from the male. Twenty-five percent of the time the sequences ended and the female followed the male back to his nest.

These statistics remind me of what I observed in the bar with my friend. Most of the time the men struck out in trying to pick up women. Either they had the wrong body language, or they weren't watching for subtle cues, or they said the wrong thing, but most of them were sent back to their chairs with their tails between their legs. My friend, however, was successful on his first attempt. But as he told me, he had to learn the hard way, through numerous rejections, the signals and cues that he had to look for. Similarly, maybe the albatrosses have to learn the cues that please their partners. At least with them, they have four or so years to practice and find a mate.

LIZARD TALK

Some lizards have a complicated visual language like the albatrosses. My house has a wooden deck that is used as a feeding ground by ornate tree lizards (*Urosaurus ornatus*) and by roadrunners who hunt the lizards. I try to shoo away the roadrunners to go elsewhere because I like watching the lizards scamper around, both on the deck and on the stucco wall of the house. They are not only friendly, but they also help to put a dent in the insect population.

Sometimes when I feel that I need a dose of animal behavior to refresh my mind, I will go out on the deck, approach within ten feet of a lizard, and stand there for a few seconds watching. Usually the lizard will turn his head around so that he can watch me. If I get closer than ten feet, the lizard will scamper off. To amuse myself, I will sometimes try to do a lizard display: I'll bend my body forward so that my head and trunk are almost parallel with the deck, and do a series of perhaps three or four head and torso bobs, moving my body up and down rapidly. Sometimes this scares the lizard, and he runs away.

Other times, however, the lizard will respond by doing three or four push-ups, raising his body up and down on his front legs. I can then respond to that by moving my head up and down several times. If I do it right, the lizard will bob his head also. After that, the lizard will lift his entire body off the ground, including his tail, by pushing up on all four legs and jerkily moving his body up and down maybe four times. If I repeat the body and head bobs, the lizard will usually repeat the up and down movements in the same sequence. However, after a few times, the lizard seems to lose interest and starts to walk around looking for small bugs on the deck. My guess is that my conversation does not prove interesting enough to hold the lizard's attention. But even if it is for a short spell, I am usually delighted to be talking to a lizard, even if neither I nor the lizard can figure out what each of us is saying. Maybe my accent is atrocious.

A related lizard, the sagebrush lizard (*Sceloporus graciosus*) has a complex grammar in its mating and territorial displays. Sagebrush lizards live in chaparral and woodland habitats of the western United States. They can often be seen basking on the ground or on low branches or rocks during the day-time, or searching for a variety of small insects and spiders. With their brown-and-yellow splotches on the upper side of their body, they can easily blend into the background of leaves and twigs, going unnoticed by predators because of their camouflage. The underside of the lizards is a whitish-cream color, with bright-blue patches along the sides of the males and some of the females, and blue or yellow coloration on the underside of the neck of both sexes.

These lizards have three components in their display. One component is the general body posture, which could have the back either arched or flattened. This exposes the bright-blue patches along their sides. The second component is the number of legs pushing the body up off the ground. That might sound funny at first, but this lizard can choose whether he wants to push up off the ground using one, two, or all four legs. The third component is the number, type, and sequence of head bobs. The lizard might bob his head quickly twice, then sit quietly. Or, he might bob his head seven times in a row, at one-second intervals. A lizard can also inflate his lower throat area, which is colored either bright blue or yellow.

If all of these displays are combined randomly there are 6,864 possible combinations of displays. However, a careful study of the displays of these lizards found that only 172 display combinations were actually used. These specific combinations comprise a type of grammar that dictates how and when a certain combination of movements should be used, just as we have grammatical rules for how words can appear in a sentence.

For example, males and females use these signals in different ways. Males use more body postures, especially during aggressive encounters, while the females use fewer body postures, but a different pattern of head bobs. Males also use a shudder-bob signal that they give only to females, signifying that they are interested in mating. Like many other species, it seems that the males start off being aggressive toward females and have to learn how to tone things down in order to mate.

COME AND SEE MY ETCHINGS

We often do not realize how visual patterns affect us. When I was in the dating phase of my life, I had a good time talking to a woman I had met at a party, so we set up a lunch date. Things went well at lunch, although in retrospect it might have been because she asked me about my work, let me talk at length, and seemed to be interested in what I had to say. We set up another date, where I was to come over to her apartment for a cup of coffee.

As soon as I walked into her apartment, I realized that we had no future together. She lived in a small apartment, a bedroom and a living room. Every place where you could put a piece of furniture, there was an overstuffed chair, a heavy end table, a lamp, a magazine rack, a shelf. The shelf had souvenirs of places she had been or wanted to go, all in cheap plastic—the Eiffel Tower, a cable car, the Golden Gate Bridge, the Statue of Liberty—interspersed with ceramic figures of elves and fairies. One corner of the living room had a large pile of stuffed animals, all with large, red paper hearts pinned to their chests. The walls had inexpensively framed inspirational sayings, such as, "Home Sweet Home" and "Home Is Where the Heart Is."

There was nothing wrong with her décor. But it was not my taste. My idea of décor at the time could perhaps be described as Asian-Scandinavian-Fusion-Minimalism adapted to the budget of a graduate student. My shelves had books on them. My furniture was functional, but unobtrusive and sparse. I had no stuffed animals. My walls had posters of abstract art bought at the local art museum. In short, it was completely different from hers. While I went through the polite motions of drinking coffee and talking about different things, I never called her after that.

At the time, I don't think that I could have verbalized to her or anyone else why I found her to be incompatible. But how we decorate our living spaces offers a profound statement of who we are and how we relate to the world. It has a syntax of items chosen to harmonize and display our worldview. If our worldview is one of chaos, then the décor of our living space reflects that chaos. If our worldview is one of peace and tranquility, that peace and tranquility is reflected in how we decorate our surroundings. And potential mates can get an instant visual picture of who we are from how we relate to our surroundings.

This is not very different from what bowerbirds do. Bowerbirds live in the tropical regions of New Guinea and Australia. The males are usually brightly colored, while the females are fairly drab, with coloration that lets them blend into the background. During mating, males build large structures called bowers out of sticks, solely for the purpose of attracting females. A bower is usually a U-shaped structure, with the sides of the U made out of strong sticks and the front and the back of the U open to allow a bird to enter inside the U. Woven into these sticks are a variety of brightly colored objects.

Of the twenty species of bowerbirds, each species designs slightly different bowers, but the general principle is the same. The male finds anything brightly colored that appeals to him. This might be iridescent beetles that the male kills and carefully places around the walls of the bower, or broken snail shells that glisten in the sun, or it might be brightly colored plastic items such as toothbrushes, toy airplanes, or plastic keyholders. Shiny metal pull-rings from the tops of soda and beer cans have also become popular in the last few decades. Everything is carefully placed to reflect the male's taste. Males from nearby bowers are known to raid each other for bright objects, just like burglars breaking into someone's house to steal their artwork.

Once a bower is properly decorated, a male sits in the bower and displays at passing females by vocalizing and stretching out his wings. His objective is to get the female to come inside his bower and be dazzled by all of the objects that he has on display. If she likes what she sees, she will allow him to mate with her in the bower. Then she goes off, builds an inconspicuous nest on the ground, lays her eggs and incubates them and raises the chicks by herself, with the male contributing nothing to the process but the initial sperm.

So the bower is not a nest. It is a structure that conveys to the female the aesthetic taste of the male, and his prowess at finding interesting and bright objects to use as wall decorations. Just as our living spaces reflect our taste and worldview, the bower reflects the taste and prowess of a potential mate. A visual statement can either induce a female to mate or cause her to reject her potential suitor.

The process of constructing bowers seems to be learned, at least to some extent. Young male bowerbirds aren't very good at designing their bowers, and as a result do not get as many matings as the older, more experienced birds. But over time they improve their decorating skills and start to attract more females. Similarly, over time, we learn to improve the décor of our houses or apartments in order to attract the kinds of mates that are compatible with our view of the world.

But the language of mating does not only involve visual signals—which in the case of bowerbirds is their architectural decorations—another important component is song.

SINGING WHALES

Like us, male humpback whales (*Megaptera novaeangliae*) sing, too. I vividly remember the day that I picked up a copy of the January 1979 issue of *National Geographic*. There, in a story called, "Humpbacks: Their Mysterious Songs," was a page with a plastic record that had the songs of the whales. I played the record right away, and was dazzled by the low-frequency rumbles, gurgles, and clicks that I was hearing. But I was even more fascinated with something else on the record. One track had the whale song speeded up some sixteen times, so that the time intervals were compressed and the song was much shorter than the multiple minutes of normal humpback whale song. And what amazed me was that the speeded-up song sounded just like bird song!

When I started analyzing prairie dog sounds, I found that I could speed up and slow down any sound that was in my computer. I sped up whale song, and found that it indeed sounded like a bird singing. But I also slowed down human speech, and found that it sounded like whale song. At sixteen times slower than normal speed, human speech has low-frequency rumbles, gurgles, and clicks, very similar to the song of a humpback whale. Speed up human speech some eight to ten times, and now it starts sounding more like the birds that you hear singing in the park in spring.

This led me to wonder how animals perceive time. Maybe whales perceive time slower than we do, and birds perceive time faster. So what sounds like a slow rumble of grunts and groans to us might be perceived by a whale the same way that we would perceive a sentence. And what sounds to us like the delightful chirping of a singing bird might be perceived by the birds the same way that we would hear a phrase or a sentence in our language. When I first started unraveling the language of prairie dogs, everyone knew that they made alarm chirps. But because the sounds were 0.1 seconds long, they sounded to us like simple chirps, with no information contained in them. People who worked with prairie dogs prior to the advent of sophisticated recording equipment assumed that all chirps were the same, with an alarm chirp for a coyote being the same as an alarm chirp for a human. Once I started stretching out the time dimension, I found that there were different chirps for different predators. This implies that prairie dogs process information faster than we can, and it also implies that other animals might process acoustic information either slower or faster than we do.

Let's take a look at humpback whale songs. I have to admit up front that no one knows what the sounds mean. All we can access are the patterns of the sound, which seem to us like songs, with a structure that is very much like language. Males are the only ones who sing, and they sing on the breeding grounds in tropical waters, and not on feeding grounds that are more distant from equatorial latitudes. Every year the whales migrate from their feeding grounds to their breeding grounds. Sometimes the males sing on the way back from their breeding grounds, but most of the song happens when they are most interested in mating and not interested in feeding.

The whales are separated into a number of different populations occupying different ocean basins. These include the Southwestern and Southeastern Atlantic populations, the North Atlantic population, the North Pacific population, the Australian population, and the Indian Ocean population. These populations have distinct differences in their DNA, suggesting that there is relatively little mixing between the different geographical groups.

At the start of the breeding season, all of the males are singing the same songs within a breeding population. Different breeding populations sing different songs, although the songs have a similar basic structure. A song contains a collection of *units* or sound types that are similar to our syllables. Units are organized into *phrases,* which could be loosely compared to our words. *Phrases* are organized into *themes,* which could be compared to our sentences. Songs last from several to thirty minutes, and are repeated over and over, sometimes for hours on end.

Over time, within a single breeding season, the songs change. Week by week, new phrases are added, old phrases are dropped, so that by the end of the breeding season the males might be singing completely different songs. Between years there are large-scale differences in songs within a breeding population. Songs that were sung some twenty years ago are no longer sung today. The phrases have changed, the timing or the *beat* of the phrases is different.

There are still unsolved mysteries about the songs. One study showed that a population of humpback whales off the coast of Kauai was changing their songs relatively similarly within a single breeding season to another population of whales off the coast of Western Mexico. Even though low-frequency sound can travel for a long way underwater, the distance that the sound can travel is estimated at tens of miles and not the couple of thousand that separated the two populations. The authors of the study suggested that perhaps the changes in the songs followed some unknown rules, or were due to some sort of neural template within the whales' brains. Of course, we don't know much about how whale song changes over broad geographic regions, so maybe the changes were coincidental. Or maybe the whales can hear each other over longer distances than we think.

A couple of studies showed that one breeding population can rapidly acquire the completely different songs of another breeding population. One study showed that in 1995 and 1996 most males within a breeding population off southeast Queensland were singing a normal song for that area, but two males out of eighty-two were singing a completely different song, which became more common in 1997, and ended up in 1998 as the only song that all of the males were singing. That new song was almost the same as the song sung by males off the west coast of Australia in 1996, so somehow that song was introduced into the southeast Queensland population and became a hit.

Another study showed that new songs can arise rapidly in one region and then invade other regions in subsequent years. In 2002 the same new song type showed up in East Australia, New Caledonia, and Tonga. The following year it was still heard in New Caledonia and Tonga, but not East Australia, and it had spread to American Samoa and the Cook Islands. By 2004 it was no longer heard in Tonga. A few whales were singing it in New Caledonia, and it was still heard in American Samoa and the Cook Islands, and had spread to French Polynesia. In 2005 a new song type arose in the East Australia population and then in the next year spread to New Caledonia, Tonga, American Samoa, and the Cook Islands. But by 2006, the East Australia population acquired yet another completely different song, which in 2007 spread to New Caledonia, Tonga, and the Cook Islands.

What accounts for these changes? The short answer is, we don't know. But we can speculate. Perhaps we can formulate a "Hip Hop" hypothesis, that says that if you want to show that you are really cool and with it, you will sing the latest songs that are popular. If you are singing older songs, others will peg you as an old fogey. Above all, you want to be novel. You want to show a female that you are creative, with a sharp mind that makes you stand out from all the others. So you improvise. Teenagers today would have little patience for someone who was singing Sinatra songs. Maybe it's the same way with the whales.

THE POETRY OF WHALES

Although I can't carry a tune, I can write poetry. I soon learned that this touched my wife's heart because no one had ever written any poetry to her before. So even though I cannot convey my thoughts and feelings through song, I can at least convey them with written or spoken words. The emotional dimension that music provides might be missing, but at least I am communicating my love for her.

Like their singing human counterparts, humpback whale males are also poets. An average of 36 percent of the themes in the songs end with the same sound, making those themes rhyme. The researchers who discovered this found something very curious about how the rhymes are distributed. There tend to be more rhymes at the end of themes if there are a lot of themes in the song. It doesn't matter if the song is long or short. What matters is the complexity of the song. As the researchers pointed out, this might mean that rhyming helps the whales remember the song more clearly, in the same way that rhyming helps us remember the words and structure of longer poems. Except that this is poetry set to music.

When I was a child growing up, my parents would often have people over to our house for what they called "literary circles." Musicians would come and play their new compositions, novelists would read selections from novels that they were writing, and poets would read some of their poetry. Most of the poetry that I heard I promptly forgot. But what stuck in my mind was when poets who were also musicians would sit down at my parents' piano and recite their poetry while playing some kind of musical tune. The combination of the music and the words made the poems so much more memorable. Maybe this is what the whales are doing—combining music with poetry, so that they can remember the songs and the songs have greater impact and meaning.

BIRDSONG

We all know that birds sing. We also know that male birds sing to attract mates and to defend their territories. And communication involved in mating is tremendously important. For us humans, bird-watching has become a popular hobby that some people take very seriously. However, both seasoned veterans and first-timers can be equally stumped trying to identify what is eventually called an LBB—little brown bird. You probably have seen them if you've walked through the woods or even a city park: little nondescript birds who flit in and out of the shrubbery and disappear before you can even get your binoculars focused. Occasionally, they will sit still long enough for you to gaze at them and try to isolate identifying features, such as a subtle eye stripe or a slight variation in the mottling of their feather patterns. However, so many small bird species look similar—especially females or birds in drab winter plumage—that it's really difficult to tell them apart.

If they look so similar, how do they tell *each other* apart when it comes time to mate? Nature has a variety of methods to keep different species from successfully mating with each other, such as preventing the wrong "plug" from fitting into the wrong "socket," or, in the cases where everything fits together and an offspring is produced, making that offspring sterile, as in the case of donkeys mating with horses and producing mules. But in both these examples, the individuals involved waste a lot of time and effort that could have been spent pursuing a member of their own species.

So nature has developed an even more efficient method of ensuring that a member of one species mates only with a member of the same species, and that's communication. In fact, the communication patterns involved in mating have been considered by evolution to be so important that they actually can become hardwired into what is called the *mating ritual*.

Mating rituals are not just preludes to sex. They also can be considered a step-by-step series where one individual presents an appropriate signal and the other individual makes an appropriate response that triggers the next set of signals. All together, these act as lock-and-key mechanisms that get the male and female of a certain species through a series of doors that start with location and recognition, and end with successful reproduction.

So if a particular little brown bird happens to be a male song sparrow, he will produce a startling variety of complex burbling songs that, to a discerning female, will immediately distinguish him from the two-note tweets of his LBB English sparrow cousin, or the different melodies produced by salt-marsh sparrows. After tens of thousands of generations of mating, the female song sparrow's ear is attuned to become interested if not downright excited by hearing this song. She might actually approach the singer and allow herself to be wooed. And so starts the ritual, and the first step of the ritual is often song.

Only about half of the nine thousand or so species of birds sing. These birds are the songbirds, technically known as the oscines (a subdivision of the passerine birds), the parrots, and hummingbirds. Like us, many songbirds learn all or part of their songs. Some have a tutor from whom they learn what to sing, either their father or some other male in the neighborhood where they grow up. Some acquire the songs of other species, as well as sounds and noises that happen to be around them, incorporating them into a repertoire of songs that can involve hundreds of sounds. The nightingale, for example, has a repertoire of one hundred to three hundred different songs, and the brown thrasher has a repertoire of more than two thousand songs. I spent one spring being awakened in the middle of the night by the mournful meowing of an obviously lost cat, and went outside on a regular basis to try to find the cat, with no luck. Finally, I happened to spot a bird in the early morning gloom, making the cat sound. It was a mockingbird, going through its song repertoire.

For a long time, people thought that most birds learned their songs at an early age, and then the song *crystallized* or became fixed in its acoustic properties as the bird got old. This crystallization was aided by a neural window, a predisposition of a particular bird to learn the sounds that were typical of its own species, and ignore the sounds of other species. So the learning was limited in scope. Some birds—the ones with large song repertoires and the ones that could

mimic sounds, like the parrots—did not have this crystallization and could acquire new sounds at any point in their life,
but most of the other birds were believed to sing their songs
with very little variation once they grew up.

However, new evidence shows that this is a very simplistic
view. A study using high-speed X-ray cinematography showed
that zebra finches (*Taeniopygia guttata*) can modulate their
songs using their beak and pharyngeal-esophageal cavity the
same way that we use our larynx, to produce subtle variations
in their songs. Another study showed that Bengalese finches
(*Lonchura domestica*) produce a considerable amount of variation in their songs when they are singing by themselves, and
only move to a more crystallized version of their song when
they are introduced to a female. And just like we correct our
speech based on the feedback that we get from hearing ourselves talk, Bengalese finches correct the pitch of their song if
they detect that it doesn't sound quite right.

There are lots of descriptions of different birdsongs, complete with sonograms that are pictorial representations of the
sounds, and word descriptions of the calls or songs (here is
the word description for the song of the American robin:
"cheerily, cheer up, cheerio"). Birders know that there is a lot
of variation in the songs. For example, an audio field guide to
birds by Donald Kroodsma provides several different song
variations for most of the species of birds represented in the
guide. Such variation has always been assumed to be inconse-
quential, more like noise rather than anything important.

But we don't know what kind of information is encoded
into the songs. Many biologists assume that the song is a complete unit, and is meaningful only in the broad context of "I
want to mate" or "I am defending my territory," rather than
assuming that there is a lot of information within the call. The
variation that is found in the songs of an individual bird is

often assumed to be due to minor fluctuations of motivation if the bird is singing the same general type of song, or perhaps due to incorrect copying of a song.

Few biologists try to match the variation with changes in context. I was listening to a talk once at an animal behavior meeting, on the vocal behavior of a group of sparrows. The speaker showed a number of sonograms of the sparrow song, and each sonogram clearly showed minor differences from all of the other sonograms. I asked the speaker if these were all sonograms of the songs of the same bird. Yes, he replied. Then I asked if there were any context differences that occurred when each song was recorded. The speaker replied—clearly annoyed that someone would ask such a stupid question—that he did not look for any context differences, and in any case, he did not expect that context differences would lead to differences in song. And that was the problem: He saw only what he expected to see, and not what might have been there.

However, such matching of variation and context might provide insight into how birds encode information. The catch is that we often lack the Rosetta Stone to unlock the meaning, or understand the kind of information that birds have in their songs.

I have a hummingbird feeder on my deck. Every morning, when I let my dog out into the dog's run, there is a male Anna's hummingbird who flies up to the feeder and sits on a clothesline nearby. He is not hungry at this point. Typically, he would have used the feeder much earlier in the morning, when the sun was just coming up. But he sits, looks at me, and starts to sing. The song is very soft, so I have to be close to him to hear it, but it is complex with a number of different syllables that I can hear clearly. So I talk to him. I tell him what a beautiful bird he is, how much I admire his bright ruby-red throat, how I hope that he will have a good day. He listens to one of my phrases, then sings a phrase in return. Then I tell him something else, and he replies, until finally he spots another male Anna's trying to get to the feeder, and he zooms off, sometimes narrowly missing my head or my arm. We talk to each other, and neither one of us has any idea of what the other saying, but that doesn't keep either of us from having a pleasant conversation to start out our morning.

Not much is known about the song of the Anna's hummingbird (*Calypte anna*), but a lot more is known about the song of the blue-throated hummingbird (*Lampornis clemenciae*) in southern Arizona. These birds have two types of songs, one that is sung by males, the other sung by females. The male song is composed of five units. We can call these units A, B, C, D, and E. The unit that begins most of the songs is A, and the songs can end with B, C, D, or E. Sometimes the songs begin with C, but not with B, D, or E. Songs are very variable in how the units are combined, but there is a definite syntax. Common triplets, or three units sung one after the other, are ABC, BCD, CDE, DEB, and EBC. These triplets can be recombined in different ways to make the song longer or shorter. The rest of the possible triplet combinations (125 combinations are possible when counting triplets) are never sung. Females sing less often than males and their song is much more variable, and correspondingly more difficult to characterize in terms of syntax.

Because hummingbirds are not oscine songbirds, fewer people have studied their vocalizations. But as more studies are being conducted, more complexity is being found in their songs. A recent study of the wedge-tailed sabrewing hummingbird (*Campylopterus curvipennis*) in southern Mexico found that the entire population of males that were studied over a four-year period had a total of 103 syllable types, and on average, each individual male had 36 syllable types in his repertoire.

The syntax of how these syllable types are used remains to be studied, as are the possible meanings of these complex songs.

I SING ALL THE BEST SONGS

Humpback whales have analogues in the bird world. Yellow-rumped caciques (*Cacius cela*) are birds that live in forested areas of western Panama, near the Pacific entrance to the Panama Canal. Colonies of up to hundred nests can occur in a single tree. During the mating season, females spend their time close to the nests, while males compete with each other to be close to the nests, where they can mate with multiple females. Each male sings between five and eight different song types, which are also sung by all of the males in the colony. Over the course of a breeding season, the song types change gradually, so that the following year, some 78 percent of the songs are different from the previous year's songs. Some of the songs are introduced to the resident males by males moving into the colony from other areas, but most of the changes in songs are due to the resident males changing their songs, just like male humpback whales change their songs during their breeding season.

Similarly, village indigobirds (*Vidua chalybeata*) living in Africa change their songs over time. These birds are small finches that live south of the Sahara in woodlands and fields, particularly close to villages. Like the caciques, the males mate with multiple females. Each male sings around twenty-three different songs, and many of these songs are shared by neighboring males. Within a breeding season, the songs change in minor ways, even though all of the males sing similar songs. By the following breeding season, the songs change, with the less successful males copying the songs of the more successful ones, the males that had more access to the females during the previous breeding season. Changes involve differences in the pitch and the timing of the notes within a song. Some songs drop out entirely the following year. Some songs persist over multiple years. Most of the songs change enough from year-to-year so that over a five-year span the songs become unrecognizable from previous ones. However, some of the songs persist for at least eight years, although the average mating lifespan for a village indigobird male is only around a year-and-a-half, and eight years is eight generations of birds. Some of the songs become a part of the singing culture of the birds, just like we still sing songs that were written over a century ago, or about five generations for us.

OF SINGING BATS AND SONGSTER MICE

Mexican free-tailed bats (*Tadarida brasiliensis*) are common on summer nights in the southwestern part of the United States. You can see them flitting around street lights, picking off the moths and beetles congregating there. They navigate and find their prey through echolocation, by putting out high-frequency sound pulses and then listening for the echoes that come back from objects in their flight path. Most of these echolocation bursts are high-frequency sound above the range of our hearing (we can hear sounds roughly between the ranges of 20 to 20,000 Hertz or cycles per second, although those of us who are much past the age of twenty only hear sounds up to about 12,000 Hertz, which is usually spelled as 12 kHz, or 12 kilohertz). But some of the echolocation calls of the Mexican free-tails drop down into our audible range, and sometimes the only way that you know that a bat is around is if you hear a series of rapid clicks as the echolocation calls drop down in their acoustic frequencies.

These bats have at least sixteen different types of vocalizations. One type is courtship songs. When it is time to mate, each adult male stakes out a territory and sings songs to attract females. Because most of these songs are well above the range of human hearing, the singing behavior of the bats has been ignored for a long time, with most investigators focusing instead on the echolocation. But now that some studies have looked at a broader aspect of the vocal signals of bats, some amazing results are turning up.

Courtship songs are composed of a number of different syllables, just like our words are made up of syllables. These syllables are organized into chirps, trills, and buzzes. Chirps have two types of syllables, A and B. The A syllables tend to be simpler in their acoustic structure, while the B syllables tend to be more complicated. Intermixed among these two types of syllables are the trills and buzzes. Within different songs, the syllables, trills, and buzzes are arranged like musical notes, with timing differences in how the notes are sounded. Some of the syllables are longer and higher in frequency, while other syllables are shorter and lower in frequency. Although the syllables are currently grouped into two categories, there is a lot of variation in the acoustic structure within each type, and we currently do not know how much of this variation is meaningful to the bats.

We do know, however, that some of these same syllables are also found in echolocation calls, as well as in calls that express irritation with other bats and alarm upon seeing a predator. Their calls are much like our sentences. We can use the same group of syllables to express our alarm, our irritation with our fellow human beings, or our attempts to sing songs to the love of our life. But unlike our vocalizations, we lack the key that would allow us to decode what the bats are really saying.

We now know that like the bats, mice sing songs. They, too, have their songs mostly in the ultrasound range, from about 20 kHz to about 100 kHz, so this is something that we humans mostly could not hear, and consequently have ignored. Generally, our tendency is that if we can't detect something, we find it very hard to believe that it is there.

I remember being out in the field one night studying the predatory habits of grasshopper mice, who are mostly carnivorous, eating a variety of insects, scorpions, and even other small mice. When a grasshopper mouse finishes eating a prey item, it stands up on its hind legs, stretches out its head toward the sky, and lets out a scream that has its lowest frequency around 15 kHz, or pretty much close to the upper level of what we can hear. There were three of us observing the mice with a night-viewing scope. Each time a mouse would scream, two of us would turn toward the sound and try to locate the mouse in the scope. The third person had somewhat poorer hearing and could not hear the mouse screams. Try as we might, we never could convince him that the mice were screaming. He didn't hear it, and as far as he was concerned, it didn't exist.

But mice really sing. One study looked at the songs of a genetic strain of laboratory mouse. When they were exposed to either a live female or the scent of a female placed into their cages on a cotton swab, male mice would start to sing. Although the mice were nearly identical genetically, the songs that they sang had a considerable amount of variation, implying that the singing was not something that was entirely determined by the mouse genes. Like the bat songs, the mouse songs contained syllables and the syllables had different intervals of time between them, depending on which mouse was singing. Each mouse had his own particular version of the songs that he sang. Another study recorded the ultrasonic songs of wild mice (*Peromyscus*). The mice had at least seven different motifs represented in their songs, consisting of different syllables and different syllable phrases.

All of this singing must surely put females into a romantic mood. This is not so different from our behavior. A study of the responses of eighteen-to-twenty-year-old single human females showed that when they were exposed to romantic lyrics in songs, they were much more likely to give out their phone numbers to males who asked, than if they heard lyrics that were nonromantic.

LANGUAGE, MATING, AND EVOLUTION

Mating signals and evolution represent a positive feedback loop. From a linguistic standpoint, mating signals show a component of syntax and grammar. The better you are as a communicator and can frame your message very precisely, the more you help your chances in mating, and the more likely it is that your language genes will be passed on to the next generation. In evolutionary terms, fitness is not how strong, rich, or powerful you are, but how many of your offspring contribute genes to the next generation's gene pool. If you cannot get your message across to a potential mate, about your virility, your attractiveness, and your desire, you are not going to breed and whatever genes you might have will die out with you. On the other hand, the genes of someone who is a master at communicating and mating will prosper, or in evolutionary terms, will be "selected," and this especially includes language ability.

Because of the importance of mating, the Discourse System

is at its optimal performance to facilitate an animal's success in mating. The more successful the Discourse System is at spreading an animal's genes, the more it is "selected" for future generations. As a part of the Discourse System, hormones affect emotions, instigate behaviors, influence desire and competitiveness to promote mating, while language allows the building of trust and a defusing of aggression. For long-lived animals, the Discourse System allows the formation of pair-bonds that last through times when the animals are not receptive to mating and times when both parents are needed to successfully raise the kids. Language, mating, and the Discourse System are all intricately tied together to promote an animal's evolutionary success.

7. BACK OFF!

I was bullied as a kid. My elementary school classroom had a long coat closet that ran along the back of the room. The closet had only one entrance, so that you had the feeling of entering a dimly lit cave festooned with coats, lunch boxes, and a variety of stuff that kids brought to school that day. When I would go into the closet to hang up my jacket, a couple of class bullies would follow me in, block the doorway, and have a few minutes of fun pushing me into jackets or onto the floor. The teacher apparently either did not believe that such things could happen in her classroom, or was too preoccupied with all of the rest of the kids, and never noticed what was going on. The rule seemed to be that as long as they didn't leave any visible marks on me, anything that they did was fair game. I put up with this for a long time. Complaining to the teacher was less than useless because she did not do anything to resolve the issue, and the bullies would take it out on me doubly hard after one of my complaints.

Finally I got tired of being bullied. I had just joined the Cub Scouts, and as a prize for some contest that I no longer remember, I received a Cub Scout knife with a five-inch blade. I was really proud of that knife. So I carried it to school one day to show it off to my friends. As I was hanging up my coat, two bullies stepped into the doorway to have some fun with me. Without thinking, I pulled out the knife, opened up the blade, and stood there with the knife held in my hand, smiling at them. I wish now in retrospect that I had said something clever, such as, "Go ahead, make my day." But I just stood there, holding the knife, without threatening them in any way.

Suddenly it wasn't as much fun for them. The knife had a respectable blade, something that could really hurt them. They didn't know if I would use it. Frankly, *I* didn't know if *I* would use it. But it changed the bullying equation. Was it worth their while to test me and possibly get hurt, or was it better to go and pick on someone else in the classroom who wouldn't fight back? We stood there for what seemed like a long time, but it was probably just only a few seconds, and then they turned around and ran out of the closet. By the time I had folded up the knife and stepped out, they were busily complaining to the teacher that I had a knife and wanted to kill them. Bless her heart, she did not believe them just like she did not believe that I was being bullied.

My reputation spread throughout the classroom. A few kids wanted to see the knife, which I took to school in my pocket every day. We would go into the coat closet and I would open up the blade, and they would stare and stare. Kids would ask me if I had ever used the knife and I would reply, "Sure," not bothering to add that it was great for cleaning the dirt from under my fingernails. If the bullies happened to be in the closet when I came in, all I had to do was put my hand in my pocket and smile, and they would scamper out as if their lives depended on it. After a while, I stopped carrying the knife because it was pretty heavy, but even then, all I had to do was put my hand in my pocket and everyone would think that I was reaching for my knife.

That taught me a lesson about the power of aggressive deterrence. My smile signaled that I was not afraid, and the knife provided a display of weaponry that represented a serious threat to my aggressors. I had communicated to my bullies that there could be serious consequences to them if they continued with their attack. And not being stupid, they evaluated the threat that I posed and decided that the risk of injury was too great to take a chance on attacking me. It was easier to move on and find a weaker and less-threatening target.

This is exactly what many species of animals do with their aggressive signals. One individual provides a challenging signal, and another individual decides on a response, either to signal an escalation of the challenge, or to signal an intention not to pursue the confrontation. There's also the possibility that one or the other individual can launch into an attack.

Aggression is one potential strategy for getting access to important resources. In human history, aggression has been a tried-and-true method for gaining land, wealth, and mates. Any book of world history is filled with stories of wars, combat, coups, and assassinations. Economic or cultural competition often seems to be resolved through warfare. We support extensive militaries and put a considerable part of our intelligence to use in trying to devise new and improved ways of slaughtering our fellow humans. At least one biologist has suggested that aggression among humans was directly responsible for the development of human intelligence. Even on an individual basis, some forms of aggressive behavior can lead to better jobs, more money, and ready access to potential mates. On the other hand, because we are social animals and live within societies, other forms of aggressive behavior can land individuals in jail, where the ability to acquire power and wealth may be severely limited.

Similarly, animals can use aggression as a means of getting access to resources. One animal could fight another, or could indicate its intention to fight, over crucial resources such as food, water, territorial space, or mates. It might display its weapons, size, or strength to an opponent, and the opponent could then evaluate whether it, too, wanted to display its own fighting strength, or its own willingness to fight. Depending on its own needs, either of the animals might escalate the contest so that an actual fight ensues.

Most of the time, we humans signal our intentions about aggressive interactions by using language. At the level of nations, diplomats use words to signal their country's displeasure with the actions of another country, or to try to defuse a potential conflict from happening. On an individual level, we will often use words to either start a fight or try to get out of one. Even if we don't use words, our body signals can be read by our opponents—staring, hand gestures, body posture, or rate of breathing can all signal information to our opponent about the likelihood of our engaging in a fight. We are surrounded by aggressive signals. From a bully verbally assaulting a child on the playground, to the driver who gives you the "one-finger salute" in traffic, to the flashing of weapons visible on every television channel, to the displays of military might shown on the nightly news—we live in a society where aggressive intent is expressed on every scale from individual to global. So it doesn't require a leap of imagination to understand the use of aggressive signals in other species.

Just about every nature program on television shows animals engaging in aggressive behavior—battling over mating rights, nesting territories, feeding grounds, or dominance. The law of "tooth and claw" envisions animals as basically aggressive, and we can relate to this. Wherever resources are limited, whether it's a child's new backpack, an international boundary, or a falcon's nesting site, there's going to be an interaction involving someone else trying to intimidate you into giving up what you have, or vice versa.

However, there is an important, if not always apparent, distinction between signaling aggressive intent and actually engaging in violent behavior. The lesson in all species who use aggressive signals is: If the aggressive display works, that's much better than having to cross the boundary into physical violence. Violent behavior—actual physical fighting—is dangerous and often costly to both parties. In our species, there are moms to stem the flow from bloody noses or to put ice on black eyes from playground battles; hospitals and emergency rooms to address more serious injuries; and attorneys to help get revenge in court. But none of these are available in other species, where an injury incurred in even the slightest tussle could become life-threatening.

So Natural Selection has promoted the development of behaviors that not only signal aggressive intent without resorting to actual aggression, but also that effectively sort out the winner without anyone becoming seriously harmed. This is a stroke of genius when you think about it. Imagine abolishing human warfare and deciding international disputes instead with, say, a chess match. Or, in a more comparative scenario, imagine settling international disputes with a football game, where planning and strategy are involved, where intimidation, strength and speed are used on the field, but there is no intent to cause serious injury and the score is settled without a single casualty. Take it one step further and imagine a situation where just flashing your feathers is enough to induce an invader to give up and go away. That's what happens in other species most often, thanks to the use of aggressive signals.

Recently, my wife and I were driving along the California coast. We stopped at an overlook along Asilomar State Beach, on the Monterey Peninsula. Our attention was drawn to an oystercatcher (*Haematopus palliatus*)—a wonderful black bird about the size of a pigeon, who has a long, red bill that it uses to forage for clams and oysters along rocky shorelines.

The oystercatcher was flying around and around in a low circle while calling "scree, scree, scree" constantly. We watched and soon figured out that the source of his upset was a turkey vulture, sitting, of all places, right on a rock near the water's edge. This is not a usual place for a vulture, and apparently the oystercatcher thought so, too. Likely the larger bird had selected a spot to sit that was too near the oystercatcher's nest, but the big bird wasn't willing to move. We found out the reason later as we started walking along the beach: The carcass of a dead seal had washed ashore, a bonanza find for a turkey vulture, who loves to eat carrion.

As we looked on, the oystercatcher continued to circle, yelling, and with each circle he swooped low and dive-bombed the vulture. Each time the vulture watched the oystercatcher approach, he responded with a typical large bird threat display: He opened his wings and lifted his head and shoulders and opened his mouth—all to look more threatening. The oystercatcher was unfazed, though, and he proceeded with his own drive-off-the-intruder display, aiming right for that raised vulture head. Each time, at the last second, the vulture closed down his wings and ducked, and the screaming oystercatcher whizzed by. Eventually, the vulture decided that this was not the best spot to be and flew off, and the triumphant oystercatcher dropped into the tangle of rocks and disappeared, probably to his nest.

Had that oystercatcher even seen a vulture before? We

don't know. Maybe not. Was the oystercatcher able to assess the risk versus the payoff of trying to drive off a large black avian trespasser? Could it tell the difference between a carrion-eating vulture and a more predatory hawk? Again, we don't know. What we do know is that a smaller bird used a combination of aggressive signals and behavior to drive off a much larger bird, all without either of them getting seriously hurt. This is the power of aggressive signals.

A clever study showed the power of aggressive signals in limiting violence. A recent mutation among a population of Pacific field crickets (*Teleogryllus oceanicus*) on the island of Kauai in the Hawaiian Islands that arose between the late 1990s and 2003 rendered the male crickets unable to produce sound. Normally, crickets rub their wings together, rubbing a scraper knob on one wing against a series of grooves called a file on the other wing. This rubbing produces a rhythmic song. Crickets use this song when they are battling with other males over territorial space, and also sing songs to attract females.

In the Kauai population, the result of the mutation is that the scraper and file disappeared, producing flat wings that are incapable of making any sounds. Crickets of this same species on the Big Island lack the mutation, and can produce normal song. When pairs of male crickets were matched in experimental chambers—some that could sing and some that could not—the pairs in which neither cricket made any sounds showed the most violent aggression, biting and head-butting each other. Where the crickets sang, usually one or the other of the pair would turn away from the encounter, while the winner would sing a victory song. Language can provide information that makes fighting unnecessary.

TALLER IS BETTER

In his book *The Expression of Emotions in Man and Animals*, published in 1872, Charles Darwin talks about the Principle of Antithesis. The basic idea is that aggression and fear are antithetical: They are at two ends of a spectrum, and visual signals reflecting these ends are going to be opposites. For example, if I am feeling particularly confident and aggressive, I will stand tall and straight, with my full height stretched out. If I am feeling afraid and lack confidence, I will slump down to the lowest height that I can manage and still stay upright. In Europe, when members of the general public meet royalty, they lower their height: Men bow, women curtsey, reflecting the higher status and greater power of a person of royal descent. When we defeat our opponents, we often say that we brought them to their knees.

Consider a dog who is confident and aggressive. This dog stands up at its full height, the tail is raised and slowly wagging, the ears are pricked up. Now contrast this with a dog who is afraid. The body is crouching, the tail is pressed downward, and the ears are flattened against the head. Both of these dogs can bite you, but for different reasons. The confident dog will bite you if you take away his resources, such as his food dish, while the fearful dog will bite you if you simply come too close and foolishly extend out your hand in an offer of friendship. Darwin thought that the Principle of Antithesis applied to many different visual signals, and his book is a treasure trove of descriptions and pictures of facial expressions and body postures of humans and animals.

Many animals have signals in which a body part is raised as a sign of aggression. One study looked at the body signals of glaucous-winged gulls (*Larus glaucescens*) that live in Puget Sound near Anacortes, Washington. When one gull confronts another in an aggressive encounter, its head, neck, and beak can be raised straight up toward the sky, or they can be lowered into a horizontal position. When the head is up, that signals to the opponent an aggressive intent, and the opponent is most likely to attack. When the head is held horizontally, parallel to the ground, it signals that there is no threat here, and the opponent is most likely to simply walk away rather than start a fight. Raised head height is a signal of an intention to fight, while lowered head height is a signal of peaceful intentions. Each bird involved in the confrontation can choose which signal to make, depending on its assessment of the strength of its opponent.

Sometimes the signals involve both raising and lowering different body parts at the same time. These combined signals usually indicate that an animal wants to play. The best-known signal of this type is the play bow of dogs. When a dog wants to play, it will lower the front part of its body, stretching out its front legs while at the same time raising the rump, and will wag its tail. This set of signals might be followed by the dog turning in a tight circle, and then doing the play bow again. Often this precipitates a chase, where the dog initiating the play gets chased by another dog, and then the two participants reverse the procedure, and the initiator is the one who chases. During the chases, the dogs can bite each other as in an aggressive encounter, but the biting is more pretend than injury-inflicting.

Darwin's Principle of Antithesis was groundbreaking at the time, but it was incomplete in that it only addressed the extremes of animal signals and did not take into account the rich complexity of the messages that these signals can convey. What Darwin missed was that changes in body postures and visual signals are a language that let others know of one's intentions. Each animal comes equipped with a toolbox of expressions and postures that it can adopt in response to changing situations around it. Darwin thought that an animal's behavior arose from some internal state or emotion, and certainly emotion has a lot to do with these signals. But I maintain that there is so much more going on.

For example, if I am walking down a dark street and see a group of thugs approaching me, I am going to experience the emotion of fear. But I also have the conscious volition to not express this fear. I can stand straight, hold my head high, walk briskly, pay no attention, and act like I am in control of the situation. Animals, too, have the option of displaying a variety of signals. Some may be an honest reflection of their emotions, some may not. Many animal behaviorists believe that animals other than humans are not capable of conscious volition in their actions, but at the moment there is not enough evidence to either support or reject their position.

We do know that other animals pay close attention to complex visual signals, because rarely are the signals simple changes in only one body part. Usually the signals involve multiple body parts that change in different combinations depending on the context. Humans spend a considerable amount of time scanning each other's faces, looking at the eyes, the nose, the mouth, and somewhat less time at the general outline of the face. With us, the eyes and eyebrows, the flaring of the nostrils, and the shape of the mouth offer excellent cues about our intentions and responses to a particular context.

Chimps, too, spend a considerable amount of time scanning chimp faces. In a study of scanning patterns of a group of chimps and a group of humans when each chimp and each human was presented with three pictures—a chimp torso and face, a human torso and face, and a lion torso and face—

the humans and chimps had some similarities and some differences. The humans scanned mostly the eyes and nose of the chimp picture; the eyes, nose, and mouth of the human picture; and the eyes and mouth of the lion picture. The chimps scanned the eyes, mouth, and shoulders of both the chimp picture and the human picture, and the eyes and mouth of the lion picture.

Like us paying attention to our visual signals, dogs pay attention to theirs. Dogs have a variety of signals that can involve using body posture, the position of the ears, the shape of the mouth, and the fur on the back of the neck and shoulders. One of the major signals is the position of the tail. But what happens when the tail is artificially shortened? Are other dogs affected by this tail shortening? In the United States at least, more than one third of all dog breeds have traditionally had their tails docked. How does this affect dog body language?

This question is a difficult one to answer scientifically because experiments have been so hard to perform. If you're using live dogs with short and long tails to study this question, you have a lot of factors other than tail length that could confuse the issue. You have all kinds of body scents, ear positions, general body posture, and behavioral interactions that can modify the response of other dogs to short or long tails.

A recent behavioral tool has been to use robots to study the behavior of other animals. With a robot you can test for specific things, such as a short tail versus a long tail on a dog, and everything else stays constant: The robot is still the same size, stays in the same position, doesn't have any confusing smells, and doesn't engage in any behaviors that could modify the response of an approaching animal. In one study, scientists used a robot about the size of a Labrador retriever, and attached to the robot either a short or a long tail. Using a servo mechanism, they could make the tail either wag or stand still. They videotaped the approaches of off-leash dogs and assessed the conditions under which the dogs either freely approached the robot or hesitated in their approach.

They found that the dogs differed in their approach to a short tail versus a long tail. Both larger and smaller dogs tended to approach the robot without hesitation when the robot had a long, wagging tail, and tended to hesitate more when the long tail was motionless. We might expect this because a wagging tail generally signals friendliness, while a motionless tail can signal potential aggression.

On the other hand, both larger and smaller dogs seemed to have a difficult time determining whether the short tail was wagging or still. Both the larger and smaller dogs tended to approach either the wagging short tail or the still short tail at about the same rate, a rate that was below the rate of approach for a long wagging tail and above the rate of approach for a motionless long tail. It was as if the dogs couldn't see the difference between a wagging short tail or a motionless one and had to make a guess as to whether to approach or not. So it seems that tail docking does introduce some confusion into dog language, making it much more difficult for dogs to determine whether a dog with a short tail is friendly or potentially aggressive.

LIZARD GRAMMARS

Previously, I talked about the ornate tree lizards living on the outside walls of my house. The lizards are all about five inches long, and sleek with a mottled pattern of brown and gray that makes them well camouflaged against a tree trunk or a tree branch.

As I sit in my study, I get to watch the behavior of the lizards through the study windows. The males are distinctively colored with one of two color patterns: either a blue stomach, a large orange spot on the chin, and an orange and blue throat; or all orange chin, throat, and stomach. There are more of the blue ones than the orange ones on my house walls. The blue ones will signal to each other by doing a series of push-ups with their head and front legs, in a jerky fashion, usually with one or two push-ups to start, followed by a couple of seconds of doing nothing, and then several more push-ups in rapid succession. Both males will do this, and then one of the males will turn tail and run.

The orange ones are not so aggressive. When a blue male confronts an orange one, the blue male does a series of push-ups while the orange one just sits there and watches. The blue male will repeat the push-ups, varying the number of push-ups he does. The orange male still does nothing. Then the blue male takes a few steps toward the orange one, and the orange lizard turns around and runs away.

In the mating signals chapter, I also talked about the signals of the sagebrush lizard that lives in sagebrush and woodland habitats of the western United States. These lizards have a more complex set of signals than my ornate tree lizards, and use these signals in aggressive territorial interactions with other males. In addition to doing push-ups and head bobs, they can modify the message by extending one or more of their legs, arching their back, or raising their tail. A similar pattern can be seen in the jacky dragon (*Amphibolurus muricatus*), a lizard that is around nine inches long, living in southeastern Australia. Like the sagebrush lizards, jacky dragons are territorial, and males give a series of complex signals to other males. Initially, a male jacky dragon goes through five body postures, one posture following another: a tail flick, a backward arm wave, a forward arm wave, a push-up, and a body rock. What happens after that is variable. A body rock can be followed by a push-up, or a backward arm wave, or a tail flick, depending on how the lizard wants to signal his aggressive intent. It is like watching a well-choreographed dance.

Although push-ups, arched backs, tail raises, and arm waves could be considered a part of Darwin's Principle of Antithesis, the message is much more complex than simply raising and lowering body parts. The message is conveyed by making certain movements in a particular, distinct sequence, with specific time intervals in between the different movements. In addition, the movements themselves can be modified depending on the context. In other words, there is a grammar in the way that the signals are combined.

SOUND

The idea that animals have the ability to select among a variety of possible signals in response to the context of a situation also applies to the sounds they can make during an encounter with an enemy or competitor. According to Darwin, though, animal sounds during an aggressive encounter are likely to be motivated solely by fear or aggression. Other researchers have agreed.

Eugene Morton of the Smithsonian Institution came up with what he called Motivation Structure Function Rules (MSFR), which is a reformulation of Darwin's principle applied to sound. Morton suggests that low-frequency sound, like low deep growls, mean aggressive threat; while high-frequency sound, like high-pitched whines, mean fear. Everything else, according to the MSFR, fits somewhere in between aggression and fear. So according to this hypothesis, the alarm calls of prairie dogs, which have an inverted V-shaped acoustic structure with some low frequency sounds and some high-frequency ones, would be a blend of aggression (the prairie dog is angry at the predator for disturbing his day) and fear (the prairie dog is afraid of the predator). The end points—low frequency and high frequency—might be valid, but we know that there is a lot more to the information contained in sound than is suggested by either the MSFR or Darwin's Principle of Antithesis.

Our human voices sound more threatening when they are low-pitched, both to us and to other animals. When I was teaching dog-training classes, I would ask my students to use their voice to reinforce the behavior that they were teaching to their dogs. I found that although clickers are the current fashion in dog-training circles (you click with the clicker when the dog does something that you want her to do, reinforcing the behavior in the dog's mind), most people would promptly lose their clickers. I preferred that people talk to their dogs, because they'll always have their voice with them. I taught them to say, "NO!" in a loud, strong, authoritative low-pitched voice, when the dog was doing something that she wasn't supposed to do, and say "Good dog!" in a lilting, high-pitched voice when the dog was being praised for doing the right thing. At the low pitch, this mimics the warning growl that dogs give to each other, causing a dog to stop what she was doing and look at her person for further instructions. Praise given at a higher pitch mimics the whines that dog moms give their pups as signs of encouragement and rewards a dog for continuing to do what she was doing.

What was a problem, however, was getting the men to say, "Good dog!" in a high-pitched voice, and the women to say,

"NO!" in a lower register. Men would typically say, "Good dog!" in something that was a cross between a growl and a snarl, while women would typically say, "NO!" in a high-pitched voice. In my classes, we practiced saying, "NO!" and, "Good dog!" to each other, with me pressing everyone to either raise or lower their voices. I would demonstrate for my class how hard it was for me to say, "Good dog!" in anything other than a growl, and then exaggerate the high pitch, putting my hand on my Adam's apple until I got the desired tone. Then we would spend about ten minutes practicing saying, "NO!" and, "Good dog!" to each other. Under my guidance, the men worked on raising their voices for the "Good dog!" while the women worked on lowering and projecting theirs strongly for the "NO!" More than once, after we did this exercise, a few women would come up to me and say, "My dog always has listened to my husband but never to me, and now I know why."

Lower-pitched voices are considered to be more dominant by both men and women. Women who have lower-pitched voices are seen by men as more dominant, but not necessarily more attractive. In one experiment, Polish women pronounced a series of vowels, and the experimenters determined the base frequency (this is called the fundamental frequency) of each woman's voice. The recordings of the vowels were then played back to both men and women, who rated each voice for dominance and attractiveness. Both the men and the women rating the voices agreed that women with lower-pitched voices were more dominant, but the men thought that higher-pitched women's voices were more attractive than lower-pitched ones. However, extremely high-pitched voices were not seen as attractive by the men raters, perhaps because the high-pitched voices resembled a child's or a baby's voice.

Conversely, women prefer lower-pitched voices in men, as

a sign of increased dominance and masculinity. Lower-pitched voices even play a role in presidential debates in the United States. In all debates from 1960 to 2000, the person with the lowest fundamental frequency went on to win the election, with the exception of the year 2000, when Gore, with the lower-base frequency voice, won the popular vote, but Bush won the electoral vote.

BUGLING ELK, ROARING DEER, AND SQUAWKING COATIS

Every autumn in the Rocky Mountain regions of the American West, you can hear the bugling of male elk around dusk. The bugling starts off as a long, eerie low-frequency screeching sound, followed by a series of three or four shorter sounds kind of like someone scratching glass on concrete. The first time one of my graduate students, newly arrived from the East Coast, heard this sound on a dark evening in the mountains, he was startled and disoriented. He later said that he thought the sound was like a banshee or goblin wailing in anticipation of the beginning of the night. After assuring him that to the best of my knowledge neither banshees nor goblins inhabited the mountains of northern Arizona, I told him that he had heard the aggressive call of a male elk (*Cervus canadensis*), advertising his presence to other males and perhaps also to any females that happened to be nearby. When you hear it for the first time, it can be pretty terrifying.

Although red deer (*Cervus elaphus*) are similar in size and shape to elk, and in fact were thought for a long time to be the same species of animal, their calls are very different. Red deer are found in Europe, Western Asia, and Northern Africa. They have a roaring call that advertises their aggressiveness toward other males, and they make this call during the mating season when they are guarding a harem of females. Depending on the size of their opponents, the males can vary the base pitch of their roars, making the roars sound deeper when they are faced with a larger opponent. This gradation in the base pitch of the roars probably conveys information to challengers about the male's willingness and ability to fight to defend his harem.

Another animal with lower- and higher-pitched calls is the coati (*Nasua narica*). These relatives of raccoons are one of my favorite animals. They have long noses and long, bushy tails, and are equally at home on the ground or in the branches of trees. When they forage on the ground they stretch out their head and long white-tipped nose, and their tail is usually held out straight in back of them, so that they look like a fat torpedo on legs. They live in social groups in Central America and the southwestern United States, and travel in small bands. Like the elk, coatis have one type of call in aggressive situations and another type of call in more friendly, social situations. The aggressive call sounds something like a "squawk" composed of several harmonic frequencies in the lower-frequency range. The other call sounds like a "chirp" and is composed of higher-pitched frequencies. "Chirps" tend to be fairly variable and perhaps encode a variety of meanings in social situations, while the "squawks" tend to be less variable and perhaps encode a meaning something like "leave me alone."

Although each of these animals has aggressive calls that are lower-pitched than more friendly ones, suggesting that Darwin's Principle of Antithesis (and the Motivation Structure Function Rules) apply, the calls have a considerable amount of complexity that is not explained by the MSFR. Aggressive calls typically contain a number of harmonics, each of which varies slightly, potentially containing information that we are still unable to decode.

Unlike the vibration of a violin string, in which the harmonics are simple multiples of the base frequency of vibration, the harmonics in these calls contain rises and falls of frequencies caused by modulation of the larynxes of the animals making the sound, as predicted by the Discourse System. These modulations probably contain more specific information about the intentions of the animals making the sounds, but we are still not at the stage where we can interpret the information and correlate the changes in frequency modulations with the subtleties of the aggressive contexts in which the animals find themselves.

LET BARKING DOGS LIE

If you want to protect your house from burglars, a good low-cost way is to get a barking-dog alarm. This device senses motion on the other side of a door or window and responds with the aggressive barking of a large guard dog such as a German shepherd. Although I have not seen any studies that document the effectiveness of such devices, anecdotally they are supposed to scare off burglars who are either afraid of large dogs, or who simply prefer not to go to the trouble of dealing with them when they can instead go on to rob some other house that's easier to break into. The broadcast barks on these recordings are deliberately low in pitch. We can only assume that burglars would not be scared off by the higher-pitched yapping of a Pomeranian or Chihuahua, although those breeds can certainly bite a burglar's ankle as well as any German shepherd.

Like barks, lower-pitched dog growls are also perceived as

more threatening by people. A study looked at whether people could identify dog growls that sounded more aggressive. The experimenters recorded the growls of thirty dogs by going into the dogs' houses, staring the dogs in the eye, and approaching them with a microphone. Then they analyzed the basic pitch (also called the fundamental frequency) of each dog's growl and the distribution of sound energy within the dog barks. Larger dogs have a longer vocal tract and make sounds that have a lower fundamental frequency, and it turns out that when people listen to dog growls, the growls that have a lower fundamental frequency are perceived as being from larger, more aggressive dogs.

Unlike us, dogs can hear subtle differences between different growls. We humans do not do so well in that department. When people were played recordings of different dog growls and asked which were aggressive and which were play growls, they had a difficult time telling them apart. Dogs appear to have no such problems. A study using forty-one dogs of various breeds tested whether dogs can tell the difference between growls given when another dog approaches food, when an unfamiliar stranger approaches, and while playing tug.

Here's how researchers set up the experiment: They left a bone on the floor of a room and allowed a subject dog to approach it. When the dog's nose was close to the bone, they played back either a food-guarding growl, or a threatening-stranger growl, or a play-tug growl, all of which they had previously recorded in real situations.

The results were striking. When the food-guarding growl was played, eleven of twelve dogs withdrew from the bone. Compare this with the other growls: two of twelve dogs withdrew from the bone when they heard the threatening stranger growl, and four of twelve dogs withdrew when they heard the play-tug growl. All three types of growls had different acoustic properties in terms of fundamental frequency and formants, and the food-guarding growls and the threatening-stranger growls were lower in pitch than the play-tug growl. Clearly, the dogs understood the meaning of the growls.

We know relatively little about the information contained in barks and growls of other species in the dog family, such as wolves and foxes. Some of the foxes, such as the gray fox, bark quite readily. One time I was doing some research along the northern California coast, and had rented for the summer a house near the beach. The house was built on a steep hill, so that the back side abutted the hill, while the front side was on tall stilts, in typical California fashion of ignoring the possibility that an earthquake would likely sever the stilts and cause the house to come tumbling down. Around the front side, some twenty feet off the ground, a door opened onto a narrow deck with a spectacular view of the ocean.

One foggy night around midnight I heard an urgent series of barks from the deck by the front door. The barks didn't sound like a dog. They were more growly snarly. My imagination promptly suggested that it was the Hound of the Baskervilles, returning from a night of hunting on the moors. But I took my flashlight, carefully opened the door a crack, and peered out. Sitting there, like a pet dog, was a gray fox (*Urocyon cinereoargenteus*)! Mind you, this fox was sitting on a narrow deck twenty feet above the ground, facing the front door, and clearly, at least in my imagination, asking to be let inside. Thoughts of rabies flashed through my mind, and I quickly shut the door, letting the fox sit there for the next couple of hours, barking. For the entire time that I lived in that house, this was a nightly ritual. The fox would show up at midnight, bark for a couple of hours, and then disappear. I often wonder now what would have happened if I had let the fox come inside. Maybe the fox simply wanted a warm bed to sleep in during the chilly, foggy coastal nights.

Another fox, the swift fox (*Vulpes velox*), barks at the edge of its territory to advertise to other foxes that this particular piece of land is taken. Swift foxes live mostly in prairie dog towns, in monogamous family groups, with mom, dad, and the kids living inside an enlarged prairie dog burrow. They are tiny animals, the adults not much bigger than housecats. I had the chance to watch a family in northern New Mexico, when the BBC team was filming my work with prairie dog language. One of the photographers had found a family of foxes, and so we all crept up to the crest of a little hillock and watched the animals through our binoculars. I found that the reason that swift foxes are called that is because they are really swift. The kids were running around chasing each other, and in my opinion they could have given a greyhound a run for its money. They seemed to accelerate from a sitting start to a high rate of speed, and then would jump on one of their playmates and tumble around in the dirt, while mom patiently sat and waited for the kids to settle down so that she could go out and hunt prairie dogs for dinner. Both mom and dad occasionally barked as they got farther away from their den, letting other foxes know that they were occupying this territory.

ANGRY BATS AND MONKEYS

A lot of people are afraid of bats. In my animal behavior classes, I have always tried to bring in as many live animals as possible, so that my students could see something that was living and breathing, rather than listen to me just talking about it. Once, I had the opportunity to bring in a bat. One of the graduate students had some Mexican free-tailed bats (*Tadarida brasiliensis*) in a cage in the laboratory, and agreed to come to my class with a live bat, and talk about bat behavior. This was in the days prior to the time when safeguards and permissions from university committees specified in stringent detail how animals were to be handled, so I made sure that we were both clear about how he was going to show the bat to the students. Prior to bringing in the bat, I went over my rules. Under no circumstances was he to let the bat go, or let anyone other than himself handle it. Picture the classroom: a large, two-story auditorium seating about 150 people, with a podium down in the front and seats going up all the way back to exits onto the second floor of the building. As class started, he took out the bat and held it up in front of the class, with the bat's wings gently outstretched. He talked for a few minutes about the biology and behavior of bats, and then asked if there were any questions.

There were lots of questions: The students knew very little about the lives of bats and were interested in finding out. Finally, one student asked, "How do they fly?" Forgetting all of the rules that we talked about, the graduate student said, "Here, let me show you." And he flipped the bat up into the air. The bat took off. Confused by the overhead lights, the bat flew toward the ceiling, and then swung down toward the seated students, making a low pass over people's heads. Screams ensued. For about five minutes the bat swooped down toward people, with everyone trying to duck under their chairs. Finally the bat, either by luck or by chance, landed on the cage that the graduate student brought in, and was captured. Later, many students told me that it was a very scary experience, even though the chance of having the bat land on them was negligible. Somehow they thought that the bat was going to attack them.

But bats seldom attack people, and seldom attack even each other. We are now finding out that at least some bats have a rich communication system that allows them to let each other know about their aggressive intentions. One such bat is the greater false vampire bat (*Megaderma lyra*) that lives in Southeast Asia. It is a large bat, eating lizards, small birds, mice, rats, large insects, frogs, and fish, by swooping down and picking them off the surface of the ground or water. It roosts inside caves or mine shafts. As the bats interact with one another at their roosts, they produce a variety of calls in different aggressive contexts.

When one bat moves toward another, the bat being approached opens up his mouth, raises his wings, and gives a series of high-pitched clicks and warbles. The approaching bat responds with calls that have a number of harmonics and complex acoustic structure. If the approaching bat is attacked, he gives an even more acoustically complicated series of vocalizations, to which the attacking bat responds with equally complicated vocalizations. These bats have structurally complex vocalizations in at least two different contexts of aggression.

Rhesus monkeys have even more complex vocalizations in different aggressive contexts. A study of rhesus monkeys on Cayo Santiago in Puerto Rico has shown that these animals have five different screams that they give in aggressive situations. These five screams are: "noisy," "arched," "tonal," "pulsed," and "undulated." Each type of scream is distinguished by how it sounds, and any of the five can be repeated multiple times by an animal during an aggressive interaction.

The context in which these calls are given is different. "Noisy screams" are most often given by lower-ranking members of the social group when they are confronted by higher-ranking ones, and also are given when there is physical contact between the monkeys. "Undulated screams" are given by lower-ranking monkeys when they are in a dispute with a higher-ranking monkey, but there is no physical contact. "Arched screams" are given by higher-ranking monkeys when confronting lower-ranking ones. And "tonal" and "pulsed" screams are given by monkeys when they are squabbling with their relatives. The screams act as words with semantic meaning, providing information about the intentions of the monkeys.

Not all monkey screams are the same. Although we might expect that closely related monkey species would have similar calls in the same contexts, this is not the case. The pig-tailed macaque (*Macaca nemestrina*) is a close evolutionary cousin of the rhesus monkey, inhabiting much of Southwest Asia, including parts of India and China. This monkey has calls for the same kinds of contexts that the rhesus monkeys have: screams where there is physical contact, calls for disputes between higher-ranking and lower-ranking animals, and calls for disputes between relatives. But the acoustic properties of the calls are quite different from those of the rhesus monkeys. Screams have higher-peak frequencies, greater bandwidth, and more harmonics than those of the rhesus. Other vocalizations also differ in the acoustic structure of the calls. In fact, a comparison of four closely related species of monkeys shows that each species differs in the structure of their calls.

The bottom line here is two things. One is that the Motivation Structure Function Rules would not predict any of these vocalizations, because none of them are purely low-frequency sound. The other is that each species has its own language, and even though the species are closely related to one another, it is likely that one species would not understand the screams of any of the other three species of macaques.

BIRD GRAMMAR

Like mammals, many species of birds have vocalizations that they use in aggressive contexts. Territorial disputes often involve squawks and chirps as the birds face off. And prior to such potential conflict, many birds sing to advertise their territories. The divas of the natural world, birds have a huge range and complexity of songs, calls, subsongs, and what researchers call *quiet song*.

But are these songs, squawks, chatters, and chirps just random sounds, or perhaps just expressions of the emotions that the birds are feeling? Anger at another bird? A desire to fight? We are just beginning to scratch the surface of looking at these vocalizations in the context of conveying meaningful information, despite the thousands of studies that have looked at all of the general functions of birdsong.

One thing is clear: Bird vocalizations don't seem to be limited by Darwin's Principle of Antithesis and the Motivation Structure Function Rules. Both birdsongs in general, and aggressive vocalizations in particular, have a lot of different tones and sound frequency changes, so that when you look at a sonogram of an aggressive vocalization, you do not see something that has pure tones of very low frequency. Instead, you see a lot of rises and falls of frequency, suggesting that there is a considerable amount of information encoded in such calls and songs.

Some birdsong is so complex that it is still being teased apart for its meaning, but fortunately, studies of chickadees and hummingbirds have successfully shown how the information is encoded in their aggressive vocalizations.

Black-capped chickadees (*Poecile atricapillus*) are small songbirds that are found throughout the northern half of the United States and most of Canada. They are usually found around shrubs and trees in a variety of habitats. Among the many different calls that these birds have is a vocalization that is called "gargle." This name is really a misnomer. Unlike the sound of someone clearing their throat or gargling with mouthwash, the chickadee "gargle" is really a series of high-pitched, whistle-type notes that are compressed into about half a second. It sounds very musical compared to the "gurgle-gurgle-gurgle" that someone would expect from hearing the name of this vocalization.

The "gargle" is used in aggressive interactions. It is primarily given when two birds encounter each other in relatively close quarters, such as at a bird feeder. The bird that perceives itself as dominant is the one that gives the "gargle." The more subordinate bird stays silent and gives way to the gargler. As is the case with many signals, the "gargle" is sometimes accompanied by visual signals: raising a wing, ruffling the feathers, or making pecking movements.

Just as a human might yell angrily at an opponent and at the same time use body language to do something like shake a fist or extend a middle finger, a chickadee gives a series of "gargle" sounds and also provides visual cues about its intentions. Studies where "gargle" sounds alone were played back to caged birds showed that vocalizations were less effective in eliciting a response when they were not paired with video images of the gargling bird.

While at first glance it might seem that the "gargling" has little effect, think about it in a context. Suppose you heard a recording of a stranger screaming at you, "I hate you!" No big deal, right? Who knows or who cares why this person is screaming. Now suppose that you opened your front door and there, standing a short distance away, was a stranger screaming, "I hate you!" and gesticulating with his arms. You might have a much stronger response to the second situation, just like the chickadees respond more to "gargles" when they see a visual image of another chickadee.

The "gargle" is a very complex vocalization. It can contain up to thirteen different notes, and there is a syntax or appropriate order in how the notes are arranged. Some notes tend to occur together as groups, the same way that the letters in one of our words occur in a group: for example, "gargle." Nine such groups have been identified.

Other notes occur either before a group (the way that prefixes work in one of our words) or after a group (think suffixes here). So far, some eighty-four different "gargle" types have been identified. Each bird has a repertoire of multiple "gargle" types. In an aggressive encounter, the dominant bird will often vocalize one or two different gargles, and usually this has the effect of the subordinate bird yielding its space at a feeder to the dominant one. But if that doesn't work, the dominant bird will vocalize multiple different gargles, up to sixteen different ones by one count. That usually is enough to have the subordinate bird get the message that it is time to clear out.

What's interesting about this research is that it shows clearly that the vocalizations of this little bird not only have a structure and function, but also that the caller can assess how well his message is getting across and adjust his behavior accordingly. If a particular warning "gargle" is not effective in scaring off an intruder, he has the option of either giving up, attacking, or best of all, adjusting the power of his communication by deliberately escalating the complexity of his calls. Clearly this is not just a case of a knee-jerk, hardwired stimulus-response pattern.

Another tiny bird, Anna's hummingbird also sports a variety of complex aggressive vocalizations. Outside my window, a male Anna's has laid claim to one of our sugar-water feeders. He sits either on a nearby clothesline or in the branches of a nearby tree and guards the feeder all day long. When the feeder has run dry and neither my wife nor I have noticed, he will fly up to the window and hover there with his tail splayed out, bobbing up and down.

If this has no effect (and when I am writing, I tend to not pay attention to much else), he will retreat back to the clothesline and wait patiently for a few minutes, and then start the hovering display again, repeating this over and over until I start paying attention and my feeling of guilt kicks in. At that point, I'll get up and get more sugar water to refill the feeder.

Occasionally, a traveling hummingbird will fly up to the feeder, apparently not aware that it is being guarded. My hummer will instantly fly up to within a couple of feet of the intruder, hover, fan out his tail, and start a stream of vocalizations that sound like high-pitched squeaks. The hovering and the tail fanning are similar to what he does in front of my window to get me to get him some more food, so I suppose that I can interpret it as him being mad at me for failing to keep the feeder filled. He doesn't vocalize to me, however. I guess that I should be grateful for small favors.

An occasional visitor to my feeders is the black-chinned hummingbird (*Archilochus alexandri*). Both the males and the females have a complex aggressive song that has syntax, and that they can vary considerably. There are five different note types, by convention called C, Z, S, T, and E. The C note is a very short note with four harmonics. The Z and S notes are longer-duration trills that differ in their acoustic frequencies. The T note is a burst of noise, and the E note is a short note with four harmonics that differ in their acoustic frequency distributions from the C note. These note types can be recombined in different ways. Some vocalizations can start with a Z note, then have an S note followed by a T, an E, and then another S and a T. Other vocalizations can start with a C note, then combine an S and a T into a single-note group, and follow that with a T and an E. The calls can contain up to eighteen notes, mixed in different combinations. The C or S notes often begin the song, while the E note usually ends it.

These songs have the linguistic property of openness, where openness means that the call types can be recombined in many different ways. For example, we can use vowels and consonants in English to generate the approximately 500,000 English words that are known to exist, or the approximately 10,000 English words that a high-school graduate can recognize. While we don't know the specific contexts in which all of the hummingbird call types are used, it is likely that some of them convey information about the intentions of the birds to either attack and escalate an aggressive interaction, or to avoid escalation and retreat from an actual conflict.

In addition to singing a territorial song, some birds can engage in two other kinds of singing behavior that actually predict the possibility of attack: low-amplitude song and frequency matching. *Low-amplitude song* is also known as "soft song" or "quiet song" because it is not very loud. It would be like my whispering, "You're dead meat" to you. Of course, you would have to be pretty close to me to hear it. In terms of frequency matching, individual birds of the same species can sing at somewhat higher or lower frequencies, just as we have our individual voices. *Frequency matching* is when a territorial bird shifts the acoustic frequencies in its song to match those of an intruder. So if you were to say, "Hi there," in your own tone of voice, and I said, "Hi there," in exactly the same tone as you used, that would be an example of frequency matching. Male swamp sparrows (*Melospiza georgiana*) sing low-amplitude songs just prior to attacking another male. However, the message is multimodal with some body language thrown in. While they are singing the low-amplitude song, they are also raising and vibrating one or both of their wings, in much the same way that human vocalizations and body language go hand in hand. A related bird species, the song sparrow (*Melospiza melodia*) also uses low-amplitude song as an attack predictor. Frequency matching has been described as a predictor of attack in black-capped chickadees.

WHAT'S IT GOOD FOR?

Certainly there are elements of animal signals for aggression that can be explained by Darwin's and Morton's principles. People who stand tall are more highly regarded than people who slouch. Animals that growl are more likely to strike fear into our hearts than animals that whine.

One night I was walking through the southern Arizona desert. Many people think of a desert as something with endless sand dunes and no plants of any kind, like some parts of the Sahara. But the southern Arizona desert is not like that. There are large mesquite and ironwood trees, as well as saguaro cacti that can stand some twenty feet tall. Every few feet there is some kind of shrub or annual plant. Most of what you see as you look around is greenery. Sand dunes are rare. At night this desert teems with life. There are tarantulas, scorpions, centipedes, a variety of beetles, all kinds of flying insects, and snakes, mice, rats, rabbits, foxes, coyotes, bobcats, and an occasional mountain lion. As I was walking past a fairly large bush, a deep growl came from somewhere either inside or behind the bush. I jumped a couple of feet to the side and rapidly left the bush behind. I did not stop to see what had made the growl. Just hearing it was enough to tell me that some animal was upset at my being there, and if I stuck around, the animal might decide to attack and bite me.

And that is the crux of the matter. Opposites of body position and of sound frequencies might very well encode information about emotion, such as anger or fear or happiness, but there is so much more information that is encoded in both body postures and vocalizations. Birds vibrate their wings, dogs wag their tails, we skew our mouths to one side in a gesture of contempt, and these signals are often done in a predictable sequence or syntax. When we look at the signals of closely related species, such as the rhesus monkeys, the promise and hope of a common language slips away. Each species seems to have its own language, although closely related species have similar but not identical languages. Emotion might be an underlying factor behind some of the signals, but clearly looking at just emotion is not enough. We need to look at how the signals are combined together into rich languages that contain information that is relevant to each animal species.

Communicating about aggression has a lot of advantages. From a linguistic standpoint, it allows animals to express their intentions. Are they going to fight, to retreat? How motivated are they to fight? This communication is clearly not just in the form of emotional responses. There is a lot of information that is conveyed in symbolic form, through visual and acoustic signals that comprise a toolbox that animals can reach into to express their intentions and their thoughts. The symbols vary in context, and animals can control the production of the symbols according to the context.

The Discourse System explains the continuum of events that go into the production of the signals. Think of a male elk bellowing a warning challenge to other males. Prior to that, the hormones of the male have primed him for feeling like fighting, for being willing to risk injury in challenging another male, for being willing to compete with other males for access to females. His eyes, ears, and nose zero in on the sight, sound, and smell of another male. His body posture changes to a more stiff-legged, more erect one, with the head up and the antlers prominently displayed. His lungs bellow out his aggressive challenge, so that the sound can be heard up to a mile away, expending energy that could have been used for other physiological processes. Once he meets an opponent, his brain decides whether to pursue a challenge or to retreat. He might feel fear, but he also feels the urge to fight. But the heart of most aggressive encounters is not the physical fighting, it is the information conveyed by the signals. The best possible outcome is to defeat an opponent through exchanging signals about the intention to fight and to have the opponent back down without any physical contact. Fighting can lead to injury, and injury can often lead to death. Natural Selection shapes the Discourse System to provide animals with all of the necessary abilities to advertise their strength and willingness to fight, while at the same time minimizing the necessity of engaging in fights that result in injury.

8. HELLO, MY NAME IS JOE

When I take my dog for a walk in a nearby park we often meet other dogs, each walking on a leash with their owner. Usually, we have met them in previous walks, so I say hello to the people, and we stop to chat for a few minutes while our dogs greet each other. My dog and the other dog will approach each other, tails wagging. They bark once or twice, sniff each other's noses, then go and sniff each other's butts, and if they are male (as is my dog), they will sniff each other's penises.

My greeting of the people is much more subdued. I smile, sometimes raise my right hand in a wave, and as we get close, extend and shake hands if I know the other person well enough. In both cases, my dog and I each go through a process that all social animals need to do: greet another individual and recognize who they are. I remember the other person's name, and maybe the two dogs have names for each other based on their chemical smell profiles, barks, and general appearance.

My guess is that one of the first uses of the Discourse System in animals had to do with recognition and greeting. Animals encountering each other out in the wilderness had to quickly figure out whether it was friend or foe—or a potential mate—whom they were approaching, or who was approaching them. Communication quickly became a useful way of doing this, and certain signals evolved to lessen tensions between animals and convey a peaceful intent.

In social animals, members of the same family or community might have developed their own rituals for greeting, and the rituals themselves, sort of like a secret handshake, enabled individuals who ran into each other to instantly know whether they belonged to the same group. We humans still have such rituals today that vary from culture to culture.

In Morocco, for example, there are many elaborate social rituals involved in even simple transactions, and if you don't participate appropriately in the ritual, you won't be seen as "belonging" and you won't be treated as well. When my wife and I visited the city of Fez, known for its arts and crafts, we were accompanied by a young Ph.D. friend of ours who was a native Moroccan. We told him that we wanted to buy a rug, so he took us into a shop in the *souk*, or market, in the town's old quarter.

We entered the shop and spoke the traditional greeting we had learned, "*Salaam aleikum*." The salesperson gave the proper response and invited us to sit. To our surprise, we didn't do any shopping for quite a while. Instead, fragrant sweet mint tea was poured, and we sipped and chatted (our friend acting as translator) about general things, such as our visit, how we liked Morocco, etc. Only after a prerequisite amount of time had been spent socializing did the actual shopping begin. Beautiful rugs were brought out, and as we narrowed our selection down to a couple of favorites, my wife and I were left completely out of the conversation, which had shifted to pure Arabic haggling about price. Three incredible hours later, we emerged, exhausted but deeply grateful to our friend, who had negotiated a great price on an exquisite hand-woven rug. Had we just barged in and done our shopping in typical American-tourist style, we would have never, ever achieved such a bargain, and we knew it.

Animals have greeting rituals and social signaling, too. My wife is particularly good at picking up on this. For example, she says she has learned a few greeting signals in "cat." One is a "meow" that ends on an up-note, almost like someone asking a question. Another is the head-butt, where she lowers her head and aims one upper temple toward the side of the cat's face, just below one ear. This sounds much more intrusive than, say, just leaning down and patting a cat, but she believes that this is an appropriate greeting behavior.

She put it to the test with her friend's cat, Bean. Bean is one of those cats who was born cranky. She loves her owner but can be very demanding, and will often terminate a petting session with a swipe of unsheathed claws. Although Bean leads a charmed life, she often has a scowling expression on her face and basically loathes anyone but her owner. Attempts by visitors to pet her are often met with hissing snarls. She tends to hover in a room where guests are being entertained, radiating impatience for them to *"Just leave!"*

My wife had learned of Bean's reputation and was determined to win her over. The first few times she came to visit, my wife spoke sweetly and admiringly to Bean, who just glared back at first, but eventually started looking a little more receptive. My wife didn't try to pet the cat, or ask anything of her. Then, the fourth time she came over, Bean was on the kitchen counter and my wife switched from English to the cat greeting "Meow?" Bean meowed back. Knowing she might get her forehead sliced open, my wife kept her hands at her sides and lowered her head and tentatively, slowly approached Bean, who, wonder of wonders, moved *her* head toward my wife's and slid the side of her face against my wife's temple. (The area of a cat's head just below its ears contains a scent gland that cats can use to *mark* people, and other cats, that they like.) From that point on, I wouldn't go so far as to say they became best buddies, but a détente had certainly been achieved. Now when my wife comes into her friend's house, Bean comes out and approaches her, they go through their greeting ritual, and Bean even tolerates being petted for a few seconds. Progress!

WHAT'S YOUR NAME?

Another important role that language can play in a first encounter is to identify individuals, the wild version of the "Hi, My Name Is" nametag (a visual signal), or the verbal self-introduction and handshake gesture (a quaint custom that is said to have originated in the days of swordfighting: Extending your weaponless right hand toward a stranger proclaims that your intentions are peaceful).

Most of us would not be surprised to know that a variety of animals, such as a number of birds and mammals, can identify individuals within their social group. Just like we can identify individual faces, body shapes, and even the way that people walk, many animals can identify individuals by visual, acoustic, or olfactory means.

One species who might use all three is the Gunnison's prairie dogs, those chubby ground squirrels who live in the grasslands of the West. In a prairie dog colony, the animals divide up the available space into territories that contain both the food resources and burrow sites that the group needs to survive. At first, each territorial group was thought to be a highly related family unit, but recent DNA testing revealed that they are really a collection of mostly unrelated individuals who band together to cooperatively defend a particular piece of turf.

A prairie dog territorial group might have anywhere between one and twenty animals. Where there are many animals occupying a territory, there are typically several adult males, several adult females, and the young. Aboveground, prairie dogs have good distance vision and are usually on the alert for approaching predators, for whom they give alarm calls. They would also be likely to see trespassers on their property, but when two prairie dogs encounter each other, they often engage in a fascinating behavior called the *greet kiss*. Two prairie dogs approach each other with heads forward and mouths open, and when they get close enough, they turn their heads slightly, to get those big incisors out of the way, and touch their tongues together.

After such a kiss, the reaction of the prairie dogs varies, depending on who is engaging in the kiss. If they are parent and young or members of the same group, they will often move off, side by side, to forage together. But if one of the prairie dogs has strayed onto another's territory, then it's a different story that looks almost comical. Both step back after kissing and look shocked, as if each one had kissed a toad. The property owner then chases off the intruder.

So far, we don't know for sure why prairie dogs kiss. It doesn't seem to make sense that they would need taste cues to identify each other while up on the colony, because they have good vision. However, these interesting creatures spend most of their lives underground. Each coterie shares a multiroom burrow system, with rooms for sleeping, food storage, and waste management—all linked by tunnels. They spend most of the winter in their burrows, and even in summer, they are only aboveground well after sunrise and return below well before dark.

In the light of day above the ground, the prairie dogs might not need olfactory cues about an individual animal's identity, but below ground in the tunnels, smell or maybe taste might be the only way that they have of identifying friend or foe. Just as you could kiss your loved one when you got home from work in the evening and could tell they had onions at lunch, so, too, could prairie dogs tell whether someone was eating the mix of plants growing on their territory, or a different mix from somewhere else. Of course, there might be an additional reason. Just like with us, maybe it simply feels good to kiss.

Some other ground squirrels use odors to distinguish relatives from strangers. Belding's ground squirrels (*Urocitellus beldingi*) are very similar to prairie dogs in their general appearance. They live in higher elevations in the Pacific West of the United States. Small groups of females live together in a burrow, while the males typically live by themselves, also in a burrow. Like the prairie dogs, these ground squirrels have oral and dorsal scent glands that put out distinctive smells. One study has shown that the squirrels are able to discriminate between their relatives and strangers on the basis of the odors put out by these glands. Curiously, they are able to discriminate between individuals representing relatively small differences of relatedness, such as between a cousin and non-kin, or between a grandmother and an aunt. Since we humans are so bad at dealing with odors, we don't really know how these kin odors translate into what the animals actually perceive. Maybe odors are used in naming individual animals.

Think about how difficult it would be for us to assign odor

names to individual humans. The only example that I can think of from my own personal experience was a graduate student I once knew who used a particularly distinctive cologne. Odors tend to persist for a long time, and every time he would walk down the stairway of my building, for up to half an hour afterward, I could go into the stairway and instantly think, *Oh, Sam was here a little while ago.* Once I found out the name of the cologne that he was using, I would interchange Sam and the cologne name in my mind whenever I smelled his passing.

However, our Western European cultures tend to disguise odors. We wash with scented soaps and shampoos, we put on cologne or perfume, we put on deodorant, and do our best to wash away any natural body odors. When I was living in Kenya, most people did not use any scents to disguise their body odors. What you got when you went into a bus or some other crowded space was the raw smell of humanity. Sometimes it was overpowering. One time a Kenyan asked me, "How do you Europeans deal with body odors?" Thinking that he meant the overpowering body odors of people who did not use scented soaps and deodorants, I mumbled something, trying to frame a polite reply that would not insult the sensibilities of the person who asked the question. He quickly got the drift of where I was going with my reply, however, and said, "No, no, I don't mean our odors. I mean your stench. How do you put up with such foul smells as scented soaps and perfumed shampoos? You wash away all of the smells that give you clues about what people are really feeling." Maybe he had a point. Odor can be a component of language, and we wash it away.

Many species have what's called a *signature* component to their signaling, some part of the signal that is unique to that individual and identifies it in the group, just like a name. One of the most famous, and best-loved, animal to use a vocal signature is the dolphin.

Bottlenose dolphins (*Tursiops truncatus*) have individually distinct whistles that typically start with a relatively low frequency of around 5 kHz and in the space of a second rise to about 20 or more kHz. In some individual animals this rise is continuous, while in other animals there is a rise and fall in the frequency, creating an inverted-V in frequency modulation. These whistles might very well be comparable to a dolphin's name. Other dolphins will frequently copy a dolphin's signature whistle, as if they were saying that dolphin's name. One study recorded the individual whistles of dolphins, then played back the recordings to assess the dolphins' responses. The whistles of a mother's offspring were played back to the mother, as were the whistles of an unrelated young dolphin. Mothers tended to look more often at the speaker that was playing back their offspring's whistle.

Because there might be unexpected vocal cues in the whistles, another study synthesized whistles on a computer to minimize all of the acoustic features that make voices distinctive, leaving only the main acoustic structure of the whistle intact. These synthetic whistles were then played back through underwater speakers to individual dolphins. The playbacks were the whistles of a dolphin's relative and of a nonrelative, to see if each dolphin would pay more attention to a relative's synthetic whistles rather than to the synthetic whistles of a stranger. The dolphins indeed turned their heads more toward the playbacks of relatives' whistles than they did toward the playbacks of the whistles of nonrelatives. It is much like when you are at a party and there is a lot of chatter going on, and suddenly you hear your daughter's name amid all of the noise. You turn your head to see who might be talking about her and what they might be saying.

Dolphins probably learn something about signature whistles from their mothers. When a dolphin is born, its mother increases the rate of whistling from around one whistle every four minutes prior to the birth of the dolphin calf to around three whistles per minute in the first two weeks after the calf is born. Other dolphins who do not have young do not increase their rate of whistling during this period of time. Also, the mother's whistles change in their acoustic structure during this time. Because it is so difficult to record with hydrophones what is going on acoustically between different dolphins underwater, we do not know specifically what the mothers' whistles mean. Maybe they are teaching their young how to recognize their voices, and maybe they are teaching their young how to pronounce names. Maybe the mothers are naming their offspring and teaching them how to say their own names.

The whistles are not just used for names. One study looked at the contexts in which different whistles were given among seventeen adult and infant bottlenose dolphins. The adults were caught in the wild but had been confined for at least ten years, while the infants were born in captivity. The study documented whistles in fifteen different contexts. One context was either disciplining or being disciplined by another dolphin. Mothers will often discipline their infants by making a "thunk" vocalization when the infants stray too far away, causing the infant to swim back to the mother. Another context was playing with other dolphins. A third context was approaching its mother. The contexts show a full range of activities in which we would expect social animals to exchange information. While we do not know what sort of information might have been exchanged in these contexts, it is a great start. By looking at contexts, we can begin to unravel the meaning of different vocalizations, even if the unraveling at this point is done in a very gross way, missing a lot of the finer points that might be encoded in the vocalizations.

Dolphins aren't the only Cetaceans with extensive social communication. Humpback whale males are known for their extensive songs. But those are not the only sounds that the whales make. As they are traveling in social groups on their migrations, both the males and the females make sounds that have been described as "snorts," "grumbles," "wops," "thwops," "grunts," "groans," and "barks" that are used by the whales in communicating with either other whales in the same social group or with whales in other social groups that might be encountered along the migratory route. And sperm whales (*Physeter macrocephalus*) are very vocal. Sperm whales are probably the most numerous whales found in all of the Earth's oceans. The whales typically travel as groups of females who cooperate to take care of their offspring. While traveling, they produce a series of clicks called "codas" that serve as contact calls between individual whales. The "codas" differ considerably in their loudness and timing. The "coda" of one whale will frequently overlap the "coda" of another whale, as if they are simultaneously talking. Killer whales (*Orcinus orca*) produce complex whistles and pulsed calls in social situations. The calls are believed to provide information about group identity, but an inspection of the variation in the whistles and pulsed calls suggests that they are used to convey a lot more information than that.

Interestingly enough, in the northeastern Pacific Ocean there are two populations of killer whales: a resident population and a transient one. The resident population feeds on fish, who have a poor ability to hear sounds, while the transient population feeds on marine mammals, who have excellent hearing. Individuals of the resident population make a lot of pulsed sounds between the members of a group, while the transient population individuals are mostly silent except after making a kill, when they apparently use the pulsed sounds to communicate with others in their group.

Like Cetaceans who spend much of their time in water with limited visibility, another animal who relies heavily on auditory signals—primarily because it spends most of its life in darkness—is the bat. Most of the vocalizations of bats are in the ultrasonic range, between 20 and 100 kHz, well above the maximum sound frequency that we can hear. So for a long time people did not recognize that bats have a rich vocabulary in the sounds that they make.

One of my research projects in Africa involved studying the sounds of yellow-winged bats (*Lavia frons*). These bats roost as monogamous pairs in territories defended by the males. They are large bats and feed on large flying insects, often scooping a flying beetle or large moth out of the air and bringing it back to the roost to dine on at a leisurely pace. To study the vocalizations of the bats, I had to bring a tape recorder and a parabolic microphone, which looks something like a large plastic flying saucer with a rim that is about two feet in diameter. In the model that I was using, the plastic saucer fit into a backward-pointing microphone that had a pistol grip. The plastic saucer concentrated the sound at the center of the dish, and the microphone then recorded this concentrated sound. You held the grip and pointed the microphone at whatever you wanted to record. There was a little dot on the plastic of the dish and a little bead like a gunsight on the microphone so that you could line up the whole apparatus to make sure that you got the best sound. With it, you could record even faint sounds from animals that were more than a hundred feet away.

The problem was, to customs officials, it looked like something that a spy would carry. As I passed through several countries on my way to my field site at Lake Baringo, Kenya, I kept trying to explain that it was a microphone that I was using to record the sounds of bats. The customs people thought that I *was* bats. I routinely had to take apart my tape recorder and show that there was no hidden shortwave radio inside that would connect me instantly with some kind of intelligence agency. I even tried the gambit of explaining to customs people that no spy in his right mind would carry this kind of equipment openly and have such a ridiculous story about its use. To no avail. Officials would stand around for an hour or more discussing whether they should confiscate my equipment or throw me in jail. Eventually, my arguments would sink in as I pulled out notebooks of data and scientific papers that I packed for bedside reading. The conclusion usually was that I must be crazy but harmless, and I was allowed to proceed.

The male and female yellow-winged bats roost either in the same acacia tree branches or in nearby ones. Around sundown, the males begin to vocalize. If you have never seen the sunset in the tropics, it is quite a different experience from sunset in temperate regions. In the tropics, the sun sets at 6 p.m., and within ten minutes it is already dark. No long, drawn-out sunsets. It is like someone lowered a curtain and the world got dark. Same thing for sunrise. At 6 a.m., suddenly the sun is up and the world is flooded with light. The bats begin to vocalize right before sunset, with each male producing an audible high-pitched sound, so I had only a narrow window of time during the day when I could record the bats before I lost track of them in the darkness. Once I got back to my laboratory in the United States and analyzed the sound, I found that each male had his own distinctive voice and a distinct vocal signature that differed from the other males. It is very likely that each male and each female in that population of bats knew exactly who was calling and where every individual bat was roosting.

Other bats also have individual signatures in their vocalizations. Greater mouse-eared bats (*Myotis myotis*) have short echolocation calls that last around three milliseconds. The frequency drops during that time from about 100 to about 30 kHz. Individual bats can recognize other individuals based on the sound characteristics of each bat's echolocation calls. These calls have places where sound energy is more intense (these are called formants, just as we have formants in the sounds that we produce), and each bat has variation in the formants within its call. So for example, one bat might have more energy at 65 kHz, while another bat might have more energy at 45 kHz.

Based on this distribution of energy, bats can learn to identify the acoustic signatures of individuals. We know that bats can fly to feeding areas in groups of two to six animals, but previously no one knew how the bats were able to stay together as a group when flying at night at high speed. Now we know that the greater mouse-eared bats are able to communicate with each other through the individual signatures of their echolocation calls, so that each bat knows where all the other bats are located. A related species, the little brown bat (*Myotis lucifugus*) also has information encoded into its echolocation calls about individual identity, as well as information about the age and reproductive status of each bat.

One of the most crucial needs for individual recognition is in the case of a mother recognizing her young.

Nowhere is this more challenging than in large communal nesting colonies, such as in the caves of Mexican free-tailed bats. These bats roost in large numbers in caves, where mothers give birth to their pups. Although each bat has only a single pup, the number of pups jammed into small spaces can be astounding, with densities of up to five thousand pups recorded per square meter of cave. In all of this mass of juvenile bats, each mother has to find her own pup. Partly, mothers are helped by having a good spatial memory of where their pup is located. But both pups and mothers vocalize, and this helps the mothers find their young. Mothers can recognize the calls of their own pups and home in on those calls, even amid the squealing of thousands of other juveniles, while the pups can recognize the calls of their mothers and are attracted to those calls.

Some bats call back and forth to each other when they are away from their roost. White-winged vampire bats (*Diaemus youngi*) feed primarily on the blood of birds from Mexico to Argentina. Unlike their cousin the common vampire bat (*Desmodus rotundus*), they do not run around on the ground very much, but are very good at climbing branches where they can find birds. When one member of a roosting group becomes isolated from others, it calls a number of times with a social call that has a downward sweep and is structured differently than the calls they use for echolocation. Other bats from the same roosting group respond with their own social calls and fly toward the bat that has been isolated. The isolated bat and the others exchange calls until the isolated bat is found. Perhaps this is a way of making sure that a bat doesn't get lost, or gets some help if it needs it.

In most cases, we don't know if these individual-signature calls are learned or are genetically determined. However, a study of the "chuck" call of squirrel monkeys (*Saimiri sciureus*) suggests that they are probably learned. Squirrel monkeys live in the forest canopy of tropical forests in Central and South America, feeding on fruits and small insects. They have been studied in captivity for a long time, and one monkey named "Baker" had the distinction of riding into space and returning on a rocket as part of the U.S. space program. Among the vocalizations that these monkeys make is the "chuck" call that is used during social interactions. These "chuck" calls are individually distinct, with each monkey having a slightly different way of making a "chuck" call. Initially, infant monkeys do not pay attention to the "chuck" calls during social interactions, but as they get older, they start to notice the calls more and more, until finally as subadults and adults they respond strongly to the "chuck" calls of familiar members of their social group, approaching the individual making the familiar "chuck" sound.

Another animal who depends on language to function is the spotted hyena (*Crocuta crocuta*). Hyenas are excellent predators, and although most people think of them as scavengers, in parts of Kenya they kill more large mammals than lions do. You can hear their laughing-chuckling cries as they go about their hunting activities at night. I heard rumors, which I never was able to confirm, that some of the Kenyan native people would not bury their dead, but would leave them in a seated position for the hyenas to consume. This implied that hyenas ate humans as well as large ungulates.

Although I heard many hyenas, I never had any problems with them trying to get into my tents. However, one time I left out my running shoes, and by morning they were mostly gone, eaten by a hyena who left part of a sole and all of the laces. Another time, I left out a fork and a spoon. Usually all of the food, eating implements, cups, pots, and other supplies were stored in a wooden box inside my truck, so as to not attract any scavengers. But somehow I missed the fork and spoon. The next morning I awoke to find both the fork and the spoon chewed up into little balls of metal, with hyena tooth marks on them.

Hyenas live in clans in a fluid social system. Females are

dominant over males that immigrate into the social group. Curiously, females have their genitalia expanded into something that looks like a penis, so a human observer usually cannot tell whether a particular animal is a male or a female on the basis of seeing the presence of a penis. Among the females there is a dominance hierarchy with some high-ranking females and some low-ranking ones.

Around my camp, the hyenas left their scent on nearby branches. Hyena clans stake out territories and they mark their territories with scent. Both sexes rub their anal area over the stems of grass leaves or over branches, sometimes extruding their anal sacs. While many mammals have anal glands and some mammals have been known to signal their individual identity with anal gland secretions, the secretions of hyenas have been analyzed extensively and show the complexity of this signaling system. A study of the secretions identified 252 volatile compounds from among 143 anal gland secretions of individual hyenas. The composition of these volatile compounds provided a unique chemical profile for each individual hyena. There was no correlation between genetic relatedness and the chemical profile of the secretions, nor was there a correlation between dominance status and chemical profile.

The profiles of the individuals do change over time, so the hyenas have to constantly monitor the anal secretions of the members of their clan. Hyenas have frequent greeting ceremonies where they sniff each others' anuses, and this might be how they keep track of each individual chemical profile. Also, individuals within a clan often rub their bodies over the scent marks left by other clan members, mixing and mingling the scents from multiple animals as a way of signaling clan identity. Having so many chemical substances in the anal glands offers ample opportunity to code extensive information into the secretions.

But you don't have to fly to the African bush to witness animals advertising themselves using signature signals. When I walk my dog right here at home, he often stops at dog poop that inconsiderate dog people left lying around. He sniffs the poop extensively, then raises his leg and pees near the poop. Sometimes he leaves his own poop nearby (which I pick up in a plastic bag so as to not litter the landscape). We know that when dogs poop, some of the contents of the anal gland get pressed out and soak into the poop. Anyone who has had a dog probably remembers vividly a time when they had to press out the contents of a blocked anal gland, or a time when the dog got really scared and released all of the anal gland contents at once. The stench is horrible.

It turns out that anal gland secretions contain information about the individual identity of a dog, the dog's gender, and perhaps the breed of dog. Although further study is needed, it is likely that analysis of anal glands will find that dogs can vary the mix of secretions to produce specific messages. A study of the secretions of the anal glands of male and female beagles and female Labradors found that there were thirty-seven compounds containing volatile substances. The proportions of these substances varied between individual dogs, and also varied between males and females and breeds. Wolves and coyotes have similar compounds in their anal sacs. The feces of Iberian wolves ((*Canis lupus signatus*) found in Spain) contain at least seventy-seven chemical constituents that can provide information about the gender and perhaps identity of the individual wolf. Dog feces contain a similar array of chemicals. So when my dog stops to sniff poop, it is like reading the newspaper for him. It tells him who was there, probably how long ago, and what they had for lunch the last few days. All the gossip that's fit to smell.

WHERE ARE YOU?

Anthropologists postulate that human language arose out of our sociality, so it's no wonder that social animals also use language, sometimes just to keep in touch. Humans use language to keep in contact, such as when my wife and I take our dog out for a walk in the juniper forests of northern Arizona. Juniper forests can be pretty disorienting. Most juniper trees look alike, and even though most are only about ten or fifteen feet high and perhaps ten feet wide, they grow fairly close together and it is easy to lose track of where you are. We try to stay together, but sometimes one of us finds an interesting flower or rock and lags behind to look at it while the other one keeps going. This has happened to me many times. I look up and both the wife and the dog are gone, and I can't see any movement around me past the trees. When that happens to me, I resort to calling out, "Hello, where are you?" I hear in the distance, "I'm here; where are you?" and I know that I haven't lost her and the dog completely. We each call, "Hello," fairly frequently and use the direction of the sound to find each other. Other social animals use similar contact calls to locate and keep track of other individuals in their social group. In fact, we can often hear birds like chickadees or pine siskins doing similar calling out to one another as they move in loose flocks past us through the woods.

However, if my wife and I go shopping in Scottsdale, we have to use slightly different signals to keep in touch. In a crowded mall, just calling, "Hello," isn't going to work—too many people with whom we don't want to connect with will turn and respond. So if one of us spots the other across a busy food court, we have to get more specific, and call out each other's name. Animals have specialized contact calls like that, as well.

White-nosed coatis (*Nasua narica*) travel in small bands searching for small insects, vertebrates, fruits, and eggs. As they travel, they give contact calls, short "chirps" that are between 0.1 and 0.2 seconds long. These "chirps" have elements that we can hear and they also go up into the ultrasonic frequencies.

"Chirp" calls are individually distinct, with very different sound profiles for each individual animal. Coatis often forage in dense vegetation where it is relatively easy to lose track of the individuals in a group. The combination of higher and lower frequencies seems to be well adapted to the kind of habitat that the coatis prefer. High frequencies tend to drop out fairly quickly with distance and are not useful for anything other than short-distance communication, while lower frequencies tend to travel farther and can be used for longer-distance signals. Combining high and low frequencies allows the coatis to keep in touch acoustically with each other in the different kinds of environments that they might encounter.

Keeping in contact over longer distances is masterfully managed by the coyote, who travels over long distances to hunt every night. Once a symbol of the Wild West, these adaptable relatives of dogs and wolves have expanded into the rest of the country. One coyote pack must have a den in the foothills of Mingus Mountain near my house, as every morning before sunrise, we can hear them howling as they come up from hunting in the lower elevations and head home. Each coyote has his or her own style of singing, and, sure enough, research has shown that the howls provide information about the individual identity of the singer. A coyote howl typically starts with a rise in sound frequency, reaching a plateau of around 1 kHz that stays steady for several seconds, and then has a drop in sound frequency toward the end. Each coyote has its own way of increasing the sound frequency, with different individuals putting in different warbles in the rise, and then each individual varies the sound frequency during the plateau, putting in minor frequency variations in the time when the howl is fairly steady.

We have been lucky enough to see coyotes singing close up. One day a coyote stood just in front of the deck of our house (which faces a dry wash), and called and called for many minutes. Unlike the lawn ornaments, the real coyotes we've seen don't sit when they sing; they stand. If a coyote is separated from his group, his call will sound different than when they are together. Rather than a howl, the call is more like a series of barks interspersed with plaintive-sounding yips. The most amazing singing goes on when a group reunites. They will all sing, bark, howl, and huff their own songs at the same time, sounding like a joyous—if totally cacophonous— chorus. It goes on and on and it's thrilling to hear.

Wolves howl as well. Both North American and Iberian wolves have howls that contain several harmonics and frequency modulation that encodes individual identity information. When we look at the sonograms of the wolf howls, it is apparent that there is considerable opportunity for the howls to encode information about more than the identity of the animal who is howling. At this point, however, it is easiest to tease out the individual identity from the howls, because in that case we have something specific to test—the caller himself, tested against the calls of other wolves that howl.

So it appears that many species combine individual identifiers in the contact calls they use to keep in touch with one another. Another example is the pinyon jay (*Gymnorhinus cyanocephalus*). The pinyon jay is a western bird, cousin to the eastern blue jay, but with a more muted plumage of soft blues and grays. Pinyon jays forage in flocks and while they are foraging, they are constantly calling. They also call when they are flying.

I was walking my dog once in the high desert of Arizona, a habitat that is usually not inhabited by pinyon jays, when I heard a loud commotion in the distance. It sounded like a low-pitched rumble. At first I wasn't sure of the direction of the sound, but my dog turned and looked toward the north, and as I followed the direction of his gaze, I could hear that the rumble was coming from there and getting closer. Within seconds, the rumble resolved itself into multiple bird squawks, superimposed one over another so that I found it hard to know just where one squawk ended and another began. Soon a cloud of pinyon jays passed over my head, each bird calling at the top of its voice. The sound was deafening. Perhaps a minute passed before the entire flock flew over my head. Although I had heard flocks of pinyon jays forage before, I had never heard the sounds made by such a large flock when it is in flight. No one could miss it, from quite a distance away.

Pinyon jays have at least fifteen different kinds of vocalizations. Some of the calls have been described as "trills," "buzzes," "kaws," "piping," and "ricks," but the harsh, rasping ones that I heard have been described as a "rack." In addition to serving as a contact call, "rack" calls have a signature component that varies from one individual to the next and contains information about the caller's identity. This signature component probably gives each bird a good idea of the location of every other bird while the flock is moving. Plus, these individual differences in the calls allow males and females to correctly identify each other in this monogamous bird species where divorce is virtually unknown and birds that lose their mates remain alone for the rest of their lives.

Interpreting the meaning of all the other calls can be very difficult. I had a student who was interested in studying whether or not pinyon jays give calls for food while other jays were nearby. This is called the *audience effect*, and it's been shown in other bird species that some males will only call out the location of food when females are within hearing range, but they won't call if just other males are nearby, much like chickens.

When she and I looked at the vocalizations as they were displayed on a computer screen, I got an excellent appreciation of the difficulty of decoding pinyon jay vocalizations. A call might start out as a "rack" but then becomes a "multiple rack" where the two "racks" merge together with no time interval between them. Or a single "rack" might become a large number of "multiple racks," but each "rack" component has a different acoustical structure that makes the whole vocalization very difficult to tease apart. Or a vocalization might start out as a "multiple rack" and then become a "buzz" and then go back to being a "multiple rack" again. Looking at these vocalizations on the computer screen reminded me of the way that human speech looks on the screen—the patterns change within the space of seconds. But with human speech we know the code and know what it means. We don't have that yet with pinyon jays.

Other bird species go beyond the individual signature component and incorporate *group* identity into their contact calls. Mexican jays (*Aphelocoma ultramarina*) inhabit lower elevations than their pinyon jay cousins. They live mostly in scrub oak, pine, and juniper woodlands from southern Arizona to southern Mexico, in small social groups of five to fifteen birds. Like the pinyon jays, they have individual calls that serve as contact calls to keep the member of a group aware of each others' whereabouts.

Several populations of Mexican jays have been studied extensively in the Chiricahua Mountains of southern Arizona, which are a hotspot for birders from all over the United States. These mountains host occasional subtropical species that attract birding enthusiasts and scientists alike. In a study of Mexican jays, the contact calls of individual birds were played back to members of their own group and members of other flocks. Playbacks of the calls of other groups produced more interest, with birds flying to the speaker to check out who was there. Group members expected to hear the calls of one of their group on their territory, but became concerned when they heard the calls of some other group in a place where they did not belong. So either each bird in a flock memorized all the signatures of the other flock members, or there was some special flock-ID component of all the calls—whatever the mechanism was, the birds had some way of knowing when an outsider was calling.

Another bird with an intriguing vocal repertoire is the parrot. Most people think of parrots as brightly colored birds in cages whose biggest talent is imitating human words without knowing their meaning. But actually, wild parrots are highly social birds that live in flocks and have a lot of social interactions with each other, including contact call vocalizations. A study of the yellow-naped Amazon parrot (*Amazona auropalliata*) contact calls in the dry forest of Costa Rica showed that the contact calls encoded both individual information about each parrot and also information about what is called a *dialect region*. These parrots gather in nightly roosts that contain twenty to three hundred birds. The nightly roosts are traditional sites used day after day, year after year, sometimes for more than thirty years.

Based on the acoustic structure of the calls, parrot contact vocalizations can be grouped into three dialects that are learned by the birds within each dialect region, with each region including multiple roosting sites. Some birds that live on the edges of two dialects are bilingual, giving calls from both types of dialects. A genetic study of the birds showed that there was ample gene flow between the dialect regions, providing evidence that the dialects are maintained purely by learning and cultural tradition rather than by genetic diversity.

This learning aspect, and the bilingual capability of some birds, not only shows the Discourse System at work, but it also provides evidence that these animals certainly have language. It also points to the possibility that, like our human language, *facility* in the language is gained, shaped, and passed from generation to generation, through learning.

For our last illustration of contact calls and how they are evidence of language capacity and use, let's revisit the bird we saw earlier in the woods, the chickadee. All over the United States, chickadees are immediately recognizable by their small size and boldly contrasting markings of black, white, and gray.

Black-capped chickadees are cute enough to pass for Christmas tree ornaments. They are usually found around shrubs and trees in a variety of different habitats. They got their common name from the vocalizations they make that sound something like "Chick-a-dee." But calling it "Chick-a-dee" is deceptive. Included within the call is a lot of grammatical structure. Variations of these calls are often used in social contexts, but also can be used in territorial interactions or in mobbing other birds.

The "Chick-a-dee" calls of these birds can be broken down into four components that researchers have named syllable A, B, C, and D: Syllable A sounds like a short whistle, while B is shorter than A, but goes up and down in pitch. The C syllable is also short, but very harsh in tone, and the D syllable is the longest and sounds like a rasp or bark.

A black-capped chickadee call can contain anywhere

from one to several syllables, and their order and composition can vary greatly. They can be combined into strings of multiple syllables, so a call might be something like ABABCC, or AAAABBCCDD, or a longer string, such as, BCDDDDDDDDDDDDDDDDDDDDDDD. This is an example of recursion, which some linguists claim is found only in human languages.

The black-capped chickadee's cousin, the Carolina chickadee, is found in the south-central and eastern United States. Carolina chickadees also have calls that have four syllables—A, B, C, and D—and these syllables can be arranged into different combinations, usually dependent on context. Some combinations are used more often when the birds are foraging near the ground, while other combinations are used more often when the birds are flying. Most likely, the back-and-forth calling that goes on in a dense woods while a group is searching for food plays an important role in keeping flock members apprised of where everyone is at any given moment.

What is really interesting about these birds is that their calls follow a set of rules, or grammar. Playback experiments have shown that when artificially constructed songs containing inappropriate combinations of syllables are played back to the chickadees, the birds do not respond. It would be the same as if someone took our phrase, "I'm here under the fallen tree," and scrambled the syllables into something like, "Tree un the here der fal I'm en," and played back a recording of that nonsense phrase, watching our reaction. We would be totally confused, and so were the chickadees when this was done to them. This dependence upon the order of words to give a phrase or sentence meaning is what we refer to in human language as *syntax*, and chickadee calls clearly have it.

On a related note, an analysis based on the number of syllables in black-capped chickadee calls showed that the information contained in a call was somewhat comparable to the amount of information contained in a word in English, based on the number of letters that the most common words in our language contain. The average number of syllables per chickadee call is about six and the average number of letters in an English word is four. Both chickadees and humans have longer words (calls) that they can use, but primarily both species tend to stick to shorter words and calls in daily conversation.

Some would argue that even though Americans use shorter words, those words can still express pretty intricate ideas. We can talk about complex subjects, such as the national debt, or the right to bear arms, using short and simple words. So, too, with the chickadees. The complexity level of their calls might be even greater than they seem. Although superficially the D syllables all look alike when displayed on a sonogram, a closer inspection reveals that there are subtle variations in the acoustic structure of these syllables, suggesting that there might be even more information encoded in the calls than we currently suspect.

Again, the Discourse System is at work in helping social animals keep in contact. From coyotes to chickadees, animals use their senses to watch, listen for, or even sniff out signals that tell them where other members of their group are located. They respond to those signals with movements that keep them in the same area as their group, and/or they produce signature signals of their own, so that group cohesion is maintained while traveling or foraging.

THIS LAND IS MY LAND!

Occasionally, as we are walking through the woods we come across a barbed wire fence with signs that say POSTED—NO

TRESPASSING. In some places we know that we can ignore the signs, either because we know the landowners or because we know that the property has been abandoned. But sometimes there are people living behind those signs, people with guns, and trespassing is an excellent way to get yourself shot. So we respect the signs and do not go beyond the fence. Territorial animals do exactly the same thing. Once they stake out a territory, they advertise their presence on the territory either through songs or visual displays or scent piles of feces or sprays of urine. Trespassers know that if they cross the territorial borders they are likely to be attacked or at the very least confronted with an angry owner of the territory. Sometimes neighbors can trespass and not be attacked because the territorial owner knows them, but most of the time territorial advertisement is a way of saying "Keep out! This land is my land!"

Territories can be vitally important to survival and reproductive success. For many animals, their territory contains their home den, roost, or nest, and it often contains the food resources that an animal and its family need to survive. So, when you communicate about a territory, you need to be pretty specific about who owns that property, what its boundaries are, and what you are likely to do to intruders. Once again, a generic "bleep" or a general smell won't cut the mustard.

I learned firsthand about animals announcing themselves while proclaiming their territorial ownership when I was studying the calls of yellow-winged bats at Lake Baringo, Kenya. When I arrived there, I camped on a grassy area next to the lake. I set up my two tents, with their guy ropes stretched out and pounded into the ground, and prepared to stay a while. A man came by and told me to watch out for the hippos. I knew that hippos were dangerous in the water, and in fact on Lake Baringo they routinely upset the boats of fishermen by coming up out of the water underneath the boat or just bumping into the boat and knocking it over. Over the years some fishermen drowned, or were gored by the tusks that hippos have in their mouths. So I was concerned. I asked the man if the hippos were likely to tear down my tents. He laughed and said no, on the ground they were pretty gentle, but still had to be watched out for. When I asked specifically what would happen, he said, I would find out, but wouldn't give me any details.

It wasn't long before I woke up to hear a grinding noise from outside my tent. It sounded like a rusty piston working away in a cylinder that was filled with sand. It also was very loud. Taking my flashlight, I opened the flap of my tent, shone the light around, and there, not more than twenty feet away from me, was a grazing hippo. The grinding sound was the hippo's teeth as he was chewing up the grass. Let me tell you, hippos are huge! There was nothing I could do, so I zipped up the flap of the tent and hoped for the best. I listened to the grinding, but since nothing was happening, after a while I fell asleep.

Morning came. I survived. The tents survived. The hippo was gone. It was only after I went outside the tent that I realized what the man meant by my finding out about hippos. All of the guy ropes of the tents were covered with a slimy, greenish, smelly goo, as were the sides of the tents. In places it hung down from the ropes in long strings. That was the hippo introducing himself to me.

I later found out that hippos have individually distinct odors in their feces, and scatter their feces liberally. When a hippo feels the urge, he starts whirling his tail around like a propeller, as he ejects feces from his anus. Literally, the feces hits the fan. This causes the stinky goo to go flying in all directions, and advertises his presence to all of the other hippos who might wander by that area. It took me days to scrub everything clean, only to have either that hippo or some other reapply it (all hippos look alike from a distance of twenty feet at night outside your tent). I came to accept that I was just part of the hippo landscape and had to live with it. I realized that the feces also acts as a fertilizer for the grass that the hippos feed on. You might say that things come "full circle!"

Some territorial displays rely on sound. One of the most melodious grassland birds is the meadowlark, a medium-sized songster dressed for the part with a bright yellow breast garlanded by a broad ribbon of black on the chest. Both eastern (*Sturnella magna*) and western meadowlarks (*Sturnella neglecta*) have characteristic clear-tone, multinote songs, but the western meadowlark's is a bit more unusual because the males can sing two notes at once.

Meadowlark males arrive in early spring after wintering in South America. Males set up territories by *beating the bounds*— singing their songs along a proposed boundary that they want to enclose their nest sites, which are all on the ground. Every male's song is slightly different, based on singing experience and signature components. Boundary disputes are settled by song matches, where two neighboring males pick a bush on either side of the disputed line, face off, and sing at each other, and the winning male gets to choose exactly where the property line goes.

Although song battles rage all day long while boundaries are being sorted out, once the lines are settled among the birds, disputes die down and things become relatively peaceful— until the females arrive. At that point, song rates soar as males seek to outdo one another and lure females to their territories to mate. After all that is sorted out, things settle down again as the males devote themselves to helping raise a family.

What's amazing in this scenario, though, is that every resident male knows not only *his* song, he also learns all the songs of his neighbors. This was determined through an ingenious experiment. Researchers watched and recorded the individual songs and territory locations of meadowlarks on a prairie in Canada. Then they snuck in and kidnapped one of the males and replaced him with a camouflaged sound speaker. When the speaker broadcast the song of the missing male, all was well. But when the speaker broadcast the song of a different male (recorded elsewhere), an uproar ensued. It seemed that a stranger had invaded their midst, and the neighboring meadowlarks got very upset and went over to investigate and re-proclaim their territorial boundaries.

In this case, signal learning and production were augmented in the Discourse System by an additional brain function, the ability to differentiate between neighbor and stranger songs. This discernment has a clear evolutionary advantage. Neighbors who learned one another's songs and locations could save an enormous amount of energy because they didn't have to fly over and investigate every male's song that they heard. They didn't have to engage in constant, time-consuming song battles. Instead, they could attend to other aspects of their survival, such as mating, as long as they knew that their neighbors were in place and doing the same.

Just like some birds use song to proclaim territorial ownership, so do some bats. Male Mexican free-tailed bats set up territories and sing songs that contain a number of syllables and phrases (*syllables* are single notes, and *phrases* are groups of notes). These phrases can be characterized as "chirps," "buzzes," and "trills," and are as complicated as birdsong in their acoustic structure. "Chirps" are composed of two types of syllables, Type A and Type B. Each "chirp" can begin with between one and eighteen repetitions of Type A syllables, and end with a Type B syllable. Type A syllables are relatively short, about three to seven milliseconds long, and are downward sweeps in sound frequency. Type B syllables are longer, about fourteen to twenty milliseconds long, and are more complex, with the sound frequency rising and then falling. "Trills" and "buzzes" are phrases in which the syllables are repeated very rapidly and are downward sweeps of sound frequency. In addition to the territorial songs, the males mark their territory with secretions from glands on their anus, penis, and throat, and also do visual displays in which they flap their wings.

Territorial songs are only one of the sixteen different calls of the Mexican free-tailed bats. Other calls include social calls connected with irritation, protest, face-rubbing, and nose-rubbing. Face-rubbing and nose-rubbing calls are given when one bat greets another bat by rubbing its face or nose over the body of the bat. Each of these calls has a different acoustic structure of syllables. Like our words, the calls are made up of similar syllables, but the composition of the syllables differs between the calls for the different contexts. This is comparable to the way that our English words are made up of phonemes, with the same or similar phonemes used in different words, but the sequence of the phonemes differs depending on the word. When we say the words "dog" and "God," the words have the same phonemes, but the sequence of the phonemes is different.

THE LANGUAGE OF GREETING

In all of the cases in this chapter, animals use language to greet one another and identify themselves. They use language in their contact calls. They use language to communicate between parents and young. They use language in their territorial calls.

Why language and not some generic "bleet" or nonspecific smell? Because social groups have a wealth of complex relationships among their members and they need to keep all of the individuals straight. They also have to know what each member's role is in the group, and how that relates to them. Beyond that, social groups often compete with other groups, or are being preyed upon, and so it is important for them to convey information about their specific group identity and their locations. This argues for an awareness of self, and self in relation to others: I am Joe, and not Sam or Harry. I am with my mate Angela; those are my kids Bert and Arnie, and that's my next-door neighbor Frank. By extension, this implies an animal's awareness of its surroundings—being part of a group of other individuals, or being in a geographical location that could be one's own or somebody else's territory.

The Discourse System evolved to operate with heightened awareness during approaches, greetings, and social interactions. First involved are the senses, which pick up cues from around an animal—vision, scent, sound, vibration—to let that animal know that someone else is near. These cues are interpreted by the brain, which then decides whether to continue the encounter, or to run away or ignore the other animal. If there is no immediate danger to either animal, they can then choose to exchange signals revealing their sex, age, and possible purpose for being there. If they are members of the same species, they can engage in further displays to advertise their individual identity and group membership.

Some of these exchanges can be in the form of ritualized, hardwired displays, while others can be a matter of choice, which is where language comes into play. To function successfully in these situations, the Discourse System also depends upon the memory capacity of the animal, who has to remember whom it encounters, who is part of its group and who is not, and their relative status. A social animal often needs to recall where its own territory is located in relation to other territories, and who its neighbors are. Based on its store of memories, an animal can use its Discourse System to choose to respond appropriately to the signals of other animals in its social group and in its immediate vicinity, helping to maintain its status and ensuring its security and access to the group's shared resources.

9. WHAT'S THE BIG DEAL?

Language is something that helps connect us to other animals. For that reason, people have been trying to understand for a long time whether animals have language. But decoding animal language can be difficult. We need to be able to observe the context in which various signals are made, and then analyze the structure of the signals to see how much they vary by different contexts. Context provides us the Rosetta Stone for decoding the signals, but often the Rosetta Stone is just not there, so we cannot say sometimes whether something that we are observing is language or just simply communication based on instinct.

One approach to the question of animal language has been to try to teach animals some kind of language devised by humans. There are several rationales behind these attempts. One is to see if animals might have the capacity to learn a language. If they can do that successfully, then that would imply that they have the cognitive capacity in their brains to deal with a language, and by extension, that they might have a language of their own. Another is to provide a common ground for communication between an animal and humans. If an animal could be taught enough of a human language to converse with a human, perhaps we can learn something of the mind of the animal in a direct way, the same way that we can learn something about the minds of our fellow humans by talking to them. And finally, we humans see ourselves as the most intelligent beings on this planet, and we see human language as the epitome of communication. By this measure, seeing how much of a human-devised language an animal can learn can provide a yardstick for measuring the intelligence of that animal.

TEACHING LANGUAGE TO ANIMALS

Some of the more intensive efforts to teach human languages have been done with the great apes. And among the great apes, the chimpanzees have been fairly accessible to experimenters, with many chimps rounded up in the wilds of Africa for zoos and for medical research.

In the time span from the 1920s to the 1950s, two experiments indirectly tried to teach chimpanzees to speak English. In the late 1920s, W. N. Kellogg and L. A. Kellogg decided to raise a chimp at the same time as they were raising a baby son. This was the time of *behaviorism*, a school of animal behavior that put great store in the influences of the environment, compared with the influences of genes, heredity, or cognition. In 1925, one of the founders of behaviorism, John B. Watson, suggested that he could take any human child and, controlling the child's environment, make the child grow up to become whatever Watson wanted him to become—doctor, lawyer, beggar, thief.

The Kelloggs obtained a female chimp, Gua, when she was seven-and-a-half months old, and brought Gua home with them to be raised alongside their ten-month-old son Donald. For the following nine months, the Kelloggs raised Gua and Donald side by side, treating them as identically as possible. Donald and Gua ate the same food, napped at the same time, played at the same time, slept in similar cribs, and wore the same clothes. A few differences showed up—Gua liked to eat flowers and munched on the soap used for her bath. But a major difference between the two was in speech. While Donald started to articulate the sounds of human language, Gua showed no such tendency. Instead, she barked, screeched, and screamed (which is, curiously enough, what chimps do in the wild). In the end, the Kelloggs concluded that Gua was not capable of articulating human speech.

A somewhat similar experiment was done by Keith and Catherine Hayes in the 1940s with a chimp named Viki. They brought Viki into their home and raised her like a human infant until she was three years old. Viki was taken to parties and taken on automobile drives, she was exposed to a variety of people, and she was given the kind of stimulation that a human child receives. During that time, the Hayes's also tried to teach Viki to speak English. Unfortunately, after a prolonged period of training, Viki could only speak four words: "mama," "papa," "cup," and "up," and it was dubious whether "cup" and "up" were really separate words. To produce these sounds, Viki had to contort her nose and lips. She had to learn to put one hand on her nose, the other hand on her mouth, twist her lips out of shape, and whisper something that sounded vaguely like "cup." The conclusion of this experiment was that, not only would a chimp fail to pick up speech by herself (as Gua did not pick up human speech), but that it was very difficult to teach a chimp to speak a human language.

In the mid-1960s, two psychologists, Allen and Beatrix Gardner, thought that perhaps the approach of teaching spoken English was not correct. After all, it was quite possible that chimps lacked the laryngeal apparatus that humans used to produce speech. If chimps didn't have the anatomical structures to produce human sounds, then discovering that chimps can't speak English is about as significant as discovering that humans can't fly by flapping their arms in a stiff breeze. The Gardners knew that chimps use their hands when they interact with other chimps. So, they decided to capitalize on this by teaching a chimp American Sign Language, which was developed for people who could either not speak, or not hear, or both. American Sign Language (ASL) is a symbolic language, in that the signs do not necessarily represent pictures of the words that are being portrayed, and it has its own grammar. Because ASL employs a combination of hand movements and facial expressions, the Gardners thought that a chimp could possibly learn a gestural language more easily than a spoken one. In 1966, the Gardners brought a ten-month-old female chimp to the University of Nevada at Reno to begin their experiments. Because Reno is in Washoe County, they called the chimp Washoe. The Gardners raised Washoe in a suburban house, with Washoe living in a trailer in the yard. Washoe had a lot of stimulation on the theory that if she didn't have interesting things around her, what would she have to talk about? From the start, Washoe was trained to use ASL sign language. Whenever Washoe was present, all the people around her used ASL exclusively.

The Gardners and their assistants taught Washoe by either modeling the signs, for example, "This is a toothbrush," or by molding her fingers into the proper sign when an object was present. Through many such repetitions, Washoe learned to make a number of signs. Over the course of 51 months, she learned at least 132 signs. Washoe developed her own labels for some of the things around her. She called her doll, "baby mine," the refrigerator, "open eat drink," and her potty chair, "dirty good." She also leafed through magazines and picture books, making signs to herself about the pictures that were displayed in advertisements and other contexts. Washoe could request food through the appropriate signs, and could ask to play games such as "tickle" and "chase." She could generalize a sign to objects that have a different form but the same function, such as making the sign for "hat" for three different kinds of hats. And, apparently, she could come up with novel combinations of signs, such as making the signs for "water" and "bird" when she saw a picture of a swan.

I remember going to a lecture by Beatrix Gardner about the work with Washoe. She told us that Washoe loved to look through magazine pictures and make signs for the things that were happening or were displayed. For example, when she saw an advertisement for a soft drink can, she would make the sign, "drink." Once Washoe ran across an advertisement for a can of Campbell soup, and made the drink sign. Her trainer corrected her, and made the "eat" sign. Washoe became furious. Here she was, dealing with someone who clearly had no idea that you drink from cans rather than eat from them!

Once Washoe got to around the age of five, she was sent to a primate facility in Oklahoma, and the Gardners set up another experiment. This time they used chimps who were just born in various primate laboratories. Using newborn chimps was an important feature, because there could have been something in Washoe's background that could have predisposed her to learn signs the way she did. By using newborns, the Gardners could control the environment of the chimps and remove possible objections that some unknown set of circumstances influenced their results with Washoe.

More importantly, they were increasing their sample size of chimps—after all, Washoe could have been a genius and totally unrepresentative of chimps in general.

To increase their sample size, the Gardners set out to teach four chimps how to use ASL—Moja, Dar, Tatu, and Pili. Pili died of leukemia at the age of twenty-four months, but Moja eventually went to join Washoe in Oklahoma and then the entire colony, including Washoe, moved with Roger and Deborah Fouts to Ellensburg, Washington. The other chimps learned the use of signs and could identify a variety of objects projected on a screen—bugs, flowers, cats, dogs—suggesting that the ability to sign was not confined to Washoe alone.

Perhaps one of the more interesting experiments with ASL took place once the chimps were at Ellensburg. Washoe, at the age of fourteen, had just lost her newborn infant. So she adopted Loulis, a ten-month-old male chimp. At that point, the Foutses decided not to have any signing take place while Loulis was present, to see if Washoe or the other chimps would teach him how to use signs. This procedure was followed for five years. The Foutses recorded chimp conversations with remote-operated video cameras. Washoe would sign to Loulis, and would mold his hands into signs. Sometimes Loulis's signs appeared to arise through imitating Washoe or one of the other chimps when they were making signs in a particular context. When the experiment ended, Loulis was seventy-three months old and his vocabulary consisted of fifty-one signs. This shows that chimps can teach other chimps to form signs with their hands, and to use the signs correctly in the contexts of naming objects and asking for different things.

The Gardners' early work with Washoe inspired Francine Patterson to try the same thing with a gorilla. She worked out an arrangement with the San Francisco Zoo, and launched her studies with a female gorilla that became known as Koko.

As with Washoe, Koko was taught ASL. Through her conversations with the gorilla, Patterson has concluded a number of things: that the intelligence of Koko is about the same as that of a less-than-bright human, that Koko can lie to get out of trouble, that Koko is fond of cats with no tails, and that Koko is aware of herself in the mirror and likes to apply cosmetics that change her appearance.

One of the arguments that critics have used to discount the ASL studies has been the Clever Hans story. Clever Hans was a horse who lived in pre-World War I Germany. Hans was said, by his owner Herr von Osten, to be able to answer questions and read numbers from cards. Hans would nod his head for a "yes" answer, and would toss his head from side-to-side for a "no" answer. When asked to read a number from a card, or when asked a question that involved a number, Hans would tap out the number with his right hoof, and then indicate that he was finished by giving a sharp tap with his left hoof. A number of leading scientists of the day thought that Hans was clever enough to actually read numbers or do arithmetic, until zoologist Oscar Pfungst determined through careful observations that Hans was being cued by the unconscious movements of his human observers. When a question was asked, a human observer would lean forward slightly. Hans used this cue to start stamping his foot. When Hans had stamped his foot enough times to produce the answer, the human observer would lean back slightly or imperceptibly nod his head. Hans used this as a cue to stop stamping. Critics of the ASL studies suggest that, like Hans, the chimps and other apes are being cued by their trainers into giving what seem to be the right answers.

Another study with a chimp, however, sounded the death knell of the ape sign language work, at least in the minds of many scientists. Herbert Terrace started working with the chimp Nim at Columbia University, expecting to be able to teach Nim ASL and have conversations about what it was like to be a chimp. During the course of the 44 months that Nim was at Columbia, he had 57 different teachers and learned 125 signs. Unlike the Gardners, who felt that an enriched and fluid environment was conducive to chimps learning to sign, Terrace felt that the environment had to be controlled as much as possible. So, Nim was tested by his teachers in a small classroom. Although initially Terrace felt that Nim was making good progress, he later decided to analyze all the videotapes and notes that he had taken of the sessions in which a teacher was interacting with Nim. Upon analyzing this material, which represented some 19,000 sign combinations made by Nim, Terrace came to two conclusions. One was that Nim used an average of 1.1 to 1.6 signs per sentence, compared to an average of 2.6 to 4.1 signs made per sentence by a human child of comparable age. The other was that Nim responded mostly to prompting by his teachers, rather than signing independently. For example, in a sequence of photos in which Nim was filmed signing "me hug cat," Terrace points out that when Nim was signing "me" his teacher was signing "you," when Nim signed "cat" his teacher was signing "who," and when Nim signed "hug" his teacher had her hands in an N-configuration, which was their prompt for "Nim," and Nim liked hugs. All of this was enough for the skeptics to conclude that apes did not really understand sign language, and could not formulate sentences in that language. Nonskeptics, on the other hand, suggest that Terrace's experiment only showed that Nim could not formulate sentences, rather than showing that all chimps (or by extension, all great apes) could not do so. None of this means that chimps might not have a language of their own, and in fact the evidence points to chimps in the wild having both a vocal and a gestural language. Curiously enough, although some skeptics were happy to criticize the ape studies for having small sample sizes, they were happy to accept a sample size of one (Terrace's study of Nim) when it fit their preconceived opinions.

A different tack was taken by some investigators—using symbols to test the language abilities of chimpanzees. An early study was done by David and Ann Premack with several African-born chimps, the best known of which was Sarah. The Premacks used pieces of plastic that differed in size, shape, and color. These symbols became words or *lexigrams* that could be attached in a sequence by the chimp to a magnetic board, words that stood for the name of the chimp, the names of the trainers, the names of items of food, and actions, such as "Mary give Sarah apple." Some of the chimps did not learn a single word. Other chimps needed at least 1,000 repetitions to learn one word. Sarah learned to string 130 symbol-words into short sequences. Sarah had an accuracy rate of around 80 percent in constructing sequences that related to whether or not two objects were the same (for example, two keys of the same size and shape) or were different (for example, a key and a paper clip). Sarah also had about an 80 percent accuracy in responding to sequences of symbols such as: "Sarah cracker banana dish apple pail insert," involving having Sarah insert multiple objects into a pail.

The LANA Project (short for LANguage Analogue Project), started by Duane Rumbaugh, used another invented language called Yerkish. This language involved having a number of different symbols displayed on a large computer keyboard. A chimp, in this case called Lana, could then press the symbols in a particular order, and if she got the order of the symbols correct, the computer would respond appropriately. For example, Lana could say, by pressing the appropriate symbols, "Please machine open window," and the computer would open a window through which Lana could look outside her training area. The advantage of this system was that the computer could keep track of Lana's successes and errors, and Lana had available to her 255 different symbols, each of which had its own meaning and corresponded to a word in English. Unlike Sarah's having a small number of symbols to choose from during any particular experiment, Lana had a large number of symbols available to her, including the names of people, parts of her body, items of food, and actions such as "give" or "open." Yerkish had a grammar, and syntax was important to the meaning of a sentence. Lana or her trainer could signal that a particular sentence was a question (using the symbol for "?"), or a request (using the symbol for "please"), or a negation (using the symbol for "no"). Once Lana understood how to operate the keyboard and the meaning of the symbols, she could have dialogues with her trainer about food and her surroundings. These dialogues were extremely limited. There was no way that either Lana or the experimenters could touch on more abstract concepts, emotions, or a sense of self.

Critics have suggested a number of problems with these two studies. One problem that the critics have suggested is that there is no evidence that the symbols meant anything to either Lana or Sarah, beyond simple learning through association that a particular symbol was always paired with another item, such as an apple. This type of association is similar to a dog learning to sit when the trainer points to the ground with her index finger. A counter argument to this is that this is the same process by which we learn the meaning of words—someone holds up a red sweater and says "red." If we repeat back "red," we get a reward, in the form of a mother's smile, or a pat on the head, or proud parents exclaiming to everyone who will listen that their baby said "red!" Eventually, we learn to generalize "red" to other objects as well, such as tomato and sunset, and not just a sweater. Another problem that critics have pointed out is that it took a large number of training sessions to learn that a particular symbol stood for a particular item—Lana required some 1,600 training sessions to learn the symbol for "banana." This criticism of training has been applied to the ASL studies as well, where critics have pointed out that a large amount of training goes into having a chimp learn to use a particular sign. Yet another problem that the critics have suggested is that the results do not necessarily have to mean that the animals are communicating—they could simply be learning to use rules, such as "if X, do Y" and get a reward, again much the same way that trainers can get dogs to do complicated tasks. Of course, as a counter argument, we can always ask what X and Y mean to the brain of the animal, and if they are actions, are they not stored as symbols in the brain? (*Hint: We don't know the answer to this.*)

Another project with symbols and language involved two male chimps, Sherman and Austin. This project, carried out by Sue Savage-Rumbaugh, was based on the hypothesis that because language is interactive between two or more participants, Sherman and Austin might learn the language of symbols better if they had to interact with each other rather than interacting with a machine. Both chimps had to use symbols and cooperate with each other in order to get a food reward. Each chimp was in a separate room with his own keyboard of symbols, and each could see the other through a glass window between rooms. An experiment would start when an assistant would take a food item out of a refrigerator, show the food item to the chimp in the room in such a way so that the chimp in the other room couldn't see the food, and then divide the food into two containers, each of which is placed in the two rooms. The chimp who saw the food item would then use his keyboard to signal to the other chimp the name of the food that is in the container. If the other chimp, using his own keyboard, requested the correct name of the food then both chimps were allowed to open their containers and eat the food. The Sherman and Austin experiments showed that chimps could indeed use symbols to cooperate in obtaining food.

A chimp who has apparently crossed the line from manipulating lexigrams to understanding English sentences is Kanzi, a bonobo (*Pan paniscus*). Bonobos are a different species of chimp than the common chimpanzee. They are smaller, live in fairly stable social groups in the wild, the males are fairly passive, and the males and females in a group form close bonds. Kanzi was born at the Yerkes Field Station in Georgia. He was six months old when he arrived at the Georgia State University Language Research Center in 1980 with his adoptive mother, Matata, who was not his biological mother but had reared him from the time he was thirty minutes old after his biological mother had permitted Matata to hold him. Matata apparently liked Kanzi and refused to give him back to his birth mother. Matata had arrived in 1975 as a captive from the Congo in Africa. Sue Savage-Rumbaugh began working with Matata, trying to teach her to use symbols (lexigrams) similar to those that she had used with the two common chimpanzees, Sherman and Austin, and similar in design to those used by Duane Rumbaugh with Lana. At first, like the LANA Project, these symbols were arranged on a keyboard that was connected to a computer, and once the chimp touched a symbol, the computer recorded that information. Later, Savage-Rumbaugh developed a portable keyboard that could be carried around from place to place.

Matata found it very difficult to learn to use the lexigrams on a keyboard. At the end of two years of training and some thirty-thousand repetitions, using lexigrams for "banana," "juice," "raisin," "apple," "pecan," and "orange," Matata could name and ask for each food correctly, but could not pick out a picture of a food if she was shown its lexigram. Because Kanzi was always with Matata, he was always around the training sessions, although he spent much of this time playing on Matata's head and shoulders and randomly touching the keyboard while Matata was trying to learn symbols such as the one for "banana."

When Kanzi was about two-and-a-half years old, the Yerkes Center decided that Matata should become pregnant again. So, she was sedated and taken away from Kanzi. After Matata was gone, Kanzi surprised everyone by going to the keyboard and producing 120 different arrangements of lexigrams involving 13 different symbols ("banana," "juice," "raisin," "peanuts," "chase," "ball," "bite," "orange," "tickle," "swing," "cherry," "outdoors," "sweet potato"). Kanzi had apparently been passively learning how to use the keyboard and the symbols while he was hanging around watching Matata being tutored in the use of the lexigrams.

What followed was many years of work with Kanzi by Savage-Rumbaugh and her associates. Kanzi was able to initiate requests with the keyboard, and respond to sentences constructed from lexigrams by the experimenters. In addition, Kanzi would also sometimes talk to himself by picking up his keyboard, moving away from everyone, turning his back, and touching lexigrams. He could also use gestures and glances to show an experimenter what to do, such as when he wanted an experimenter to climb a vine next to a tree that he wanted to climb. Savage-Rumbaugh's observations suggest that Kanzi could understand a variety of complex sentences spoken in English, as when asked, "Would you put some grapes in the swimming pool?", Kanzi got out of the swimming pool, walked over to some grapes, and threw them into the water. Savage-Rumbaugh suggests that understanding spoken sentences means that Kanzi would have to grasp the concept of syntax, and that correctly responding to sentences is just as complex an ability as producing sentences. Kanzi has also been recorded producing different vocalizations in different contexts, such as for "banana," "grape," "juice," and "yes." He was not vocalizing the English words, but was producing different sounds, each of which corresponded with a different English word.

Sue Savage-Rumbaugh has also been working with two other chimps, Panbanisha and Panzee. Panbanisha is a bonobo like Kanzi, and Panzee is a common chimp, like Sherman and Austin. Both chimps have been kept in the same environment as Kanzi, and have been spoken to in English in the same way that everyone spoke to Kanzi. Like Kanzi, both chimps have had access to the keyboard containing 256 symbols or lexigrams. Both chimps have learned to respond to spoken English and also to use the keyboard of symbols, suggesting that Kanzi's abilities are not unique but are something that other chimps can learn to do.

Another set of studies in teaching animals human-invented languages has involved dolphins. In the 1960s, John Lilly popularized the concept that dolphins could possibly have a language of their own, which we might eventually be able to decipher. Louis Herman of the University of Hawaii worked with two Atlantic bottlenose dolphins, Akeakamai (a Hawaiian term meaning lover of great wisdom) and Phoenix (as in the bird who rises up from its own ashes), in an attempt to test their linguistic abilities. Herman was using two different kinds of artificial languages—a visual language with Ake (the short form of Akeakamai) and an acoustic language with Phoenix. Herman was particularly interested in whether the dolphins could understand syntax. To that end, he devised tasks that test for the dolphin's ability to understand the sequences of signs. For example, in the visual language, a trainer makes five gestures that stand for "bottom frisbee fetch surface hoop," meaning "Go to the frisbee on the bottom of the tank and take it to the hoop at the surface." The syntax can be reversed, to say "surface hoop fetch bottom frisbee," meaning "Go to the hoop at the surface and take it to the frisbee at the bottom." Ake was then assessed for the accuracy with which he performed these tasks. The syntax for the two dolphins was different. If Phoenix were asked to place a hoop in a basket, the acoustic signs would be "hoop in basket." For the same task for Ake, the visual gestures would be "basket hoop in."

By teaching two forms of syntax to two different dolphins, Herman hoped to show that the dolphins could learn arbitrary rules, just as humans learn arbitrary rules of syntax and grammar for different languages. The use of either visual or acoustic signs in the form of sentences also allowed Herman to test whether the dolphins could understand novel sentences, asking them to do things that they have never done before. Herman and his associates also tested whether the dolphins could understand sentences that asked them to do a task in the immediate future, such as when they were asked to take an object that was not yet in the tank, and only later the object was thrown into the tank along with several other objects. In general, Herman's results showed that the dolphins could perform the tasks asked by the different sentences with an accuracy level of 60 to 100 percent.

Although she was not specifically trying to teach language, the work that Irene Pepperberg did with Alex the grey parrot (*Psittacus erithacus*) showed that the bird had a good concept of the cognitive aspects of language. Alex learned to say in English whether something was the same as, or different from, an object that was presented to him. He could announce the colors of objects, and could count how many objects were displayed. One time in my animal behavior class, Pepperberg showed a video of Alex interacting with a new parrot that she had brought into her laboratory. Alex loved to have the feathers on his neck rubbed, a normal part of parrot grooming behavior. Sometimes he would bite the fingers of whoever was rubbing his neck, and when that happened, the person would say, "Gently, gently now." If Alex persisted, the person would say, "That's all" and walk away. In the video, Alex is grooming the neck feathers of the new parrot when the bird starts to bite. Alex says, "Gently, gently now." The bird continues to bite, and Alex says, "That's all" and walks away.

Other studies suggest that dogs can learn either artificial or human languages. Dogs are being taught K9 Sign Language, which is a gestural language devised by Sean Senechal, in which the human makes a sign with a hand or an arm gesture, and the dog can respond with a body movement. A dog can use body movements to make requests, such as raising up the front left paw and lowering it again to request chicken for dinner. A border collie named Rico knows some three hundred words in German, and when she is given a task of fetching an item whose name she does not know, if that item is among other items whose names she knows, she will fetch the unknown item by the process of deduction. Another border collie named Chaser knows the names of over one thousand objects in English and can fetch one of those objects upon spoken request.

The results of these studies suggest that animals can learn human languages. However, we have to be cautious in interpreting these results. Issues of sample size, extensive training schedules, and possibilities of inadvertent cueing are difficulties that must always be kept in mind. This is not to detract from the extensive work that the above investigators have done with their animals, putting their heart and soul into their projects and risking their scientific careers in the process. Methodologically, the difficulties involved in teaching animals human-generated languages are vast, and considering these methodological difficulties the results have been very impressive. But the difficulties allow the skeptics to point to one or another problem and suggest that these problems invalidate the conclusion that some animals can learn human languages.

Perhaps for these reasons a better approach is to study the signals of animals under natural conditions in wild populations, trying to deduce whether or not the signals constitute a language. In wild populations the sample sizes are larger, there are no training schedules, and cueing is usually not an issue. As we have seen, we have abundant evidence that we can decode the natural languages of animals, if we have the appropriate contexts as our Rosetta Stone.

LANGUAGE AS EMPOWERMENT

Let's consider one feature that has been mentioned before— language as empowerment. With language, we can describe the external world, we can describe our feelings and thoughts, and we can make requests and demands of others. We can get positive feedback from others about very specific things that we do. We can get building blocks for understanding the world around us. Language is a tool for interaction. Without language, we are individuals drifting along the waves of solitude, never able to communicate our thoughts to anyone, never able to share any experiences, never able to pass along any knowledge that we have accumulated. With language, we can progress from naming objects—answering the "What's that?" questions—to building up a philosophy of how the world works. Without language, none of this is possible.

So, do animals have this empowerment? Conventional wisdom says no. But, as we have seen, a number of animal languages have some of the same design features as human languages. Can it be that we are truly alone and special? Again, conventional wisdom rushes in with a resounding "Yes!" But conventional wisdom may be wrong. Our emphasis on technology has set us apart from nature, has lulled us into thinking that we have no direct connection to the natural world around us. Occasional hurricanes and other natural disasters remind us that we are not separate from the rest of the world, but human memory tends to be short, and we assume that these are merely blips that can be fixed with better technology. We conveniently forget that we are the products of the same evolutionary processes that resulted in many of the animal species that we see around us today, and that many of the same kinds of cells, neurons, muscles, tissues, and organs are found in us, in horses, in dogs, and in birds. The rattlesnake that slithers past my house every night looking for wood rats has a brain that is structurally similar to a part of my brain, and the wild pigs that come to eat my cactus garden have physiological processes that are similar to those of humans.

Let's do a thought experiment. In this experiment, I am lecturing on some topic of animal behavior to the students in my class. Some of the students are taking notes. Others are looking at me with varying gazes ranging from complete comprehension to complete blankness. Still others are looking at their watches to see how much time is left before they get to go and eat their lunch. A few are busily trying to count the number of bricks that make up the walls of my classroom.

Now let's introduce an alien observer who focuses an electron telescope on my classroom from his flying saucer that is buzzing around the Earth outside the limits of detection of our radar screens. The alien is doing his Ph.D. work at Buzzoff University on the planet Tishtosh, and he is studying the question of whether humans have language. He has chosen my classroom as his study site. He knows absolutely nothing about humans, beyond what he can see with his telescope. Nothing about human culture, intelligence, or abilities. The prevailing view of the scholars at Buzzoff University is that humans are programmed by instinct to build large structures that we would call cities, and have societies that are similar to those that we see in ants. Blindly following instinct, humans build and build until they have used up all of their natural resources, and then they disappear from an area until the resources grow back and the cycle repeats itself. Any communication that occurs is entirely programmed by instinct.

Our alien wants to prove that humans have language. He dutifully records all of the responses of the students to my speaking (Remember the Operational Definition of Communication? A signal must have a predictable response for communication to be recognized by the observer as having taken place.) He documents how many students are taking notes, how many are gazing at their watches, how many are looking at bricks. He does this day after day for my lectures. Some days more students are writing in their notebooks. Other days more students are gazing at me. Then, after monitoring thirty lectures, he does a statistical analysis of the numbers. And, guess what? He finds no relationship between my speaking and the activities of the students. Statistics fail to show that whenever I am speaking, the students are always performing one type of activity. Chagrined, the alien reports to his academic advisor that he was unable to document that humans have a language, and tries to ignore the triumphant "I told you so, but you wouldn't listen" look from his advisor. He writes in his Ph.D. thesis that the evidence best supports the hypothesis that I am vocalizing because I must be emotionally excited due to some unknown physiological quirk, and the students are merely present because of a social instinct to congregate in groups.

This thought experiment is similar to where we are today with animal language research. We have only a limited understanding of the nuances of animals' lives—of what is important to them, of how they perceive the world around them—but we make assumptions based on our very limited knowledge.

Once I had a discussion with a person who was a professional philosopher. This person heard me speak about some of my research with prairie dogs. After my lecture, he came up to me and told me that he was intrigued, but he did not believe that prairie dogs had anything approaching language. When I asked him why he thought that way, he told me that he saw no evidence that prairie dogs had any kind of moral philosophy or body of ethics, and without such evidence he was unwilling to grant them the possibility of language. When I asked him how he knew that they didn't, he asserted that no animal is capable of understanding a moral philosophy or having a body of ethics. I was completely unable to make any headway with my argument that this may or may not be so, but we don't have enough evidence, or even ways to test, whether or not this assumption is true.

One assumption that we make is that if animals had language, they would use it the same way that we would. But even that assumption may not be true. An animal signal may be equivalent to a concept, rather than a word. So, for example, a single vocalization directed by a territorial bird toward another bird intruding into the first bird's territory may be equivalent to something like, "This is my territory, and if you persist in intruding, I intend to attack you and fight." For humans, this might be similar to thinking in pictures, as described by Temple Grandin in her book, *Thinking in Pictures*. As a person who has suffered from autism, Grandin points out that her thought processes are not in words, but in pictures showing different situations. Some of us who are visually oriented may have experienced this—we might have a picture that flashes through our mind, and then we spend a brief instant translating the picture into words in our thought stream. For some animals, a concept might be in the form of a picture, and the signal might be an external manifestation of the picture or concept.

An example of this might be the response of horses to the join-up signals described by Monty Roberts in his book *The Man Who Listens to Horses*. In training horses to accept humans as riders, Roberts parts company with the traditional and somewhat violent methods of "breaking" horses by tying them up and immobilizing them on the ground and destroying their spirit. Instead, he has found by watching wild horses that they have a series of signals that indicate something along the lines of, "Hello, I want to join you and be friends, and I don't want to hurt you or otherwise abuse you." These signals are in the form of body orientation, of either a horse or of Roberts. A *body orientation* stands for what we would call a concept, and this concept is recognized by another horse, who can then make a decision to either accept or reject the premise that is expressed in that concept.

In human languages, words can delineate and describe concepts, but they can also obscure what we mean as well. Take philosophy, for example. The words written by your favorite philosopher might be crystal clear to you. On the other hand, the semantic values of the words might be so ambiguous that you might have to go to an interpretive work written by someone else to find out what your favorite philosopher really meant when he or she was talking about rational deconstruction.

We humans also have simple signals that stand for concepts. Some aspects of body language show this quite nicely. For example, extending the right hand for someone to shake is almost universally seen as a sign of friendship, but it also exemplifies a concept, that my right hand does not have a weapon (an important point for the 80 percent of the human population who are right-handed), and because my right hand does not have a weapon, I come to you in friendship. We have to be cautious with body language, because some aspects are clearly motivational, expressing our inner emotions, often without our knowledge, to the point that if body language and spoken language conflict in their signals, the listener will usually believe the body language rather than what was said. Other aspects of body language are under our conscious control, such as waving good-bye to someone who is leaving. Some linguists have suggested that body language is not a true language because it lacks a grammar, but if signals stand for concepts, a grammar might be entirely irrelevant and not very useful.

The signals-as-concepts theory might explain the difficulties that Herbert Terrace found with the chimp Nim, who did not string ASL signs into sentences. ASL is a visual language, and many of the signs stand for concepts, although the people who use ASL can also use finger spelling to spell out words if there is not a sign for a particular name or situation. Controversy still exists as to whether ASL has a grammar, but most linguists seem to accept that ASL is a genuine human language with its own grammar. This grammar is different from

English grammar. For example, in English, the usual sentence construction is subject, verb, object, such as, "Kathy lost her keys." In ASL, the object often precedes the subject, so the sentence would be, "Her keys, Kathy lost." As mentioned earlier, Nim was taught a number of ASL signs by a multitude of teachers, but when Herbert Terrace analyzed the film and video tapes that he had of Nim interacting with the humans, he found that Nim was not able to string more than one or two signs together into a sentence. By comparison, human babies who were taught ASL could string four or more signs together into a sentence by the time they reached Nim's age. This result led Terrace to conclude that chimps can't really use signs as a language, the way that he initially expected that they could.

However, we are now finding out that chimps have both a vocal language and they use meaningful gestures in the wild. A study of the different calls that chimps make in the wild found that there were eighty-eight different call combinations, where different sounds were combined for different contexts, much like we combine different words into sentences. Another study documented sixty-six different gestures that were used by wild populations of chimps in different contexts. Even chimps in captivity understand the concept of meaningful gestures. In one study with forty-nine captive chimps, a human experimenter held a banana and knelt about three feet in front of each chimp's cage, either facing toward the chimp or facing away from the chimp. Most of the time, when the experimenter was turned away from the chimps, they vocalized to get the person's attention. However, when the experimenter was holding the banana and facing toward the cage, most of the chimps used gestures to indicate that they wanted the banana. Similarly, when four chimps that knew ASL were tested individually in a laboratory setting, they were able to change their behavior depending on whether the experimenter was sitting with his back toward them or was sitting facing them. When the experimenter's back was turned, the chimps either made attention-getting sounds or turned away and left. When the experimenter was facing the chimps, they immediately started to make ASL signs to him. If chimps use sounds and gestures in the wild to stand for concepts, much like our body language, then stringing signs together into a sentence would be completely meaningless— one sign can express the intention of the chimp just as well as a series of words or ASL signs. So Nim may not have learned to string signs together because that is not particularly meaningful to chimps.

One of the complaints about the ASL work with chimps and other primates is that they mostly make signs about food, and not too much else. But one possibility is overlooked here: If you simplify the communication system to the bare basics, this may be all that the animals have in common with their human experimenters to talk about.

Let's do another thought experiment. Let's imagine that a human who is a Wall Street stockbroker is taking a well-deserved vacation in the wilds of Canada, hiking and taking pictures in blessed solitude. While he is asleep in his sleeping bag, an alien spaceship appears and abducts him (aliens are great for thought experiments). He is taken to the planet Xylo, where he is put into a small room. He sees no other humans anywhere. There are no sources of outside stimulation. No TV. No internet. No friends, no lunchtime martinis at the neighborhood pub. All he sees is an occasional bug-eyed alien. He tries speaking English to them, but it quickly becomes apparent that they do not understand English and act as if these are just meaningless noises. Then the aliens start teaching him their language, which involves using their arms to semaphore signals. So he learns some signs. What is he going to talk about with his captors? He lacks the enormous enculturation that goes into the subtleties of his captors' behavior. They lack the enormous enculturation that goes into his behavior. How could he ever explain to them what a Wall Street broker does for a living? How could he explain to them the concepts of stocks and bonds, buying and selling, money, power, and status, using a few basic signs? Ah, you might say, humans are smart, and in no time he would not only know the language, but he would be running the place. Having had to struggle with learning another language where I could get instant feedback and explanations, I would submit to you that if that is your answer, you would be wrong. He would be left with the basics: I want an apple (or whatever the alien equivalent of an apple would be), or I want out of my room. Just like the chimps, he would be unlikely to learn anything beyond very basic communication.

Another assumption that we make when we look at the communication system of animals is that the time scale of their signals is exactly the same as the time scale that we perceive. For example, a bird makes a vocalization that sounds like "squaak" to us. We assume that another bird perceives the "squaak" exactly the way that we hear it. But what if the perceiving bird had a different time scale of perception, and the "squaak" actually was registered by the bird's brain as a long communication equivalent to our sentence or paragraph? This kind of time-compression technology is available to us in military transmissions of message. For example, submarines can transmit a considerable amount of information in a single burst of radio transmission by speeding up the encoding of the message, and the receiver of the transmission can decode the message by slowing it down. The alarm calls of prairie dogs sound like a simple "cheep" to us, yet my colleague John

Placer and I are showing that if you slice up this "cheep"—which lasts about one-tenth of a second—into twenty time slices, each lasting five-thousandths of a second, we find significant acoustic structures of information in each time slice. The sound that we hear as a very brief "cheep" packs in as much information to prairie dogs as a long, drawn-out sentence would for us.

Another unanswered question is about grammar. As we have seen, some animals have grammar. These animals include a diverse group: lizards, honeybees, chickadees, and cephalopods such as squid. Grammar is very difficult to establish in studies of animal communication. In order to establish that grammar is present, we have to understand all the possible nuances and subtleties involved in the communication system. A simple assertion that there are no nuances and subtleties is not sufficient, because once again we really don't know the answer, nor do we have sufficient experimental evidence to make any kind of judgment at this point. We can, of course, assume that if we find evidence of syntax, the syntax will reflect an underlying grammatical structure.

Understanding the intricacies of a human language depends on being able to communicate with the native speakers of the language and ask them why certain kinds of constructions make sense while others do not. We can't do this with animals, but we can approach animal communication systems with an open mind and allow for the possibility that there might be a language that has an underlying grammatical structure. With an open mind, we can start decoding animal communication systems much the same way as code breakers decode encrypted human communications—looking for patterns that are repeated and analyzing the structure of those patterns in particular contexts. With the Discourse System as a conceptual framework, we can begin to see the continuity of language in different animal groups.

Not too long ago, I was having a conversation with a colleague who has thought a lot about communication in animals. He said, "Why do you insist on calling it language? Don't you realize that this is a Red Flag for many people? Why don't you simply call it communication, and leave it at that?"

My response was that the evidence for language in animals is extensive, and it is time for all of us to acknowledge that. I don't want to continue the myth that we humans are so special that only we have language. That keeps alive the idea of "Us" versus "Them"—that we are not part of the evolutionary process that shaped us all. And the Discourse System shows how language and all of the structures and processes that go into its production are modified by evolution and natural selection.

LANGUAGE AS A BRIDGE

Let's consider the implications of animals having language. One of the cornerstones of dogmatic thought about animals is that they cannot think because they do not have language. In his presidential address to the American Philosophical Association in 1973, Norman Malcolm said: "The relationship between language and thought must be so close that it is really senseless to conjecture that people may *not* have thoughts, and also really senseless to conjecture that animals *may* have thoughts." Malcolm titled this address "Thoughtless Brutes."

Thinking is another one of the areas that is currently out of favor with animal behavorists, as a legacy of the behaviorism school of thought popularized by B. F. Skinner. From the 1930s to the 1980s, behaviorism shaped the thinking of many psychologists and biologists who were studying the behavior of animals. The essence of behaviorist thought says that we can't know anything about what is going on inside an animal—it is a black box, an unknown quantity. But what is going on inside the animal really doesn't matter according to the behaviorists, because everything that is important about the behavior of the animal is embodied in two things—an outside stimulus and the response of the animal to that outside stimulus. Both the stimulus and the response can be measured, while anything going on inside the animal, such as thinking, cannot be detected or measured. An animal could learn to change its response to a particular stimulus, and this changed response could be measured in terms of how long (or how many repetitions, called trials) it took for the animal to change its response. What the animal thought about the situation, if anything, was considered to be irrelevant. This view mutated into the position that animals did not think at all, and in fact were incapable of thinking, as yet another way to keep humans and animals apart.

I sometimes ask my students in my animal behavior class the following questions: First, I ask, "Who thinks that humans can think?" Everybody raises their hand. Next, I ask, "Who thinks that dogs can think?" About two-thirds of the students raise their hands. Then I ask, "Who thinks that cats can think?" Maybe one-third of the students raise their hands. Finally, I ask, "Who thinks that ants can think?" No one raises their hand. But the bottom line is, we really don't know, one way or the other. And, interestingly, we have a clear idea of how to differentiate between those species that we assume think and those that don't, but none of this is based on science, it is all just gut feeling.

Other than through our own experience, we have no good quantitative way of knowing whether humans think, but we assume that if we ourselves think, all other people can think as well. Some of us think in pictures and not in words, as Temple Grandin describes. But whether we think in pictures or in words, ultimately many of us translate what we are thinking into words.

Can other animals do this? My guess is that they can, in ways that are relevant to them and their language. I do not expect a bat to produce a high-pitched English rendition of Shakespeare's sonnets, but maybe the bat is producing a high-pitched version of sonnets that are relevant to bats.

Think of the implications of animals using language to think. If they think, that means that they have mental representations of the world around them. These representations might be different for different species. The world might be a vast soundscape for a bat, a sea of ultraviolet colors for a bee, and a mosaic of odors for an ant. Other animals see the world very differently from us. But if they have mental representations of their world, and can use symbolic language to communicate those representations to others, then perhaps they can also have two things that we take for granted among ourselves: consciousness and self-awareness.

Yes, scientists might say that this is nonsense. But how many scientists understood how bats were able to navigate in the dark before Donald Griffin did his classic experiments in the 1950s? He once told me that when he proposed the idea of bats using sound to navigate as the subject of his Ph.D. work, he was told by fellow scientists that it was a completely ridiculous idea and he shouldn't waste his time. He persisted, and now we know that bats use a dimension of sound that we cannot begin to appreciate.

I don't think that the vast gulf between humans and other

species exists, in either consciousness or intentions. I think it's time to rise above the gridlock and think about animals from an entirely new perspective. In my view, animal language provides the flexibility to signal information, and provides the flexibility to respond according to the context. The signaler might want to influence another animal's behavior, or might want to inform someone of an external situation, or might even want to tell someone that he isn't feeling well. The recipient interprets the signal through the filter of his experience, emotions, and the context in which the signal is given.

For us, the idea that other animals have language is a bridge back to the natural world. We can begin to cross the vast chasm that we have set up between "Us" and "Them," and start to see that we are not very different after all. We are all part of this natural world. We certainly have a lot of talents that other animals do not have. But they have a lot of talents that we do not have. The one thing that we all have is that we are all in this natural world together, and the quicker we realize that we are all interdependent on one another— and one species is not any better than any other—the quicker we can bring harmony to our lives.

ACKNOWLEDGMENTS

I thank my agent, Laura Wood, for her outstanding help and tireless efforts in guiding me through the process of writing this book. I also thank my editor, Daniela Rapp of St. Martin's Press, for her clarity of vision and excellent editing in shaping the structure of the book. I thank my wife, Dr. Judith Kiriazis, for her creativity, ideas, and help with editing the manuscript. Finally, I thank all of my students who over the years helped me decode prairie dog language, spending countless hours in the field and in the laboratory documenting prairie dog behaviors and analyzing the results of time-consuming experiments.

BIBLIOGRAPHY

1. Doctor Dolittle and Animal Language

Lofting, H. *Doctor Dolittle in the Moon*. Philadelphia: J. B. Lippincott, 1928.

———. *Doctor Dolittle's Caravan*. New York: Frederick A. Stokes, 1926.

———. *Doctor Dolittle's Circus*. New York: Frederick A. Stokes, 1924.

———. *Doctor Dolittle's Garden*. New York: Frederick A. Stokes, 1927.

———. *Doctor Dolittle's Return*. Philadelphia: J. B. Lippincott, 1933.

———. *Doctor Dolittle's Zoo*. New York: Frederick A. Stokes, 1925.

———. *The Story of Doctor Dolittle*. New York: Frederick A. Stokes, 1920.

———. *The Voyages of Doctor Dolittle*. New York: Frederick A. Stokes, 1922.

2. What Is Language?

Anderson, S. R. *Doctor Dolittle's Delusion: Animals and the Uniqueness of Human Language.* New Haven, CT: Yale University Press, 2004.

Chomsky, N. "Three factors in language design." *Linguistic Inquiry* 36 (1) (2005): 1–22.

Fitch, W. T., M. D. Hauser, and N. Chomsky. "The evolution of the language faculty: clarifications and implications." *Cognition* 97 (2) (2005): 179–210; discussion 211–25.

Gentner, T. Q., K. M. Fenn, D. Margoliash, and H. C. Nusbaum. "Recursive syntactic pattern learning by songbirds." *Nature* 440 (7088) (2006): 1204–7.

Hailman, J. P., and M. S. Ficken. "Combinatorial animal communication with computable sythax: Chick-a-dee calling qualifies as 'language' by structural linguistics." *Animal Behaviour* 34 (1986): 1899–1901.

Hauser, M. D., N. Chomsky, and W. T. Fitch. "The faculty of language: What is it, who has it, and how did it evolve?" *Science* 298 (2002): 1569–79.

Hockett, C. F. "Logical considerations in the study of animal communication." In *Animal Sounds and Communication,* ed. W. E. Lanyon and W. N. Tavolga, 392–430. Washington, DC: American Institute of Biological Sciences, 1960.

Kiriazis, J., and C. N. Slobodchikoff. "Anthropocentrism and the study of animal language." In *Anthropomorphism, Anecdotes, and Animals,* edited by R. W. Mitchell and N. S. Thompson, 365–69. Albany, NY: State University of New York Press, 1997.

Otte, D. "Effects and functions in the evolution of signaling systems." *Annual Review of Ecology and Systematics* 5 (1974): 385–417.

Owren, M. J., D. Rendall, and M. J. Ryan. "Redefining animal signaling: influence versus information in communication." *Biology & Philosophy* 25 (5) (2010): 755–80.

Penn, D. C., K. J. Holyoak, and D. J. Povinelli. "Darwin's mistake: Explaining the discontinuity between human and nonhuman minds." *Behavioral and Brain Sciences* 31 (2008): 109–78.

———., and D. J. Povinelli. "On the lack of evidence that non-human animals possess anything remotely resembling a 'theory of mind.'" *Philosophical Transactions of the Royal Society B: Biological Sciences* 362 (2007): 731–44.

Rendall, D., M. J. Owren, and M. J. Ryan. "What do animal signals mean?" *Animal Behaviour* 78 (2) (2009): 233–40.

Seyfarth, R. M., D. L. Cheney, T. Bergman, J. Fischer, K. Zuberbühler, and K. Hammerschmidt. "The central importance of information in studies of animal communication." *Animal Behaviour* 80 (1) (2010): 3–8.

Shannon, C. E., and W. Weaver. *The Mathematical Theory of Communication.* Urbana, IL: University of Illinois, 1949.

Soltis, J. "What do animal signals do?" *Animal Behaviour* 78 (6) (2009): 1485–86.

3. A New Theory of Language

Balter, M. "First gene linked to speech identified." *Science* 294 (2001): 32.

Enard, W., M. Przeworski, S. E. Fisher, C. S. L. Lai, V. Wiebe, T. Kitano, A. P. Monaco, and S. Paabo. "Molecular evolution of FOXP2, a gene involved in speech and language." *Nature* 418 (2002): 869–72.

Fisher, S. E., and C. Scharff. "FOXP2 as a molecular window

into speech and language." *Trends in Genetics* 25 (4) (2009): 166–77.

Haesler, S., K. Wada, A. Nshdejan, E. E. Morrisey, T. Lints, E. D. Jarvis, and C. Scharff. "FoxP2 expression in avian vocal learners and non-learners." *Journal of Neuroscience* 24 (2004): 3164–175.

Hewes, G. W. "Language origin theories." In *Language Learning By a Chimpanzee: The LANA Project,* edited by D. M. Rumbaugh, 3–53. New York: Academic Press, 1977.

Krause, J., C. Lalueza-Fox, L. Orlando, W. Enard, R. E. Green, H. A. Burbano, J-J. Hublin, C. Hanni, J. Fortea, M. de la Rasilia, J. Bertranpetit, A. Rosas, and S. Paabo. "The derived FOXP2 variant of modern humans was shared with Neandertals." *Current Biology* 17 (2007): 1908–12.

Lai, C. S. L., S. E. Fisher, J. A. Hurst, F. Vargha-Khadem, and A. P. Monaco. "A forkhead-domain gene is mutated in a severe speed and language disorder." *Nature* 413 (2001): 519–23.

Pinker, S. "Talk of genetics and vice versa." *Nature* 413 (2001): 465–66.

Shu, W., J. Y. Cho, Y. Jiang, M. Zhang, D. Weisz, G. A. Elder, J. Schmeidler, R. De Gasperi, M. A. Gama Sosa, D. Rabidou, A. C. Santucci, D. Perl, E. Morrisey, and J. D. Buxbaum. "Altered ultrasonic vocalization in mice with a disruption in the FoxP2 gene." *Proceedings of the National Academy of Sciences (USA)* 102 (2005): 9643–648.

Webb, D. M., and J. Zhang. "FoxP2 in song-learning birds and vocal-learning mammals." *Journal of Heredity* 96 (3) (2005): 212–16.

4. Watch Out!

Ackers, S. H., and C. N. Slobodchikoff. "Communication of stimulus size and shape in alarm calls of Gunnison's prairie dogs, Cynomys gunnisoni." *Ethology* 105 (1999): 149–62.

Armstrong, D. F. *Original Signs: Gesture, Sign, and the Sources of Language.* Washington, DC: Gallaudet University Press, 1999.

Balderrama, N., J. Nunez, F. Guerrieri, and M. Giurfa. "Different functions of two alarm substances in the honeybee." *Journal of Comparative Physiology A* 188 (6) (2002): 485–91.

Blumstein, D. T., and K. B. Armitage. "Alarm calling in yellow-bellied marmots: I. The meaning of situationally variable alarm calls." *Animal Behaviour* 53 (1997): 143–71.

Burke Da Silva, K., D. L. Kramer, and D. M. Weary. "Context-specific alarm calls of the eastern chipmunk, Tamias striatus." *Canadian Journal of Zoology* 72 (1994): 1087–92.

Cheney, D. L., and R. M. Seyfarth. *How Monkeys See the World: Inside the Mind of Another Species.* Chicago: University of Chicago Press, 1990.

Chomsky, N. "Three factors in language design." *Linguistic Inquiry* 36 (1) (2005): 1–22.

Collier, T. C., D. T. Blumstein, L. Girod, and C. E. Taylor. "Is alarm calling risky? Marmots avoid calling from risky places." *Ethology* 116 (12) (2010): 1171–178.

Collins, A. M, T. E. Rinderer, H. V. Daly, J. R. Harbo, and D. Pesante. "Alarm pheromone production by two honeybee (Apis mellifera) types." *Journal of Chemical Ecology* 15 (6) (1989): 1747–56.

Evans, C. S. "Referential signals." In *Perspectives in Ethology:Communication*, edited by D. H. Owings, M. D. Beecher, and N. S. Thompson, 99–143. New York: Plenum Press, 1997.

———. L. Evans, and P. Marler. "On the meaning of alarm calls: functional reference in an avian vocal system." *Animal Behaviour* 46 (1993): 23–38.

———. J. M. Macedonia, and P. Marler. "Effects of apparent size and speed on the response of chickens, Gallus gallus, to computer-generated simulations of aerial predators." *Animal Behaviour* 46 (1993): 1–11.

Fichtel, C. "Reciprocal recognition of sifaka (Propithecus verreauxi verreauxi) and redfronted lemur (Eulemur fulvus rufus) alarm calls." *Animal Cognition* no. 7 (1) (2004): 45–52.

Ficken, M. S., and J. Popp. "A comparative analysis of passerine mobbing calls." *Auk* no. 113 (2) (1996): 370–80.

Frederiksen, J. K., and C. N. Slobodchikoff. "Referential specificity in the alarm calls of the black-tailed prairie dog." *Ethology Ecology & Evolution* 19 (2007): 87–99.

Furrer, R. D., and M. B. Manser. "The evolution of urgency-based and functionally referential alarm calls in ground-dwelling species." *American Naturalist* 173 (3) (2009): 400–10.

Greene, E., and T. Meagher. "Red squirrels, Tamiasciurus hudsonicus, produce predator-class specific alarm calls." *Animal Behaviour* 55 (1998): 511–18.

Jones, K. J., and W. L. Hill. "Auditory perception of hawks and owls for passerine alarm calls." *Ethology* 107 (2001): 717–26.

Kiriazis, J., and C. N. Slobodchikoff. "Perceptual specificity in the alarm calls of Gunnison's prairie dogs." *Behavioural Processes* 73 (1) (2006): 29–35.

Manser, M. B. "Response of foraging group members to sentinel calls in suricates, Suricata suricatta." *Proceedings of the Royal Society B: Biological Sciences* 266 (1999): 1013–19.

————. M. B. Bell, and L. B. Fletcher. "The information that receivers extract from alarm calls in suricates." *Proceedings of the Royal Society B: Biological Sciences* 268 (1484) (2001): 2485–491.

Marler, P. "Characteristics of some animal calls." *Nature* 176 (1955): 6–8.

————. C. S. Evans, and M. D. Hauser. "Animal signals: Motivational, referential, or both?" In *Nonverbal vocal communication: Comparative and Developmental Approaches,* edited by H. Papousek, U. Jurgens, and M. Papousek, 66–86. Cambridge: Cambridge University Press, 1992.

Oda, R. "The responses of Verreaux's sifakas to anti-predator alarm calls given by sympatric ring-tailed lemurs." *Folia Primatologica* 69 (1998): 357–60.

Ouattara, K., A. Lemasson, and K. Zuberbuhler. "Campbell's monkeys use affixation to alter call meaning." *PLoS ONE* 4 (11) (2009): e7808.

Owings, D. H., and D. F. Hennessy. "The importance of variation in sciurid visual and vocal communication." In *The Biology of Ground-Dwelling Squirrels,* edited by J. O. Murie and G. R. Michener, 169–200. Lincoln, NE: University of Nebraska Press, 1984.

————. and W. J. Loughry. "Variation in snake-elicited jump-yipping by black-tailed prairie dogs: Ontogeny and snake specificity." *Zeitschrift fur Tierpsychologie* 70 (1985): 177–200.

Placer, J., C. N. Slobodchikoff, J. Burns, J. Placer, and R. Middleton. "Using self-organizing maps to recognize acoustic units associated with information content in animal vocalizations." *Journal of the Acoustical Society of America* 119 (5) (2006): 3140–146.

Seeley, T. *Honeybee Ecology: A Study of Adaptation in Social Life.* Princeton, NJ: Princeton University Press, 1985.

Shalter, M. D. "Localization of passarine seet and mobbing calls by goshawks and pygmy owls." *Zeitschrift fur Tierpsychologie* 46 (1978): 260–67.

Slobodchikoff, C. N., J. Kiriazis, C. Fischer, and E. Creef. "Semantic information distinguishing individual predators in the alarm calls of Gunnison's prairie dogs." *Animal Behaviour* 42 (1991): 713–19.

———. A. Paseka, and J. L. Verdolin. "Prairie dog alarm calls encode labels about predator colors." *Animal Cognition* 12 (3) (2009): 435–39.

———. B. S. Perla, and J. L. Verdolin. *Prairie Dogs: Communication and Community in an Animal Society.* Cambridge, MA: Harvard University Press, 2009.

Soard, C. M., and G. Ritchison. "'Chick-a-dee' calls of Carolina chickadees convey information about degree of threat posed by avian predators." *Animal Behaviour* 78 (6) (2009): 1447–453.

Templeton, C. N., and E. Greene. "Nuthatches eavesdrop on variations in heterospecific chickadee mobbing alarm calls." *Proceedings of the National Academy of Sciences (USA)* 104 (13) (2007): 5479–482.

———. E. Greene, and K. Davis. "Allometry of alarm calls: Black-capped chickadees encode information about predator size." *Science* 308 (2005): 1934–37.

Thompson, A. B., and J. F. Hare. "Neighbourhood watch: multiple alarm callers communicate directional predator movement in Richardson's ground squirrels, Spermophilus richardsonii." *Animal Behaviour* 80 (2) (2010): 269–75.

Wager, B. R., and M. D. Breed. "Does honey bee sting alarm pheromone give orientation information to defensive bees?" *Annals of the Entomological Society of America* 93 (6) (2007): 1329–32.

Zuberbühler, K. "Interspecies semantic communication in two forest primates." *Proceedings of the Royal Society B: Biological Sciences* 267 (2000): 713–18.

———. "A syntactic rule in forest monkey communication." *Animal Behaviour* 63 (2) (2002): 293–99.

5. What's for Dinner?

Allen, T., and J. Clarke. "Social learning of food preferences by white-tailed ptarmigan chicks." *Animal Behaviour* 70 (2) (2005): 305–10.

Anderson, M. G., D. H. Brunton, and M. E. Hauber. "Reliable Information Content and Ontogenetic Shift in Begging Calls of Grey Warbler Nestlings." *Ethology* 116 (4) (2010): 357–65.

———. "Species specificity of grey warbler begging solicitation and alarm calls revealed by nestling responses to playbacks." *Animal Behaviour* 79 (2) (2010): 401–9.

Bugnyar, T. "Food calling in ravens: are yells referential signals?" *Animal Behaviour* 61 (5) (2001): 949–58.

———. and B. Heinrich. "Ravens, Corvus corax, differentiate between knowledgeable and ignorant competitors." *Proceedings of the Royal Society B: Biological Sciences* 272 (2005): 1641–46.

Burns, F. L. "Crow Language." *Wilson Bulletin* 13 (1) (1901): 5–9.

Caine, N. G., R. L. Addinton, and T. L. Windfelder. "Factors affecting the rates of food calls given by red-bellied tamarins." *Animal Behaviour* 50 (1995): 53–60.

Chamberlain, D. R., and G. W. Cornwell. "Selected vocalizations of the common crow." *Auk* 88 (3) (1971): 613–34.

Clarke, J. A. "White-tailed ptarmigan food calls enhance chick diet choice: learning nutritional wisdom?" *Animal Behaviour* 79 (1) (2010): 25–30.

Conner, R. N. "Vocalizations of common ravens in Virginia." *Condor* 87 (3) (1985): 379–88.

Contrera, F. A. L., and J. C. Nieh. "Effect of forager-deposited odors on the intra-patch accuracy of recruitment of the stingless bees Melipona panamica and Partamona peckolti (Apidae, Meliponini)." *Apidologie* 38 (2007): 584–94.

Crockford, C., and C. Boesch. "Context-specific calls in wild chimpanzees, Pan troglodytes verus: analysis of barks." *Animal Behaviour* 66 (2003): 115–25.

Denault, L. K., and D. A. McFarlane "Reciprocal altruism between male vampire bats, Desmodus rotundus." *Animal Behaviour* 49 (3) (1995): 855–56.

Dornhaus, A., and L. Chittka. "Evolutionary origins of bee dances." *Nature* 401 (1999): 38.

Enggist-Dueblin, P. "Cultural transmission of vocalizations in ravens, Corvus corax." *Animal Behaviour* 64 (6) (2002): 831–41.

Evans, C. S., and L. Evans. "Chicken food calls are functionally referential." *Animal Behaviour* 58 (1999): 307–19.

———. "Representational signalling in birds." *Biology Letters* 3 (1) (2007): 8–11.

———. J. M. Macedonia, and P. Marler. "Effects of apparent size and speed on the response of chickens, Gallus gallus, to computer-generated simulations of aerial predators." *Animal Behaviour* 46 (1993): 1–11.

———. and P. Marler. "Food calling and audience effects in

male chickens, Gallus gallus: their relationship to food availability, courtship and social facilitation." *Animal Behaviour* 47 (1994): 1159–170.

Frederiksen, J. K., and C. N. Slobodchikoff. "Referential specificity in the alarm calls of the black-tailed prairie dogs." *Ethology, Ecology & Evolution* 19 (2007): 87–99.

Frisch, K. von. *The Dance Language and Orientation of Bees.* Translated by L. E. Chadwick. Cambridge, MA: Belknap Press, 1967.

———. "Decoding the Language of the Bee." *Science* 185 (4152) (1974): 663–68.

Hauser, M. D., C. S. Evans, and P. Marler. "The role of articulation in the production of rhesus monkey, Macaca mulatta, vocalizations." *Animal Behaviour* 45 (1993): 423–33.

———., and P. Marler. "Food-associated calls in rhesus macaques (Macaca mulatta): I. Socioecological factors." *Behavioral Ecology* 4 (3) (1993): 194–205.

———. "Food-associated calls in rhesus macaques (Macaca mulatta): II. Costs and benefits of call production and suppression." *Behavioral Ecology* 4 (3) (1993): 206–12.

Holldobler, B. "Multimodal signals in ant communication." *Journal of Comparative Physiology A* 184 (1999): 129–41.

———. U. Braun, W. Gronenberg, W. Kirchner, and C. Peeters. "Trail communication in the ant Megaponera foetens (Fabr.) (Formicidae, Ponerinae)." *Journal of Insect Physiology* 40 (1994): 585–93.

———., and E. O. Wilson. *The Leafcutter Ants.* New York: Norton, 2011.

Kirchner, W., and C. Dreller. "Acoustical signals in the dance language of the giant honeybee, Apis dorsata." *Behavioral Ecology and Sociobiology* 33 (1993): 67–72.

Kitzmann, C. D., and N. G. Caine. "Marmoset (Callithrix

geoffroyi) Food-Associated Calls are Functionally Referential." *Ethology* 115 (5) (2009): 439–48.

Magrath, R. D., B. J. Pitcher, and A. H. Dalziell. "How to be fed but not eaten: nestling responses to parental food calls and the sound of a predator's footsteps." *Animal Behaviour* 74 (5) (2007): 1117–29.

Marler, P., A. Dufty, and R. Pickert. "Vocal communication in the domestic chicken: I. Does a sender communicate information about the quality of a food referent to a receiver?" *Animal Behaviour* 34 (1986): 188–93.

Marzluff, J. M., B. Heinrich, and C. S. Marzluff. "Raven roosts are mobile information centers." *Animal Behaviour* 51 (1996): 89–103.

———. J. Walls, H. N. Cornell, J. C. Withey, and D. P. Craig. "Lasting recognition of threatening people by wild American crows." *Animal Behaviour* 79 (3) (2010): 699–707.

Michelsen, A. B. B. Andersen, J. Storm, W. Kirchner, and M. Lindauer. "How honeybees perceive communication dances, studies by means of a mechanical model." *Behavioral Ecology and Sociobiology* 30 (1992): 143–50.

Munz, T. "The bee battles: Karl von Frisch, Adrian Wenner and the honey bee dance language controversy." *Journal of the History of Biology* 38 (2005): 535–70.

Nieh, J. C. "The honey bee shaking signal: function and design of a modulatory communication signal." *Behavioral Ecology and Sociobiology* 42 (1998): 23–36.

———. "The food recruitment dance of the stingless bee, Melipona panamica." *Behavioral Ecology and Sociobiology* 43 (1998): 133–45.

———. "A negative feedback signal that is triggered by peril curbs honey bee recruitment." *Current Biology* 20 (2010): 310–15.

———. "Recruitment communication in stingless bees (Hymenoptera, Apidae, Meliponini)." *Apidologie* 35 (2) (2004): 159–82.

———. "Stingless bee communication." *American Scientist* 87 (1999): 428–35.

———. "Variation in the ability to communicate three-dimensional resource location by stingless bees from different habitats." *Animal Behaviour* 66 (6) (2003): 1129–39.

———. "The stop signal of honey bees: reconsidering its message." *Behavioral Ecology and Sociobiology* 33 (1993): 51–56.

———. L. S. Barreto, F. A. L. Contrera, and V. L. Imperatriz-Fonseca. "Olfactory eavesdropping by a competitively foraging stingless bee, Trigona spinipes." *Proceedings of the Royal Society B: Biological Sciences* 271 (1548) (2004): 1633–640.

———. F. A. L. Contrera, R. R. Yoon, L. S. Barreto, and V. L. Imperatriz-Fonseca. "Polarized short odor-trail recruitment communication by a stingless bee, Trigona spinipes." *Behavioral Ecology and Sociobiology* no. 56 (5) (2004).

———. F. A. L. Contrera, and P. Nogueira-Neto. "Pulsed mass recruitment by a stingless bee, Trigona hyalinata." *Proceedings of the Royal Society B: Biological Sciences* 270 (1529) (2003): 2191–196.

———. S. Ramirez, and P. Nogueira-Neto. "Multi-source odor-marking of food by a stingless bee, Melipona mandacaia." *Behavioral Ecology and Sociobiology* 54 (6) (2003): 578–86.

Richards, D. B., and N. S. Thompson. "Critical properties of the assembly call of the common American Crow." *Behaviour* 64 (1978): 184–203.

Robinson, G. E. "Chemical communication in honeybees." *Science* 271 (1996): 1824–825.

Roush, R. S., and C. T. Snowdon. "Food transfer and development of feeding behavior and food-associated vocalizations in Cotton-Top Tamarins." *Ethology* 107 (2001): 415–29.

Seeley, T. D. "Born to dance." *Natural History* 6/99 (1999): 54–57.

———. *Honeybee Democracy*. Princeton, NJ: Princeton University Press, 2010.

———. *Honeybee Ecology: A Study of Adaptation in Social Life*. Princeton, NJ: Princeton University Press, 1985.

———. S. Kuhnholz, and A. Weidenmuller. "The honey bee's tremble dance stimulates additional bees to function as nectar receivers." *Behavioral Ecology and Sociobiology* 39 (1996): 419–27.

Slocombe, K. E., T. Kaller, L. Turman, S. W. Townsend, S. Papworth, P. Squibbs, and K. Zuberbühler. "Production of food-associated calls in wild male chimpanzees is dependent on the composition of the audience." *Behavioral Ecology and Sociobiology* 64 (12) (2010): 1959–966.

Stahler, D. "Common ravens, Corvus corax, preferentially associate with grey wolves, Canis lupus, as a foraging strategy in winter." *Animal Behaviour* 64 (2) (2002): 283–90.

Thompson, N. S. "A comparison of cawing in the European Carrion Crow (Corvus corone) and the American Common Crow (Corvus brachyrhynchos)." *Behaviour* 80 (1982): 106–17.

Trivers, R. L. "The evolution of reciprocal altruism." *Quarterly Review of Biology* 46 (1971): 35–37.

Wilkinson, G. S. "Reciprocal food sharing in the vampire bat." *Nature* 308 (5955) (1984): 181–83.

6: Let Me Love You

Bohn, K. M., B. Schmidt-French, S. T. Ma, and G. D. Pollak. "Syllable acoustics, temporal patterns, and call composition vary with behavioral context in Mexican free-tailed bats." *Journal of the Acoustical Society of America* 124 (3) (2008): 1838–848.

Catchpole, C. K., and P. J. B. Slater. *Bird Song: Biological Themes and Variations.* Cambridge: Cambridge University Press, 1995.

Cerchio, S., J. K. Jacobsen, and T. F. Norris. "Temporal and geographical variation in songs of humpback whales, Megaptera novaeangliae: synchronous change in Hawaiian and Mexican breeding assemblages." *Animal Behaviour* 62 (2) (2001): 313–29.

Ekman, P. *Telling Lies: Clues to Deceit in the Marketplace, Politics, and Marriage.* New York: Norton, 1992.

Ficken, M. S., K. M. Rusch, S. J. Taylor, and D. R. Powers. "Blue-throated hummingbird song: A pinnacle of nonoscine vocalizations." *Auk* 117 (2000): 120–28.

Garland, E. C., A. W. Goldizen, M. L. Rekdahl, R. Constantine, C. Garrigue, N. D. Hauser, M. M. Poole, J. Robbins, and M. J. Noad. "Dynamic horizontal cultural transmission of humpback whale song at the ocean basin scale." *Current Biology* 21 (8) (2011): 687–91.

Gittleman, J. L., and S. D. Thompson. "Energy allocation in mammalian reproduction." *American Zoologist* 28 (1988): 863–75.

Gonzalez, C., and J. F. Ornelas. "Song Variation and Persistence of Song Neighborhoods in a Lekking Hummingbird." *Condor* 111 (4) (2009): 633–40.

Gueguen, N. , C. Jacob, and L. Lamy. " 'Love is in the air': Effects of songs with romantic lyrics on compliance with a courtship request." *Psychology of Music* 38 (3) (2010): 303–7.

Guinee, L. N., and K. B. Payne. "Rhyme-like repetitions in songs of humpback whales." *Ethology* 79 (1988): 295–306.

Holy, T. E., and Z. Guo. "Ultrasonic songs of male mice." *PLoS Biology* 3 (12) (2005): e386.

Kalcounis-Rueppell, M. C., J. D. Metheny, and M. J. Vonhof. "Production of ultrasonic vocalizations by Peromyscus mice in the wild." *Frontiers in Zoology* 3 (2001): 3.

Kelso, E. C., and E. P. Martins. "Effects of two courtship display components on female reproductive behaviour and physiology in the sagebrush lizard." *Animal Behaviour* 75 (2) (2008): 639–46.

Kroodsma, D. *The Backyard Birdsong Guide: A Guide to Listening.* San Francisco: Chronicle Books, 2008.

Madden, J. R. "Do bowerbirds exhibit cultures?" *Animal Cognition* 11 (2008): 1–12.

Martins, E. P. "Contextual use of the push-up display by the sagebrush lizard, Sceloporus graciosus." *Animal Behaviour* 45 (1993): 25–36.

———. "Structural complexity in a lizard communication system: The Sceloporus graciosus 'push-up' display." *Copeia* 4 (1994) 944–55.

Moynihan, M. *Communications and Noncommunication by Cephalopods.* Bloomington, IN: Indiana University Press, 1985.

Noad, M. J., D. H. Cato, M. M. Bryden, M-N. Jenner, and K. C. S. Jenner. "Cultural revolution in whale songs." *Nature* 408 (2000): 537.

Ohms, V. R., P. C. Snelderwaard, C. ten Cate, and G. J. L. Beckers. "Vocal tract articulation in Zebra finches." *PLoS ONE* (2010) 5 (7): e11923.

Payne, K., and R. S. Payne. "Large scale changes over 19 years in songs of humpback whales in Bermuda." *Zeitschrift fur Tierpsychologie* 68 (1985): 89–114.

Payne, R. B. "Behavioral continuity and change in local song populations of Village indigobirds Vidua chalybeata." *Zeitschrift fur Tierpsychologie* 70 (1985): 1–44.

Payne, R. S., and S. McVay. "Songs of humpback whales." *Science* 173 (1971): 585–97.

Pickering, S. P. C., and S. D. Berrow. "Courtship behaviour of the Wandering Albatross Diomedea exulans at Bird Island, South Georgia." *Marine Ornithology* 29 (2001): 29–37.

Pruett-Jones, M., and S. Pruett-Jones. "The bowerbird's labor of love." *Natural History* 92 (9) (1983): 48–55.

Rosenbaum, H. C., C. Pomilla, M. Mendez, M. S. Leslie, P. B. Best, K. P. Findlay, G. Minton, P. J. Ersts, T. Collins, M. H. Engel, S. L. Bonatto, D. P. Kotze, M. Meyer, J. Barendse, M. Thornton, Y. Razafindrakoto, S. Ngouessono, M. Vely, and J. Kiszka. "Population structure of humpback whales from their breeding grounds in the South Atlantic and Indian Oceans." *PLoS ONE* 4 (10) (2009): e7318.

Sakata, J. T., C. M. Hampton, and M. S. Brainard. "Social modulation of sequence and syllable variability in adult birdsong." *Journal of Neurophysiology* 99 (4) (2008): 1700–11.

Sober, S. J., and M. S. Brainard. "Adult birdsong is actively maintained by error correction." *Nature Neuroscience* 12 (7) (2009): 927–31.

Trainer, J. M. "Cultural evolution in song dialects of Yellow-rumped caciques in Panama." *Ethology* 80 (1989): 190–204.

Wedell, N. "Sperm competition and ejaculate evolution." *Society of Reproduction and Fertility Supplement* 65 (2007): 115–35.

7. Back Off!

Baker, M. C., T. T. Tracy, and L. E. Miyasato. 1996. "Gargle vocalizations of black-capped chickadees: Test of repertoire and video stimuli." *Animal Behaviour* 52 (1996): 1171–175.

Ballentine, B., W. A. Searcy, and S. Nowicki. "Reliable aggressive signalling in swamp sparrows." *Animal Behaviour* 75 (2) (2008): 693–703.

Bastian, A., and S. Schmidt. "Affect cues in vocalizations of the bat, Megaderma lyra, during agonistic interactions." *Journal of the Acoustical Society of America* 124 (1) (2008): 598–608.

Bekoff, M. "Play signals as punctuation: The structure of social play in canids." *Behaviour* 132 (1995): 419–29.

Bigelow, R. S. *The Dawn Warriors: Man's Evolution Toward Peace*. Boston: Little, Brown, 1969.

Borkowska, B., and B. Pawlowski. "Female voice frequency in the context of dominance and attractiveness perception." *Animal Behaviour* 82 (1) (2011): 55–59.

Compton, L. A., J. A. Clarke, J. Seidensticker, and D. R. Ingrisano. "Acoustic characteristics of white-nosed coati vocalizations: A test of motivation-structural rules." *Journal of Mammalogy* 82 (2) (2001): 1054–58.

Darden, S. K., and T. Dabelsteen. "Acoustic territorial signalling in a small, socially monogamous canid." *Animal Behaviour* 75 (3) (2008): 905–12.

Darwin, C. *The Expression of Emotions in Man and Animals*. London: John Murray, 1872.

Feighny, J. A., K. E. Williamson, and J. A. Clarke. "North American elk bugle vocalizations: Male and female bugle call structure and context." *Journal of Mammalogy* 87 (6) (2006): 1072–77.

Feinberg, D. R., B. C. Jones, A. C. Little, D. M. Burt, and D. I. Perrett. "Manipulations of fundamental and formant frequencies influence the attractiveness of human male voices." *Animal Behaviour* 69 (3) (2005): 561–68.

Ficken, M. S., C. M. Weise, and J. A. Reinartz. "A complex vocalization of the black-capped chickadee. II. Repertoires, dominance and dialects." *Condor* 89 (1987): 500–9.

Foote, J. R., L. P. Fitzsimmons, D. J. Mennill, and L. M. Ratcliffe. "Male chickadees match neighbors interactively at dawn: support for the social dynamics hypothesis." *Behavioral Ecology* 19 (6) (2008): 1192–199.

Galusha, J. G., and J. F. Stout. "Aggressive communication by Larus glaucescens. Part IV. Experiments on visual communication." *Behaviour* 62 (1977): 222–35.

Gouzoules, H., and S. Gouzoules. "Design features and developmental modification of pigtail macaque, Macaca nemestrina, agonistic screams." *Animal Behaviour* 37 (1989): 383–401.

———. "Agonistic screams differ among four species of macaques: the significance of motivation-structural rules." *Animal Behaviour* no. 59 (3) (2000): 501–12.

Gouzoules, S., H. Gouzoules, and P. Marler. "Rhesus monkey (Macaca mulatta) screams: Representational signalling in the recruitment of agonistic aid." *Animal Behaviour* 32 (1984): 182–93.

Gregory, S. W., Jr., and T. J. Gallagher. "Spectral analysis of candidates' nonverbal vocal communication: Predicting U.S. presidential election outcomes." *Social Psychology Quarterly* 65 (3) (2002): 298–308.

Hailman, J. P., and C. K. Griswold. "Syntax of black-capped chickadee (Parus atricapillus) gargles sorts many types into few groups: Implications for geographic variation, dialect drift, and vocal learning." *Bird Behavior* 11 (1996): 39–57.

Kano, F., and M. Tomonaga. "Face scanning in chimpanzees and humans: continuity and discontinuity." *Animal Behaviour* 79 (1) (2010): 227–35.

Leaver, S. D. A., and T. E. Reimchen. "Behavioral responses of Canis familiaris to different tail lengths of a remotely-controlled life-sized dog replica." *Behaviour* 145 (2008): 377–90.

Logue, D. M., I. O. Abiola, D. Rains, N. W. Bailey, M. Zuk, and W. H. Cade. "Does signalling mitigate the cost of agonistic interactions? A test in a cricket that has lost its song." *Proceedings of the Royal Society B: Biological Sciences* 277 (1693) (2010): 2571–575.

Morton, E. S. "On the occurrence and significance of motivation-structural rules in some bird and mammal sounds." *American Naturalist* 111 (1977): 855–69.

Parr, L. A., and M. Heintz. "Facial expression recognition in rhesus monkeys, Macaca mulatta." *Animal Behaviour* 77 (6) (2009): 1507–513.

Peters, R. A., and C. S. Evans. "Design of the Jacky dragon visual display: signal and noise characteristics in a complex moving environment." *Journal of Comparative Physiology A* 189 (6) (2003): 447–59.

Piaskowski, V. D., C. M. Weise, and M. S. Ficken. "The body ruffling display of the black-capped chickadee." *Wilson Bulletin* 103 (3) (1991): 426–34.

Reby, D., K. McComb, B. Cargnelutti, C. Darwin, W. T. Fitch, and T. Clutton-Brock. "Red deer stags use formants as assessment cues during intrasexual agonistic interactions." *Proceedings of the Royal Society B: Biological Sciences* 272 (1566) (2005): 941–47.

Rusch, K. M., C. L. Pytte, and M. S. Ficken. "Organization of agonistic vocalizations in black-chinned hummingbirds." *Condor* 98 (1996): 557–66.

Searcy, W. A., R. C. Anderson, and S. Nowicki. "Bird song as a signal of aggressive intent." *Behavioral Ecology and Sociobiology* 60 (2) (2006): 234–41.

Taylor, A. M., D. Reby, and K. McComb. "Context-Related Variation in the Vocal Growling Behaviour of the Domestic Dog (Canis familiaris)." *Ethology* 115 (10) (2009): 905–15.

———. "Human listeners attend to size information in domestic dog growls." *Journal of the Acoustical Society of America* 123 (5) (2008): 2903–909.

8. Hello, My Name Is Joe

Arnould, C., C. Malosse, J-P. Signoret, and C. Descoins. "Which chemical constituents from dog feces are involved in its food repellent effect in sheep?" *Journal of Chemical Ecology* 24 (3) (1998): 559–76.

Balcombe, J. P. "Vocal recognition of pups by mother Mexican free-tailed bats, Tadarida brasiliensis mexicana." *Animal Behaviour* 39 (1990): 960–66.

———. and G. F. McCracken. "Vocal recognition in Mexican free-tailed bats: Do pups recognize mothers?" *Animal Behaviour* 43 (1992): 79–87.

Berger, L. R., and J. D. Ligon. "Vocal communication and individual recognition in the pinyon jay, Gymnorhinus cyanocephalus." *Animal Behaviour* 25 (1977): 567–84.

Bohn, K. M., B. Schmidt-French, S. T. Ma, and G. D. Pollak. "Syllable acoustics, temporal patterns, and call composition vary with behavioral context in Mexican free-tailed bats." *Journal of the Acoustical Society of America* 124 (3) (2008): 1838–848.

Burgener, N., M. Dehnhard, H. Hofer, and M. L. East. "Does anal gland scent signal identity in the spotted hyaena?" *Animal Behaviour* 77 (3) (2009): 707–15.

Carter, G. G., M. B. Fenton, and P. A. Faure. "White-winged vampire bats (Diaemus youngi) exchange contact calls." *Canadian Journal of Zoology* 87 (7) (2009): 604–8.

Clucas, B. A., T. M. Freeberg, and J. R. Lucas. "Chick-a-dee call syntax, social context, and season affect vocal responses of Carolina chickadees (Poecile carolinensis)." *Behavioral Ecology and Sociobiology* 57 (2) (2004): 187–96.

Dahlin, C. R., R. P. Balda, and C. Slobodchikoff. "Food, audience and sex effects on pinyon jay (Gymnorhinus cyanocephalus) communication." *Behavioural Processes* 68 (1) (2005): 25–39.

Deecke, V. B., J. K. B. Ford, and P. J. B. Slater. "The vocal behaviour of mammal-eating killer whales: communicating with costly calls." *Animal Behaviour* 69 (2) (2005): 395–405.

Dunlop, R. A., D. H. Cato, and M. J. Noad. "Non-song acoustic communication in migrating humpback whales (Megaptera novaeangliae)." *Marine Mammal Science* 24 (3) (2008): 613–29.

Falls, J. B. "Song matching in western meadowlarks." *Canadian Journal of Zoology* 63 (1985): 2520–24.

———. and L. G. D'Agincourt. "A comparison of neighbor-stranger discrimination in eastern and western meadowlarks." *Canadian Journal of Zoology* 59 (1981): 2380–385.

Ferrer-i-Cancho, R., and B. McCowan. "A law of word meaning in dolphin whistle types." *Entropy* 11 (4) (2009): 688–701.

Freeberg, T. M. "Complexity in the chick-a-dee call of Carolina chickadees (Poecile Carolinensis): Associations of context and signaler behavior to call structure." *Auk* 125 (4) (2008): 896–907.

Fripp, D., and P. Tyack. "Postpartum whistle production in bottlenose dolphins." *Marine Mammal Science* 24 (3) (2008): 479–502.

Hailman, J. P., M. S. Ficken, and R. W. Ficken. "The 'chick-a-dee' calls of Parus atricapillus: A recombinant system of animal communication compared with written English." *Semiotica* 56 (1985): 191–224.

Hopp, S. L., P. Jablonski, and J. L. Brown. "Recognition of group membership by voice in Mexican jays, Aphelocoma ultramarina." *Animal Behaviour* 62 (2) (2001): 297–303.

Janik, V. M., L. S. Sayigh, and R. S. Wells. "Signature whistle shape conveys identity information to bottlenose dolphins." *Proceedings of the National Academy of Sciences (USA)* 103 (21) (2006): 8293–297.

Kazial, K. A., S. Pacheco, and K. N. Zielinski. "Information content of sonar calls of little brown bats (Myotis lucifugus): Potential for communication." *Journal of Mammalogy* 89 (1) (2008): 25–33.

Martín, J., I. Barja, and P. López. "Chemical scent constituents in feces of wild Iberian wolves (Canis lupus signatus)." *Biochemical Systematics and Ecology* 38 (6) (2010): 1096–102.

Marzluff, J. M. "Vocal recognition of mates by breeding pinyon jays, Gymnorhinus cyanocephalus." *Animal Behaviour* 36 (1988): 296–98.

Mateo, J. M. "Kin recognition in ground squirrels and other rodents." *Journal of Mammalogy* 84 (4) (2003): 1163–181.

Maurello, M. A., J. A. Clarke, and R. S. Ackley. "Signature characteristics in contact calls of the white-nosed coati." *Journal of Mammalogy* 81 (2) (2000): 415–21.

McCowan, B., and J. D. Newman. "The role of learning in chuck call recognition by squirrel monkeys (Saimiri sciureus)." *Behaviour* 137 (3) (2000): 279–300.

———. and D. Reiss. "Maternal aggressive contact vocalizations in captive bottlenose dolphins (Tursiops truncatus): Wide-band, low-frequency signals during mother/aunt-infant interactions." *Zoo Biology* 14 (1995): 293–309.

Mitchell, B. R., J. M. Makagon, M. M. Jaeger, and R. H. Barrett. "Information content of coyote barks and howls." *Bioacoustics* 15 (2006): 289–314.

Natynczuk, S., J. W. S. Bradshaw, and D. W. MacDonald. "Chemical constituents of the anal sacs of domestic dogs." *Biochemical Systematics and Ecology* 17 (1) (1989): 83–87.

Olivier, R. C. D., and W. A. Laurie. "Habitat utilization by hippopotamus in the Mara River." *East African Wildlife Journal* 12 (1974): 249–71.

Palacios, V., E. Font, and R. Marquez. "Iberian wolf howls: Acoustic structure, individual variation, and a comparison with North American populations." *Journal of Mammalogy* 88 (3) (2007): 606–13.

Sayigh, L. S., H. C. Esch, R. S. Wells, and V. M. Janik. "Facts about signature whistles of bottlenose dolphins, Tursiops truncatus." *Animal Behaviour* 74 (6) (2007): 1631–642.

———. P. L. Tyack, R. S. Wells, A. R. Solow, M. D. Scott, and A. B. Irvine. "Individual recognition in wild bottlenose dolphins: A field test using playback experiments." *Animal Behaviour* 57 (1998): 41–50.

Schulz, T. M., H. Whitehead, S. Gero, and L. Rendell. "Overlapping and matching of codas in vocal interactions between sperm whales: insights into communication function." *Animal Behaviour* 76 (6) (2008): 1977–988.

Tibbetts, E. A., and J. Dale. "Individual recognition: it is good to be different." *Trends in Ecology & Evolution* 22 (10) (2007): 529–37.

Verdolin, J. L., and C. N. Slobodchikoff. "Resources, not Kinship, Determine Social Patterning in the Territorial Gunnison's prairie Dog (Cynomys gunnisoni)." *Ethology* 115 (1) (2009): 59–69.

Wright, T. F. "Regional dialects in the contact call of a parrot." *Proceedings of the Royal Society B: Biological Sciences* 263 (1996): 867–72.

———. C. R. Dahlin, and A. Salinas-Melgoza. "Stability and change in vocal dialects of the yellow-naped amazon." *Animal Behaviour* 76 (3) (2008): 1017–27.

———. and G. S. Wilkinson. "Population genetic structure and vocal dialects in an amazon parrot." *Proceedings of the Royal Society B: Biological Sciences* 268 (1467) (2001): 609–16.

Yovel, Y., M. L. Melcon, M. O. Franz, A. Denzinger, and H-U. Schnitzler. "The voice of bats: How greater mouse-eared bats recognize individuals based on their echolocation calls." *PLoS Computational Biology* 5 (6) (2009): e1000400.

9. What's the Big Deal?

Armstrong, D. F. *Original Signs: Gesture, Sign, and the Sources of Language.* Washington, DC: Gallaudet University Press, 1999.

Bodamar, M. D., and R. A. Gardner. "How cross-fostered chimpanzees (Pan troglodytes) initiate and maintain conversations." *Journal of Comparative Psychology* 116 (1) (2002): 12–26.

Candland, D. K. *Feral Children and Clever Animals: Reflections on Human Nature.* Oxford: Oxford University Press, 1993.

Crockford, C., and C. Boesch. "Call combinations in wild chimpanzees." *Behaviour* 142 (2005): 397–421.

Fouts, R., and S. T. Mills. *Next of Kin: My Conversations with Chimpanzees.* New York: William Morrow, 1997.

Gardner, R. A., B. T. Gardner, and T. E. Van Cantfort. *Teaching Sign Language to Chimpanzees.* Albany, NY: State University of New York Press, 1989.

Grandin, T. *Thinking in Pictures, and Other Reports from My Life with Autism.* New York: Vintage Books, 1995.

Herman, L. M. "Cognition and language competencies of bottlenosed dolphins." In *Dolphin Cognition and Behavior: A Comparative Approach*, edited by R. J. Shusterman, J. A. Thomas and F. G. Woods, 221–52. Hillsdale, NJ: Lawrence Erlbaum Associates, 1986.

———. D. G. Richards, and J. P. Wolz. "Comprehension of sentences by bottlenosed dolphins." *Cognition* 16 (1984): 129–219.

Hobaiter, C., and R. W. Byrne. "The gestural repertoire of the wild chimpanzee." *Animal Cognition* 14 (2011): 745–67.

Hostetter, A. B., M. Cantero, and W. D. Hopkins. "Differential use of vocal and gestural communication by chimpanzees (Pan troglodytes) in response to attentional status of a human (Homo sapiens)." *Journal of Comparative Psychology* 115 (4) (2001): 337–43.

Kaminski, J., J. Call, and J. Fischer. "Word learning in a domestic dog: Evidence for 'Fast Mapping'." *Science* 304 (2004): 1682–683.

Lilly, J. C. *Communication Between Man and Dolphin: The Possibilities of Talking with Other Species.* New York: Crown Publishers, 1978.

Malcolm, N. "Thoughtless brutes." *Proceedings and Addresses of the American Philosophical Association* 46 (1973): 5–20.

Patterson, F., and E. Linden. *The Education of Koko.* New York: Holt, Rinehart and Winston, 1981.

Pepperberg, I. M. *The Alex Studies: Cognitive and Communicative Abilities of Grey Parrots.* Cambridge, MA: Harvard University Press, 1999.

Pfungst, O. *Clever Hans (The Horse of Mr. van Osten).* New York: Henry Holt, 1911.

Pilley, J. W., and A. K. Reid. "Border collie comprehends object names as verbal referents." *Behavioural Processes* 86 (2) (2011): 184–95.

Premack, D. *Gavagai!, or the Future History of the Animal Language Controversy.* Cambridge, MA: MIT Press, 1986.

———. and A. J. Premack. *The Mind of an Ape.* New York: W. W. Norton, 1983.

Roberts, M. *The Man Who Listens to Horses: The Story of a Real-Life Horse Whisperer.* New York: Random House, 1997.

Rumbaugh, D. *Language Learning by a Chimpanzee: The LANA Project.* New York: Academic Press, 1977.

Savage-Rumbaugh, E. S. *Ape Language: From Conditioned Response to Symbol.* New York: Columbia University Press, 1986.

———. and R. Lewin. *Kanzi: An Ape at the Brink of Human Mind.* New York: Wiley, 1994.

Savage-Rumbaugh, S., S. G. Shanker, and T. J. Taylor. *Apes, Language, and the Human Mind.* Oxford: Oxford University Press, 1998.

———. W. M. Fields, and J. Taglialatela. "Ape consciousness-human consciousness: A perspective informed by language and culture." *American Zoologist* 49 (2000): 910–21.

Senechal, S. *Dogs Can Sign, Too: A Breakthrough Method for Teaching Your Dog to Communicate to You.* Berkeley, CA: Celestial Arts, 2009.

Slobodchikoff, C. N., and J. Placer. "Acoustic structures in the alarm calls of Gunnison's prairie dogs." *Journal of the Acoustical Society of America* 119 (5) (2006): 3153–160.

Taglialatela, J. P., S. Savage-Rumbaugh, and L. A. Baker. "Vocal production by a language-competent Pan paniscus." *International Journal of Primatology* 24 (1) (2003): 1–17.

Terrace, H. S. *Nim*. New York: Knopf, 1979.

———. L. A. Petitto, R. J. Sanders, and T. G. Bever. "Can an ape create a sentence?" *Science* 206 (1979): 891–902.

Wallman, J. *Aping Language*. Cambridge: Cambridge University Press, 1992.

INDEX